THIRD EDITION

COMMUNICATION
Concepts and Processes

Joseph A. DeVito
Queens College
of the City University of New York

PRENTICE-HALL, INC., Englewood Cliffs, New Jersey 07632

Library of Congress Cataloging in Publication Data

DeVito, Joseph A   (date)   comp.
    Communication, concepts and processes.

    Includes index.
    1. Communication—Addresses, essays, lectures.
I. Title.
P91.25.D48 1980   001.51   80-22846
ISBN 0-13-153411-4

PRINTED IN THE UNITED STATES OF AMERICA

10 9 8 7 6 5 4 3 2 1

*Prentice-Hall International, Inc., London
Prentice-Hall of Australia Pty. Limited, Sydney
Prentice-Hall of Canada, Ltd., Toronto
Prentice-Hall of India Private Limited, New Delhi
Prentice-Hall of Japan, Inc., Tokyo
Prentice-Hall of Southeast Asia Pte. Ltd., Singapore
Whitehall Books Limited, Wellington, New Zealand*

For the Third Time,
to Boo

Contents

Topic Index

The following index lists the articles under the more common basic communication course topics or units. Since some of the articles are applicable to more than one topic or unit of the course they are listed in several places. This topic index should allow for greater ease and flexibility in coordinating these readings with the course topics.

EFFECTIVENESS IN COMMUNICATION

INTERPERSONAL COMMUNICATION

INTRAPERSONAL COMMUNICATION

LANGUAGE

LISTENING

MODELS AND THEORIES OF COMMUNICATION

NONVERBAL COMMUNICATION

ORGANIZATIONAL COMMUNICATION

PERCEPTION

PERSUASION

PUBLIC SPEAKING

RELATIONAL COMMUNICATION

SELF CONCEPT

SELF DISCLOSURE

SILENCE

SMALL GROUP COMMUNICATION

Coordinating Readings with Standard Textbooks

The following matrix keys the articles in *Communication: Concepts and Processes* with the chapters or units in various textbooks in fundamentals of communication, interpersonal communication, and public speaking. The articles in *Communication* are identified by the author's name (and in some instances a short title) in the left column. The numbers within the matrix boxes identify the unit or chapter numbers in the various textbooks. The texts are identified at the top of the matrix by the author's name and title and more fully in the list presented below.

Each article in *Communication* can be understood by itself and so instructors may rearrange the articles to coordinate with the text chapters in any way that seems most effective for their classes and students.

Textbooks Keyed

BARKER, LARRY L. *Communication*. Englewood Cliffs, New Jersey: Prentice-Hall, 1978.

BROOKS, WILLIAM D. *Speech Communication*, 3e. Dubuque, Iowa: Wm. C. Brown, 1978.

BURGOON, MICHAEL AND MICHAEL RUFFNER. *Human Communication*. New York: Holt, Rinehart and Winston, 1978.

CRONKHITE, GARY. *Communication and Awareness*. Menlo Park, California: Cummings, 1976.

DEVITO, JOSEPH A. *Communicology*. New York: Harper & Row, 1978.

PACE, R. WAYNE, BRENT D. PETERSON, AND M. DALLAS BURNETT. *Techniques for Effective Communication*. Reading, Massachusetts: Addison-Wesley, 1979.

TAYLOR, ANITA, TERESA ROSEGRANT, ARTHUR MEYER, AND B. THOMAS SAMPLES. *Communicating*, 2e. Englewood Cliffs, New Jersey: Prentice-Hall, 1980.

TUBBS, STEWART L. AND SYLVIA MOSS. *Human Communication*, 3e. New York: Random House, 1980.

ADLER, RONALD B., LAWRENCE B. ROSENFELD, AND NEIL TOWNE. *Interplay: The Process of Interpersonal Communication*. New York: Holt, Rinehart and Winston, 1980.

ADLER, RONALD B. AND NEIL TOWNE. *Looking Out/Looking In: Interpersonal Communication*, 2e. New York: Holt, Rinehart and Winston, 1978.

DEVITO, JOSEPH A. *The Interpersonal Communication Book*, 2e. New York: Harper & Row, 1980.

SMITH, DENNIS R. AND L. KEITH WILLIAMSON. *Interpersonal Communication: Roles, Rules, Strategies, and Games*. Dubuque, Iowa: Wm. C. Brown, 1977.

VERDERBER, RUDOLPH F. AND KATHLEEN S. VERDERBER. *Inter-Act: Using Interpersonal Communication Skills*, 2e. Belmont, California: Wadsworth, 1980.

WEAVER, RICHARD L., II. *Understanding Interpersonal Communication.* Glenview, Illinois: Scott, Foresman, 1978.

DEVITO, JOSEPH A. *The Elements of Public Speaking.* New York: Harper & Row, 1981.

EHNINGER, DOUGLAS, BRUCE E. GRONBECK, AND ALAN H. MONROE. *Principles of Speech Communication,* 8e. Glenview, Illinois: Scott, Foresman, 1980.

EHNINGER, DOUGLAS, ALAN H. MONROE, AND BRUCE E. GRONBECK. *Principles and Types of Speech Communication,* 8e. Glenview, Illinois: Scott, Foresman, 1978.

HUNT, GARY. *Public Speaking.* Englewood Cliffs, New Jersey: Prentice-Hall, 1981.

JEFFREY, ROBERT C. AND OWEN PETERSON. *Speech: A Text with Adapted Readings,* 3e. New York: Harper & Row, 1980.

ROSS, RAYMOND S. *Essentials of Speech Communication.* Englewood Cliffs, New Jersey: Prentice-Hall, 1979.

Table — Cross-reference of readings by source. Columns grouped under three categories: **Public Speaking**, **Interpersonal Communication**, and **Fundamentals of Communication**.

	Public Speaking						**Interpersonal Communication**						**Fundamentals of Communication**							
	Ross, *Essentials of Speech Communication*	Jeffrey and Peterson, *Speech*	Hunt, *Public Speaking*	Gronbeck, *Principles and Types of Speech Communication* (Ehninger, Monroe, and Gronbeck)	Ehninger, Gronbeck, and Monroe, *Principles and Types of Speech Communication*	DeVito, *The Elements of Public Speaking*	Weaver, *Understanding Interpersonal Communication*	Verderber and Verderber, *Inter-Act*	Smith and Williamson, *Interpersonal Communication*	DeVito, *The Interpersonal Communication Book*	Adler and Towne, *Looking Out/Looking In*	Adler, Rosenfeld, and Towne, *Interplay*	Tubbs and Moss, *Human Communication*	Taylor, *Communicating*	Pace, Peterson, and Burnett, *Techniques for Effective Communication*	DeVito, *Communicology*	Cronkhite, *Communication and Awareness*	Burgoon and Ruffner, *Human Communication*	Brooks, *Speech Communication*	Barker, *Communication*
Schramm	1	1, 2	1	1	1	1, 2	1	1	1, 2, 4, 12	1	1, 2	1	1, 2	1	1	1, 2	1, 2, 3	1, 2	1, 2	1
Satir	1, 2	3	1, 2	2	2	2, 3	2, 3, 4	2	4, 12	2	1, 2, 4	1, 4	1, 2, 4	1, 2, 6	1	3	1, 2, 3	2, 3, 13	2, 5	3
Bois	3	3	2	2	2	4	8	5, 6	4	3	4	4	4	3	1	18	1, 2, 3	4, 13	1	2
Greening and Hobson	3	3	2	2	2	4	8, 10	5	10	14	4	4, 5	6	3	1	11	1, 2, 3	4, 13	1	2
McCroskey and Wheeless	4	3	1	3	1	6	9	2	10	8	2	4, 5	3	2	1	21	4, 5	2	10	5
Gibb	1, 2	3	1, 3	3	2	4	9	5	3, 6	3, 15	3	4, 5, 7, 8	6	6	1	18	4, 5	6	10	3, 5
DeVito, "Language"	3	14, 15	10	13	8	21, 22, 23	5	3	11	11, 12, 13	7	10	7	3	2	10, 11, 32	11	4	4	2
Newsweek	3	14, 15	10	13	8	21	5	3	6	14	7	10	7	3	2	11	11	4	4	2
Marcus	3	14, 15	10	13	8	21, 23	5	3	6	12	7	10	7	3	2	10	11	4	4	2
Royko	3	14, 15	10	13	8	21	5	3	11	14	7	10	7	3	2	11	11	4	4	2
Eakins and Eakins	3	14, 15	10	13	8	22	5	3, 11	6, 9	30	7	10	7	3	2	34	11	4	4	2
Polin	3	14, 15	10	13	8	22	5	3	9, 11	30	7	10	7	3	2	11	11	4	4	2

	Public Speaking						Interpersonal Communication						Fundamentals of Communication							
	Ross, Essentials of Speech Communication	Jeffrey and Peterson, Speech	Hunt, Public Speaking	Ehninger, Monroe, and Gronbeck, Principles and Types of Speech Communication	Ehninger, Gronbeck, and Monroe, Principles and Types of Speech Communication	DeVito, The Elements of Public Speaking	Weaver, Understanding Interpersonal Communication	Verderber and Verderber, Inter-Act	Smith and Williamson, Interpersonal Communication	DeVito, The Interpersonal Communication Book	Adler and Towne, Looking Out/Looking In	Adler, Rosenfeld, and Towne, Interplay	Tubbs and Moss, Human Communication	Taylor, Communicating	Pace, Peterson, and Burnett, Techniques for Effective Communication	DeVito, Communicology	Cronkhite, Communication and Awareness	Burgoon and Ruffner, Human Communication	Brooks, Speech Communication	Barker, Communication
New York Times	3	14, 15	10	13	8	21	5	3	9, 11	30	7	10	7	3	2	11	11	4	4	2
Lalanne	3	3, 14, 15	10	13	1, 15	21	5	3	10, 11	3	7	10	7	3	2	21, 28	11	4	7	2
Miller	5	12	8, 11	14	4	24	6	4	7, 8	16, 18	6	9	8	4	2	12, 14	12	5	6	4, 11
Cuthill	5	12	8, 11	14	4	24, 26	6	4	7, 8	17	6	9	8	4	2	13	12	5	6	4, 11
Leathers	5	13	8, 11	14, 15	5	25	6	4	7, 8	19	6	9	8	4	2	15	12	5	6	4, 11
Jensen	5	13	8, 11	14, 15	5	25	6	4	7, 8	19	6	9	8	4	2	15	12	5	6	4, 11
Levy	2	2	9	3	1, 2	4	2	10, 11	10	5, 6, 7	2	2, 3	6, 9	2, 5, 7	2	4, 5, 18, 19	4	6	2, 3, 7	5, 6
Rogers and Farson	1	2	2	2	2	3	4, 10	7	10	22	5	8	2, 9, 12	6, 7, 8	2	8, 9	3	6	5	3, 5, 6
Barker	1	2	2	2	2	3, 4	4	7	1	25	5	1, 8	3, 9	7, 8	1, 2	9	3, 4, 13	6	7	3, 5, 6
Weaver	8	11	6	5, 6, 9, 10	12	7, 8	8	9	11	30	8	11	9, 10	7, 8	2	20, 34	4, 15	6, 14	8	5, 6
Haney	9	2	16	20	14, 15	17	10, 11	12, 13	4	21	7	6	10, 12	9, 10, 11	3	23	7, 8, 14	7	9	7
Yerkovich	9	2	6, 16	20	14, 15	5, 20	11	12, 13	4	23, 30, 32	7	6	10	9, 10, 11	3	23	7, 8, 14	7	9	7

	Ross, Essentials of Speech Communication	Jeffrey and Peterson, Speech	Hunt, Public Speaking	Ehninger, Monroe, and Gronbeck, Principles and Types of Speech Communication	Ehninger, Gronbeck, and Monroe, Principles and Types of Speech Communication	DeVito, The Elements of Public Speaking	Weaver, Understanding Interpersonal Communication	Verderber and Verderber, Inter-Act	Smith and Williamson, Interpersonal Communication	DeVito, The Interpersonal Communication Book	Adler and Towne, Looking Out/Looking In	Adler, Rosenfeld, and Towne Interplay	Tubbs and Moss, Human Communication	Taylor, Communicating	Pace, Peterson, and Burnett Techniques for Effective Communication	DeVito, Communicology	Cronkhite, Communication and Awareness	Burgoon and Ruffner, Human Communication	Brooks, Speech Communication	Barker, Communication
	Public Speaking						**Interpersonal Communication**						**Fundamentals of Communication**							
Bales	9	2	16	20	14, 15	7, 8	11	12	4	9, 23	5	6	10	9, 10, 11	3	23, 24, 25	7, 8, 14	7	9	7
DeVito, "Groupthink"	9	2	16	20	14, 15	7, 8	11	12	4	21, 23	5	6	10	9	3	23	7, 8, 14	7	9	7
Gouran	9	2	16	20	14, 15	7, 8	11	12	4	26, 27	5	6	10	9, 10, 11	3	22, 23, 24, 25	7, 8, 14	7	9	7
DeVito, "Risky-Shift"	9	2	16	20	14, 15	7, 8	11	12	4	29, 30	5	6	10	9	3	23	7, 8, 14	7	9	7
Ross, "General Purposes"	6, 7, 10	5, 6, 8, 9, 10	12, 15	3, 4, 17, 18, 22	11	9, 10, 11, 17	7	8, 9	12	24, 10	8	11	11	12, 13, 14, 15, 16	4	26, 27, 28	9, 10, 13	8, 9	10	8
Ross, "Organizing a Speech"	6, 7, 10	7, 8, 9	7, 12, 5, 15, 3	5, 6, 7, 8, 9, 10, 11, 12	9, 11	7, 8, 13, 14, 15, 16	7	8, 9	12	24, 10	8	11	11	12, 13, 14, 15, 16	4	26, 27, 28	9, 10, 13	8, 9	11, 12, 13	9, 10
Thompson, "Compendium"	6, 7, 10	11	13, 14	18, 19	12	18, 19, 20	7	8, 9	12	24, 4	8	11	11	12, 13, 14, 15, 16	4	6, 7, 16, 17	9, 10, 13	8, 9, 11, 12	14	8, 9
Thompson, "Decalogue"	6, 7, 10	11	13, 14	18, 19	12	10	7	8, 9	12	24, 10	8	11	11	12, 13, 14, 15, 16	4	6, 7	9, 10, 13	8, 9, 11, 12	14	8, 9
Washburne	10	11	11	21	12, 15	4	4, 9	13	12	4, 25	7	7	11	6, 16	2	28	13	6	14	12

xvii

Preface

This third edition gives me the opportunity to update the previous edition—to incorporate readings dealing with new developments and more recent emphases in the field of communication and to eliminate those readings which proved less effective. As with the previous two editions, this one continues to be based on a humanistic view of communication, but it is one which recognizes and incorporates the insights and developments derived from the scientific study of messages. It is only with this union that any meaningful and comprehensive view of communication may be presented.

This book is designed primarily for the student beginning her or his study of communication. Although the reader may also be used for the undergraduate course in communication theory, it is primarily designed as an introductory textbook—to introduce students to the varied concepts and processes of communication. The articles cover most of the topics normally covered in introductory courses in fundamentals of communication. I continue to emphasize readings that stress those universals of communication that form the basis for any meaningful introduction to communication—whether theory or practice, whether interpersonal, public speaking, or fundamentals.

The articles included here cover the broad range of communication: communication theories and models, listening, communication barriers, communication motivations, defensiveness, verbal and nonverbal messages, male-female communication, intrapersonal and interpersonal communication, conflict, serial and small group communication, gossiping, public speaking, and persuasion. More specifically, the readings are organized into six parts. Part One focuses on preliminaries covering communication models and theories and some of the essential concepts concerning communication in all its forms: listening, communication barriers, and communication apprehension. Part Two deals with verbal messages: the nature of language and its major characteristics and the principles of verbal interaction, the communication function of names; the differences between male and female communication; and formulating, asking, and answering questions—a most important but sorely neglected aspect of verbal behavior. In Part Three I consider nonverbal messages, beginning with a general overview of the nature and function of nonverbal communication and following with articles dealing with more specific aspects of nonverbal behavior: paralanguage, silence, and interpretation of the nonverbal signals of others. Intrapersonal and interpersonal communication constitute Part Four. Here I deal with self-concept and self-awareness, interpersonal listening, feedback, and conflict—topics that are at the core of interpersonal communication but are also basic to an understanding of communication in all its forms and functions. Serial and small group communication are focused on in Part Five. Beginning with a general orientation to serial communication, I then consider gossiping—a little studied but much practiced form of serial communication, the structure and function of small group communication, and some of the principles of effective small group interaction. In Part Six, public communication is considered. Here the essentials of public speaking and persuasion are considered—the purposes of public speaking, methods of organization, the nature and means of achieving persuasion and retortmanship—how to (not) avoid answering questions. As can be appreciated, these readings provide a most comprehensive introduction to the fundamentals of communication.

The questions and suggestions for projects following each of the articles should enable the student to relate the content of the readings to his or her own unique communicative experiences.

This collection, like its predecessors, was designed to serve either of two basic purposes. As a supplement it may be used with any of the standard textbooks in fundamentals of communication to provide a broader view of the field. As a supplement it may also be used in courses concentrating on interpersonal communication or public speaking. In these cases, this reader will serve to introduce students to areas of communication outside of this interpersonal or public speaking specialty, and it will enable them to see more clearly the place of interpersonal or public speaking within this broad field of communication.

This book may also be used as the main text for a course in fundamentals of communication. The readings cover as much—in most cases more—material as any of the standard texts in fundamentals. The connecting introductions prefacing each of the major parts of the text will prove more than sufficient in tying the various articles together and the collection as a whole will prove as unified as any of the more traditional texts. If a still more comprehensive course is desired, these readings may be supplemented by any of the various paperbacks currently available or by the brief and excellent pamphlets available in the Modcom series (Modules in Speech Communication), published by Science Research Associates, Chicago, Illinois or the CommComp series (Components in Speech Communication), published by Gorsuch Scarisbrick, Dubuque, Iowa. In this way an extremely thorough course, but one of maximum flexibility, may be designed.

To further aid the instructor in using this reader as a supplement to a standard textbook, I have included a key to some of the standard textbooks in fundamentals of communication, interpersonal communication, and public speaking so that the relationship between these readings and the chapters in these textbooks may be seen more clearly. Following the standard index, a topic index is presented that lists the articles under some of the more common topics as they might normally appear in a standard syllabus for an introductory course.

I have built into this edition a more practical orientation to communication than existed in the previous editions. Here there is more "how to do it" articles—papers dealing with how to remove communication blocks, how to structure a public speech, how to listen more efficiently, and how to participate in small group communication situations with greater effectiveness. Although I agree that there is nothing so practical as a good theory, I also think that the beginning student is greatly aided by specific guidance in what to do and how to do it. And so this edition, to a much greater extent than the previous editions, incorporates a blend of both theoretical and practical insights. I have retained from the previous editions the standard of including only articles that are well-written and interesting to read. There is little sense in including theoretically sound articles that never get read because they are so dull. The readings included here are all written in a lively and engaging style.

PRELIMINARIES

The articles in this first section cover a number of *preliminaries*, the foundations of the study of human communication concepts and processes. In "How Communication Works," Wilbur Schramm presents an interesting view of communication and identifies elements and processes that are common to all forms of communication—communication with ourselves, communication with one person or with a group of persons, or communication with a mass audience of thousands or millions. The concepts that Schramm introduces—encoder, decoder, redundancy, feedback, and the like—provide a useful beginning vocabulary for conceptualizing and talking about communication and communication processes. This article should clarify the structure and function of communication and should provide a framework through which the other more specialized articles may be viewed. Each of the remaining articles may be viewed as an elaboration of one or more of the components discussed by Schramm.

Virginia Satir, in a deceptively simple article, "Communication: Talking and Listening," focuses on communication as a means for creating and maintaining relationships. Satir cleverly blends theoretical insights into communication with the practical day-to-day experiencing and improving of communication. By experimenting with the games or exercises suggested by Satir you should find that your own insights into communication will increase substantially.

J. S. Bois, in his brief "How to Communicate Effectively," covers some of the essential guidelines to effective communication. In reading this article, operationalize Bois' suggestions and particularize them for yourself. Seeing the guidelines operate in your own communications will enable you to better understand their significance and the ways to go about internalizing them and making them an integral part of your own communication behaviors.

In "Communication Blocks," Tom Greening and Dick Hobson further explore the ways to effective communication by explaining some of the ways in which communication barriers or blocks may be removed or lessened. Like the suggestions by Bois, those by Greening and Hobson should be particularized by yourself. See your own experiences, your own interactions, your own every day communications in these suggestions.

One of the greatest blocks to effective communication comes from a person's shyness or what has come to be called "communication apprehension," a tendency to withdraw from communication situations and interactions. The research and theory bearing on this question—as well as on the related tendencies to approach communication situations—is reviewed by James McCroskey and Lawrence Wheeless in their "Communication Motivations."

The concept of defensiveness owes most of its formulation to the work of Jack Gibb. In "Defensive Communication" Gibb outlines in more detail the nature of defensiveness and its alternative, supportiveness. Regardless of how closely messages may adhere to the standards of correctness or persuasiveness set down by the experts, they will fail if they are seen as threats and if they arouse defensive behavior. This article should help a great deal in eliminating that possibility.

These articles provide background into the structure of, functions of, and ways to communication effectiveness. The remaining sections address more specific issues such as verbal and nonverbal messages, interpersonal communication, serial and small group communication, and public speaking.

How Communication Works

Wilbur Schramm

Communication comes from the Latin *communis*, common. When we communicate we are trying to establish a "commonness" with someone. That is, we are trying to share information, an idea, or an attitude. At this moment I am trying to communicate to you the idea that the essence of communication is getting the receiver and the sender "tuned" together for a particular message. At this same moment, someone somewhere is excitedly phoning the fire department that the house is on fire. Somewhere else a young man in a parked automobile is trying to convey the understanding that he is moon-eyed because he loves the young lady. Somewhere else a newspaper is trying to persuade its readers to believe as it does about the Republican Party. All these are forms of communication, and the process in each case is essentially the same.

Communication always requires at least three elements—the source, the message, and the destination. A *source* may be an individual (speaking, writing, drawing, gesturing) or a communication organization (like a newspaper, publishing house, television station, or motion picture studio). The *message* may be in the form of ink on paper, sound waves in the air, impulses in an electric current, a wave of the hand, a flag in the air, or any other signal capable of being interpreted meaningfully. The *destination* may be an *individual* listening, watching, or reading; or a member of a *group*, such as a discussion group, a lecture audience, a football crowd, or a mob; or an individual member of the particular group we call the *mass audience*, such as the reader of a newspaper or a viewer of television.

Now what happens when the source tries to build up this "common-

Wilbur Schramm, "How Communication Works," in *The Process and Effects of Mass Communication,* ed. Wilbur Schramm (Urbana, Illinois: University of Illinois Press, 1954), pp. 3–10. Reprinted by permission of University of Illinois Press.

ness" with his intended receiver? First, the source encodes his message. That is, he takes the information or feeling he wants to share and puts it into a form that can be transmitted. The "pictures in our heads" can't be transmitted until they are coded. When they are coded into spoken words, they can be transmitted easily and effectively, but they can't travel very far unless radio carries them. If they are coded into written words, they go more slowly than spoken words, but they go farther and last longer. Indeed, some messages long outlive their senders—the *Iliad,* for instance; the Gettysburg address; Chartres cathedral. Once coded and sent, a message is quite free of its sender, and what it does is beyond the power of the sender to change. Every writer feels a sense of helplessness when he finally commits his story or his poem to print; you doubtless feel the same way when you mail an important letter. Will it reach the right person? Will he understand it as you intend him to? Will he respond as you want him to? For in order to complete the act of communication the message must be decoded. And there is good reason, as we shall see, for the sender to wonder whether his receiver will really be in tune with him, whether the message will be interpreted without distortion, whether the "picture in the head" of the receiver will bear any resemblance to that in the head of the sender.

We are talking about something very like a radio or telephone circuit. In fact, it is perfectly possible to draw a picture of the human communication system that way:

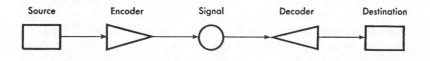

Substitute "microphone" for encoder and "earphone" for decoder and you are talking about electronic communication. Consider that the "source" and "encoder" are one person, "decoder" and "destination" are another, and the signal is language, and you are talking about human communication.

Now it is perfectly possible by looking at those diagrams to predict how such a system will work. For one thing, such a system can be no stronger than its weakest link. In engineering terms, there may be filtering or distortion at any stage. In human terms, if the source does not have adequate or clear information; if the message is not encoded fully, accurately, effectively in transmittable signs; if these are not transmitted fast enough and accurately enough, despite interference and competition, to the desired receiver; if the message is not decoded in a pattern that corresponds to the encoding; and finally, if the destination is unable to handle the decoded message so as to produce the desired response—then, obviously, the system is working at less than top efficiency. When we realize that *all* these steps must be accomplished with relatively high efficiency if any communication is to be successful, the everyday act of explaining something to a stranger, or writing a letter, seems a minor miracle.

A system like this will have a maximum capacity for handling information and this will depend on the separate capacities of each unit on the chain—for example, the capacity of the channel (how fast can one talk?) or the capacity of the encoder (can your student understand something explained quickly?). If the coding is good (for example, no unnecessary words) the capacity of the channel can be approached, but it can never be exceeded. You can readily see that one of the great skills of communication will lie in knowing how near capacity to operate a channel.

This is partly determined for us by the nature of the language. English, like every other language, has its sequences of words and sounds governed by certain probabilities. If it were organized so that no set of probabilities governed the likelihood that certain words would follow certain other words (for example, that a noun would follow an adjective, or that "States" or "Nations" would follow "United") then we would have nonsense. As a matter of fact, we can calculate the relative amount of freedom open to us in writing any language. For English, the freedom is about 50 percent. (Incidentally, this is about the required amount to freedom to enable us to construct interesting crossword puzzles. Shannon has estimated that if we had about 70 percent freedom, we could construct three-dimensional crossword puzzles. If we had only 20 percent, crossword puzzle making would not be worthwhile.)

So much for language *redundancy*, as communication theorists call it, meaning the percentage of the message which is not open to free choice. But there is also the communicator's redundancy, and this is an important aspect of constructing a message. For if we think our audience may have a hard time understanding the message, we can deliberately introduce more redundancy; we can repeat (just as the radio operator on a ship may send "SOS" over and over again to make sure it is heard and decoded), or we can give examples and analogies. In other words, we always have to choose between transmitting more information in a given time, or transmitting less and repeating more in the hope of being better understood. And as you know, it is often a delicate choice, because too slow a rate will bore an audience, whereas too fast a rate may confuse them.

Perhaps the most important thing about such a system is one we have been talking about all too glibly—the fact that receiver and sender must be in tune. This is clear enough in the case of a radio transmitter and receiver, but somewhat more complicated when it means that a human receiver must be able to understand a human sender.

Let us redraw our diagram in very simple form, like this:

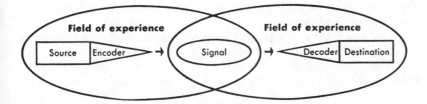

Think of those circles as the accumulated experience of the two individuals trying to communicate. The source can encode, and the destination can decode, only in terms of the experience each has had. If we have never learned any Russian, we can neither code nor decode in that language. If an African tribesman has never seen or heard of an airplane, he can only decode the sight of a plane in terms of whatever experience he has had. The plane may seem to him to be a bird, and the aviator a god borne on wings. If the circles have a large area in common, then communication is easy. If the circles do not meet—if there has been no common experience— then communication is impossible. If the circles have only a small area in common—that is, if the experiences of source and destination have been strikingly unlike—then it is going to be very difficult to get an intended meaning across from one to the other. This is the difficulty we face when a non-science-trained person tries to read Einstein, or when we try to communicate with another culture much different from ours.

The source, then, tries to encode in such a way as to make it easy for the destination to tune in the message—to relate it to parts of his experience which are much like those of the source. What does he have to work with?

Messages are made up of signs. A sign is a signal that stands for something in experience. The word "dog" is a sign that stands for our generalized experience with dogs. The word would be meaningless to a person who came from a dog-less island and had never read of or heard of a dog. But most of us have learned that word by association, just as we learn most signs. Someone called our attention to an animal, and said "dog." When we learned the word, it produced in us much the same response as the object it stood for. That is, when we heard "dog" we could recall the appearance of dogs, their sound, their feel, perhaps their smell. But there is an important difference between the sign and the object: the sign always represents the object at a reduced level of cues. By this we mean simply that the sign will not call forth all the responses that the object itself will call forth. The sign "dog," for example, will probably not call forth in us the same wariness or attention a strange dog might attract if it wandered into our presence. This is the price we pay for portability in language. We have a sign system that we can use in place of the less portable originals (for example, Margaret Mitchell could re-create the burning of Atlanta in a novel, and a photograph could transport world-wide the appearance of a bursting atomic bomb), but our sign system is merely a kind of shorthand. The coder has to be able to write the shorthand, the decoder to read it. And no two persons have learned exactly the same system. For example, a person who has known only Arctic huskies will not have learned exactly the same meaning for the shorthand sign "dog" as will a person who comes from a city where he has known only pekes and poms.

We have come now to a point where we need to tinker a little more with our diagram of the communication process. It is obvious that each person in the communication process is both an encoder and a decoder. He receives and transmits. He must be able to write a readable shorthand,

and to read other people's shorthand. Therefore, it is possible to describe either sender or receiver in a human communication system thus:

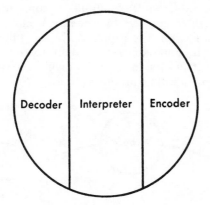

What happens when a signal comes to you? Remember that it comes in the form of a sign. If you have learned the sign, you have learned certain responses with it. We can call these mediatory responses, because they mediate what happens to the message in your nervous system. These responses are the *meaning* the sign has for you. They are learned from experience, as we said, but they are affected by the state of your organism at the moment. For example, if you are hungry, a picture of a steak may not arouse exactly the same response in you as when you are overfed.

But subject to these effects, the mediatory responses will then determine what you do about the sign. For you have learned other sets of reactions connected to the mediatory responses. A sign that means a certain thing to you will start certain other processes in your nerves and muscles. A sign that means "fire," for example, will certainly trigger off some activity in you. A sign that means you are in danger may start the process in your nerves and muscles that makes you say "help!" In other words, the meaning that results from your decoding of a sign will start you *en*coding. Exactly *what* you encode will depend on your choice of the responses available in the situation and connected with the meaning.

Whether this encoding actually results in some overt communication or action depends partly on the barriers in the way. You may think it better to keep silent. And if an action does occur, the nature of the action will also depend on the avenues for action available to you and the barriers in your way. The code of your group may not sanction the action you want to take. The meaning of a sign may make you want to hit the person who has said it, but he may be too big, or you may be in the wrong social situation. You may merely ignore him, or "look murder at him," or say something nasty about him to someone else.

But whatever the exact result, this is the process in which you are constantly engaged. You are constantly decoding signs from your environment, interpreting these signs, and encoding something as a result. In fact, it is misleading to think of the communication process as starting somewhere and ending somewhere. It is really endless. We are little switchboard centers handling and rerouting the great endless current of communication. We can accurately think of communication as passing through us—changed, to be sure, by our interpretations, our habits, our abilities and capabilities, but the input still being reflected in the output.

We need now to add another element to our description of the communication process. Consider what happens in a conversation between two people. One is constantly communicating back to the other, thus:

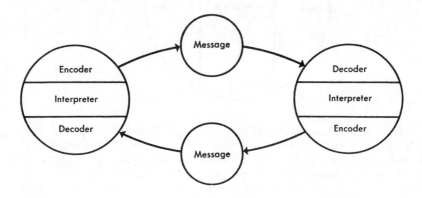

The return process is called *feedback,* and plays a very important part in communication because it tells us how our messages are being interpreted. Does the hearer say, "Yes, yes, that's right," as we try to persuade him? Does he nod his head in agreement? Does a puzzled frown appear on his forehead? Does he look away as though he were losing interest? All these are feedback. So is a letter to the editor of a newspaper, protesting an editorial. So is an answer to a letter. So is the applause of a lecture audience. An experienced communicator is attentive to feedback, and constantly modifies his messages in light of what he observed in or hears from his audience.

At least one other example of feedback, also, is familiar to all of us. We get feedback from our own messages. That is, we hear our own voices and can correct mispronounciations. We see the words we have written on paper, and can correct misspellings or change the style. When we do that, here is what is happening:

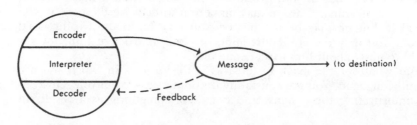

It is clear that in any kind of communication we rarely send out messages in a single channel, and this is the final element we must add to our account of the communication process. When you speak to me, the sound waves from your voice are the primary message. But there are others: the expression on your face, your gestures, the relation of a given message to past messages. Even the primary message conveys information on several levels. It gives me words to decode. It emphasizes certain words above others. It presents the words in a pattern of intonation and timing which contribute to the total meaning. The quality of your voice (deep, high, shrill, rasping, rich, thin, loud, soft) itself carries information about you and what you are saying.

This multiple channel situation exists even in printed mass communication, where the channels are perhaps most restricted. Meaning is conveyed, not only by the words in a news item, but also by the size of the headline, the position on the page and the page in the paper, the association with pictures, the use of boldface and other typographical devices. All these tell us something about the item. Thus we can visualize the typical channel of communication, not as a simple telegraph circuit, in which current does or does not flow, but rather as a sort of coaxial cable in which many signals flow in parallel from source toward the destination.

These parallel relationships are complex, but you can see their general pattern. A communicator can emphasize a point by adding as many parallel messages as he feels are deserved. If he is communicating by speaking, he can stress a word, pause just before it, say it with a rising inflection, gesture while he says it, look earnestly at his audience. Or he can keep all the signals parallel—except *one*. He can speak solemnly, but wink, as Lowell Thomas sometimes does. He can stress a word in a way that makes it mean something else—for example, "That's a *fine* job you did!" And by so doing he conveys secondary meanings of sarcasm or humor or doubt.

The same thing can be done with printed prose, with broadcast, with television or films. The secondary channels of the sight-sound media are especially rich. I am reminded of a skillful but deadly job done entirely with secondary channels on a certain political candidate. A sidewalk interview program was filmed to run in local theaters. Ostensibly it was a completely impartial program. An equal number of followers of each candidate were interviewed—first, one who favored Candidate A, then one who favored Candidate B, and so on. They were asked exactly the same questions, and said about the same things, although on opposite sides of the political fence, of course. But there was one interesting difference. Whereas the supporters of Candidate A were ordinary folks, not outstandingly attractive or impressive, the followers of Candidate B who were chosen to be interviewed invariably had something slightly wrong with them. They looked wildeyed, or they stuttered, or they wore unpressed suits. The extra meaning was communicated. Need I say which candidate won?

But this is the process by which communcation works, whether it is mass communication, or communication in a group, or communication between individuals.

FOR DISCUSSION

1. Schramm cites Chartres cathedral as an example of a communication message. What properties does this cathedral possess that would qualify it as a message? In what ways does it differ from speeches, letters, books, and what we would traditionally classify as messages? Do you agree with Schramm that it should be considered a "message"?

2. "We always have to choose," says Schramm, "between transmitting more information in a given time, or transmitting less and repeating more in the hope of being better understood. . . . it is often a delicate choice, because too slow a rate will bore an audience, whereas too fast a rate may confuse them." Analyze the communication patterns and habits of the instructors you have this term. Do some try to communicate too much while others communicate too little? Are these instructors aware of the capacity of their students for taking in information? From observing their communication, what assumptions do you think these different instructors have made about their students' abilities?

3. In discussing the importance of the fields of experience between source and receiver, Schramm notes that communication is possible only to the degree that these fields overlap. Relate this concept to the problems of children communicating with their parents. How might parent-child communication be improved? Are these same problems present in teacher-student communication? How might such communication be improved?

4. During a class lecture observe the role of feedback. What kinds of feedback do the students give the instructor? What kinds does the instructor give the students? Is the instructor aware of the feedback from students? Does he modify his messages on the basis of this feedback? In what ways? Might the ability to perceive and act on the basis of feedback be used as one standard by which to measure effectiveness in communicating and teaching? Why?

5. What elements that Schramm has not included would you include in a model of communication? Diagram the process of communication as you understand it at present. Of what value is your model?

Communication

Talking and Listening

Virginia Satir

I see communication as a huge umbrella that covers and affects all that goes on between human beings. Once a human being has arrived on this earth, *communications is the largest single factor determining what kinds of relationships he makes with others and what happens to him in the world about him.* How he manages his survival, how he develops intimacy, how productive he is, how he makes sense, how he connects with his own divinity—all are largely dependent on his communication skills.

Communication is the gauge by which two people measure one another's "pot level," and it is also the tool by which that level can be changed for them both. Communication covers the whole range of ways people pass information back and forth; it includes the information they give and receive, and the ways that that information is used. Communication covers how people make meaning of this information.

All communication is learned. By the time we reach the age of five, we probably have had a billion experiences in sharing communication. By that age we have developed ideas about how we see ourselves, what we can expect from others, and what seems to be possible or impossible for us in the world. Unless we have some exceedingly unusual experiences, those ideas will become fixed guides for the rest of our lives.

Once a person realizes that all of his communication is learned, he can set about changing it if he wants to. It will be helpful to remember that every baby who comes into this world comes only with raw materials. He has no self-concept, no experience of interacting with others, and no experience in dealing with the world around him. He learns all these

From Virginia Satir, *Peoplemaking* (Palo Alto, Calif.: Science and Behavior Books, Inc., 1972), pp. 30–58.

things through communication with the people who are in charge of him from his birth on.

First, I want to review the elements of communication. At any point in time, with few exceptions such as blindness and deafness, everyone brings the same elements to his communication process.

He brings his *body*—which moves, has form and shape.

He brings his *values*—those concepts that represent his way of trying to survive and live the "good life" (his "oughts" and "shoulds" for himself and others).

He brings his *expectations* of the moment, gleaned from past experience.

He brings his *sense organs*—eyes, ears, nose, mouth, and skin, which enable him to see, hear, smell, taste, touch, and be touched.

He brings his *ability to talk*—his words and voice.

He brings his *brain*—which is the storehouse of his knowledge, including what he has learned from his past experience, what he has read, and what he has been taught.

Communication is like a film camera equipped with sound. It works only in the present, right here, right now, between you and me.

This is how it works. You are face to face with me; your senses take in what I look like, how I sound, what I smell like, and, if you happen to touch me, how I feel to you.

Your brain then reports what this means to you, calling upon your past experience, particularly with your parents and other authority figures, your book learning, and your ability to use this information to explain the message from your senses. Depending upon what your brain reports, you feel comfortable or uncomfortable—your body is loose or tight.

Meanwhile, I am going through something similar. I too, see, hear, feel something, think something, have a past, have values and expectations, and my body is doing something. You don't really know what I am sensing, what I am feeling, what my past is, what my values are and exactly what my body is doing. You have only guesses and fantasies, and I have the same about you. Unless the guesses and fantasies are checked out, they become "the facts" and as such can often lead to traps and ruptures.

To illustrate the sensory message, the brain's interpretation of it, and the consequent feelings and feelings *about* the feelings, let's consider the following.

I am in your presence; you are a man. I think, "Your eyes are very wide apart, you must be a deep thinker." Or, "You have long hair, you must be a hippie." To make sense out of what I see, drawing on my experience and knowledge, what I tell myself influences me to have certain feelings both about myself and about you before a word is spoken.

For example, if I tell myself you're a hippie, and I'm afraid of hippies, then I might feel fear in myself and anger at you. I might get up and leave this frightening situation, or I might slug you. Perhaps I would tell myself you look like a scholar. Since I admire smart people, and I feel you are like me, I might want to start a conversation. On the other hand, if I felt myself to be stupid, your being a scholar would make me feel ashamed, so I would bend my head and feel humiliated.

Meanwhile you are also taking me in and are trying to make sense out of me. Perhaps you smell my perfume, decide I am a nightclub singer, which is offensive to you, so you turn your back. On the other hand, maybe my perfume would make you decide I am a neat gal, and you would search for ways to contact me. Again, all this takes place in a fraction of a second before anything is said.

I have developed a set of games or exercises that will help deepen your awareness and appreciation of communication with the emphasis in this chapter on looking, listening, paying attention, getting understanding, and making meaning.

It is best to try these games with a partner. Choose any member of your family that you wish. If no one feels free to join you, then try it alone in your imagination, but you will all learn and grow if you all take part in these exercises.

Sit directly in front of your partner, close enough to be able to touch him easily. You may not be used to doing what I'm going to ask you to do; it may even seem silly or uncomfortable. If you feel that way, try to go along anyway and see what happens.

Now imagine you are two people, each with a camera, photographing the other. This is how it is when two people are face-to-face. There may be other people present, but at any moment in time, only two people can be eye-to-eye.

A picture must be processed to see what was actually photographed. Human beings process their pictures in the brains, which interpret them, and then *maybe* people know what the picture is.

First, sit back comfortably in your chair and just look at the person in front of you. Forget what Mama or Papa said about its being impolite to stare. Give yourself the luxury of fully looking, and don't talk. Notice each movable part of his face. See what the eyes, eyelids, eyebrows, nostrils, facial and neck muscles are doing, and how the skin is coloring. Is it turning pink, red, white, blue? You'll observe the body, its size, form and the clothing on it. And you'll be able to see how the body is moving— what the legs and arms are doing, how the back is held.

Do this for about one minute and close your eyes. See how clearly you can bring this person's face and body to your mind's eye. If you've missed something, open your eyes and pick up on the details you may have missed.

This is the picture-taking-process. Our brains could develop the picture as follows: "His hair is too long; he should sit up straight. He is just like his mother." Or, "I like his eyes. I like his hands. I don't like the color of his shirt. I don't like his frown." Or you may ask yourself, "Does he frown all the time? Why doesn't he look at me more? Why is he wasting himself?" You may compare yourself to him. "I could never be as smart as he is." You may remember old injuries. "He had an affair once; how can I trust him?"

This is part of your internal dialogue. Are you aware that dialogue of some kind is going on in your head all the time? When your senses are focused on something, this inner dialogue is emphasized.

As you become aware of your thoughts, you may notice some of them make you feel bad, and your body responds. It may stiffen, your stomach could get butterflies, your hands become sweaty, your knees weak, and your heart beat faster. You could get dizzy or blush. If, on the other hand, you're having thoughts that make you feel good, your body may relax.

> All right. We're ready to go on with the exercise. You have really looked at your partner. Now close your eyes. Does he remind you of anyone? Almost everyone reminds one of someone else. It could be a parent, a former boy or girl friend, a movie star—anybody. If you find a resemblance, let yourself be aware of how you feel about that person. Chances are that if the reminders are strong, you could sometimes get that person mixed up with the one in front of you. You could have been reacting to him as someone else. Should this happen the other person will be in the dark and feel unreal about what is happening.

> After about a minute open your eyes and share what you've learned with your partner. If you found another person while your eyes were closed, tell your partner who it was and what part of him reminded you of your partner. Add how you feel about this. Of course, your partner will do the same thing.

When this kind of thing goes on, communication is taking place with shadows from the past, not real people. I have actually found people who lived together for thirty years treating one another as someone else and constantly suffering disappointment as a result. "I am not your father!" cries the husband in a rage.

As mentioned, all of these responses take place almost instantly as you look. What words come out depend upon how free you and your partner feel with one another, how sure you are about yourself and how aware you are in expressing yourself.

So you have looked at your partner, and you have become aware of what is going on inside of you.

> Close your eyes for a minute. Let yourself become aware of what you were feeling and thinking as you looked—your body feelings and also how you felt about some of your thoughts and feelings. Imagine telling your partner all that you can about your inner space activity. Does the very thought of it make you quake and feel scared? Are you excited? Do you dare? Put into words all you want to and/or can about your inner space activity, talking quietly about what went on within you with a sharing attitude.

How much of your inner space activity were you willing to share with your partner? The answer to this question can give you a pretty good idea of where you stand in terms of freedom with your partner. If you quaked at the thought of sharing, you probably didn't want to tell much. If you had negative feelings, you probably wanted to hide them. If there is very much of this negative kind of response, you've probably been troubled about your relationship. If you felt you had to be careful, could you let yourself know why? Could you be honest and direct?

If you keep too much of your inner space to yourself, barriers are quickly built up, which often leads to loneliness and a first step toward emotional divorce. Emotional divorces can exist between parents and children and between siblings as well as the married pair. If you can risk sharing your insides, some of the barriers may begin to tumble.

Now we are ready for the sound part of your camera to become active. When your partner starts breathing heavily, coughing, making sounds or talking, your ears report it to you. Your hearing stimulates inner space experience just as seeing does.

The other person's voice usually puts other sounds in the background except to someone who has broadened his ability to hear. His voice is loud, soft, high, low, clear, muffled, slow, fast. Again, you have thoughts and feelings about what you hear. Almost everyone notices and reacts to voice quality—sometimes to the extent that the words may escape you and you have to ask your partner to repeat.

I'm convinced that few people would talk as they do if they knew how they sounded. Voices are like musical instruments—they can be in or out of tune. But the tunes of our voices are not born with us; so we have hope. If people could really hear themselves, they could change their voices. I am convinced that people don't hear how they really sound, but how they *intend* to sound.

Once a woman and her son were in my office. She was saying in loud tones to him, "You are always yelling!" The son answered quietly, "You are yelling now." The woman denied it. I happened to have my tape recorder on, and I asked her to listen to herself. Afterward she said rather soberly, "My goodness that woman sounded loud!" She was unaware of how her voice sounded; she was aware only of her thoughts, which were not getting over because her voice drowned them out. You all probably have been around people whose voices were high-pitched and harsh, or low and barely audible, who talked as if they had a mouthful of mush, and you have experienced the resultant injury to your ears. A person's voice can help you or hinder you in understanding the meaning of his words.

Share with your partner how his voice sounds to you, and ask him to do the same.

When more of us know how to hear our voices, I think they will change considerably. If you have a chance to hear yourself on a tape recorder, by all means do it. Prepare yourself for a surprise. If you listen to it in the presence of others, you will probably be the only one who feels

your recorded voice sounds different. Everyone else will say it's right on.
There is nothing wrong with the tape recorder.

We're ready for another exercise.

Again sit within touching distance of your partner, and look at each other
for one minute. Then take each other's hands and close your eyes. Slowly
explore the hands of your partner. Think about their form, their texture.
Let yourself be aware of any attitudes you have about what you're
discovering in these hands. Experience how it feels to touch these hands
and be touched by them. See how it feels to feel the pulses in your
respective fingertips.

After about two minutes open your eyes and continue touching at the
same time you are looking. Let yourself experience what happens. Is
there a change in your touching experience when you look? After about
thirty seconds close your eyes, continuing to touch and experience any
possible changes. After a minute disengage your hands with a "parting
but not a rejection" and sit back and let yourself feel the impact of the
whole experience. Open your eyes and share your inner space with your
partner.

Try this variation: one closes his eyes, and the other uses his hands to
trace all the parts of the other's face, keeping awareness on touch.
Reverse this and share your experience.

At this point in the experiment many people say they become
uncomfortable. Some say their sexual responses get stirred up, and it is
like having intercourse in public. My comment at this point is, "It was
your *hands* and *faces* you were touching!" Some say they feel nothing; the
whole thing seems stupid and silly. This saddens me as it could mean these
people have constructed walls around themselves so they never can get
the joy of physical comfort. Does anyone ever really outgrow his wish and
need for physical comforting?

I have noticed that when couples with these feelings gradually let
down and begin to enjoy touching, their relationship improves in all areas.
The taboo against touching and being touched goes a long way to explain
sterile, unsatisfying, monstrous experiences many people have in their
sexual lives.

This taboo also does much to explain to me why the younger person
gets into so much premature sex. They feel the need for physical
comforting and think the only proper avenue open to them is intercourse.

As you went through all these experiments, you probably also realized
that they are subject to individual interpretation. When our hands touch,
you and I each feel the touch differently. I think it is so important for
people to tell each other how the touch of the other feels. If I intend a
loving touch and you experience it as harsh, I think it is pretty important
for me to know that. This not knowing how we look, sound, or how our
touch feels to someone else is very common, and it is also responsible for
much disappointment and pain in relationships.

Now try smelling each other. This may sound a little vulgar. However, any woman who has ever used perfume knows that the sense of smell is important in the way she is perceived. Many a potentially intimate relationship has been aborted or remained at a distance because of bad odors or scents. See what happens as you break your taboos against smelling, and let yourself tell and be told about your smells.

By this time it is possible that as you made contact with your eyes, ears, skin, and sharing one another's inner space activities you already have a heightened appreciation of each other. It is equally possible that as you first looked, memories of old hurts were so strong that that was all you could see. I call this "riding the garbage train." As long as you look now, but see yesterday, the barriers will only get higher. If you encounter the "garbage train," say so and dump it.

What is so important to remember is to look at one another in the present, in the here and now. Eyes clouded with regret for the past or fear for the future limit your vision and offer little chance for growth or change.

Believe it or not, I have met hundreds and hundreds of family pairs who have not touched each other except in rage or sex, and who have never looked at one another except in fantasy or out of the concerns of their eyes.

The next set of exercises are concerned with physical positions and how they affect communication.

Turn your chairs around back to back, about eighteen inches apart, and sit down. Talk to each other. Very quickly you will notice some changes. You become physically uncomfortable, your sense of enjoyment of the other decreases, and it's hard to hear.

Add another dimension to the exercise and move your chairs about fifteen feet apart, remaining back to back. Notice the drastic changes in your communication. It is even possible to "lose" your partner entirely.

One of my first discoveries after beginning the study of families in operation was how much of their communication was carried on in precisely this way. The husband is in the den behind his newspaper; the wife is doing the ironing. Each has his attention elsewhere, yet they are talking about something important. "I hope you made the mortgage payment today." The other one grunts. Two weeks later there is the eviction notice. You can probably think of many, many examples of your own.

Don't be fooled by thinking that in order to be polite there must be great physical distances between people. I think if there is more than three feet between people, a great strain is put on their relationship.

Now let's try something else.

Decide which of you will be A and which B. In the first round A stands and B sits on the floor directly in front of him. Talk about how this feels.

Stop after two minutes. Share how it feels to talk in this position. Then change places and share again.

At one time we were all in the on-the-floor position in relation to the adults around us. It is the position any young children in your family are in right now.

Still in these positions let yourselves become aware of how your bodies feel. The sitter has to look up. Within thirty seconds his neck and shoulders will begin to ache, his eyes and eye muscles will become strained and his head will probably begin to ache. You, the stander, will have to arch your back to look down, and your back and neck muscles will begin to ache. It will probably become more difficult to see as the strain grows.

(Give yourself just thirty seconds in these positions so you'll know what I'm talking about. They become really horrible by sixty seconds.)

Everyone was born little, and each of us spends from ten to fifteen years (sometimes longer) being shorter than our parents. Considering the fact that most of our communication takes place in the positions described above, there is little wonder so many people *feel* so little all their lives. Understanding this, we can also understand why so many grow up with distorted views about themselves and their parents as people.

Let's look at this exercise from a slightly different perspective.

Again, in the position of the last exercise, both of you look straight ahead and notice the scenery. From the floor you see knees, legs, and if you look down, you see feet and very big ones. Look up and you see all the protrusions—genitals, bellies, breasts, chins, and noses.

So often I have heard reports from people about their parents' mean looks, huge breasts, bellies, huge genitals and chins, and so on. Then when I met the parents I often saw quite the opposite. The child had formed his menacing picture from his out-of-perspective position.

The parent sees the child out of perspective as well. He could always envision you as little. These images, formed early in childhood, become bases upon which other experiences follow and which, for many, many people, never change.

Try this variation. You are in the same up and down positions. Make hand contact. The one on the floor obviously has to hold his hand and arm up; the one standing has his arm down. Thirty seconds is enough time for the upraised arm to get numb.

Inasmuch as the adult enjoys a more comfortable position with his arm down, he might find it difficult to realize the discomfort he is inflicting on the child. The child might struggle to get away, and the adult could become irritated at this "negative behavior" when all the poor kid wants is to get comfortable.

How many times have you seen a child, both arms up, being virtually dragged along between his parents? Or a hurrying mother dragging along her offspring by one arm on the bias?

Get into your standing and sitting positions for thirty seconds again. Then break eye contact, and notice how quickly this change in position will give your neck, eyes, shoulders, and back some relief.

Again, imagine how easy it would be for an adult to interpret this action on the part of a child as disrespectful. On the other hand, the child trying to contact his parent could interpret his glancing away as indifference or even rejection.

It would be natural for him to tug at his parent for attention. This could annoy the parent to the extent that he could slap the pesky child or box his ears. All of this would be humiliating, "pot lowering," and the child could get hurt. This whole interaction is fertile breeding ground for engendering feelings of fear and hate in the child and rejection on the part of the adult.

Suppose the parent responds to the tugging by what he supposes is a reassuring pat on the head but doesn't gauge his force very well?

You the stander give the sitter a rather obvious pat on the head. Is it experienced as comforting or as a "cranial explosion"?

The significance of eye contact can be seen in this last set of exercises. In order for people to really contact one another successfully, they need to be on eye level, each supported by his own two feet and facing one another. I hope we've established how essential eye level contact is between adults and children when images and expectations of one another are being formed. We must never forget that first experiences have great impact and unless something happens to change it, that experience will be the reference point for all of the future.

If you have young children, work it out so you contact them at eye level. Most of the time this means that adults will have to squat and build eye level furniture.

Now I would like to undertake some exercises that will help deepen understanding and make meaning between two people.

Good human relations depend a great deal on people's getting one another's meaning, whatever words they happen to use. Also, since our brains work so much faster than our mouths, we often use a kind of "shorthand," which might have an entirely different meaning for the other person than what we intended.

We learned from the seeing exercise that although we *thought* we were seeing, we were actually making up much of what we "saw." This same kind of thing is possible with words. Let's try this exercise.

Make what you believe to be a true statement to your partner. He is then to repeat it to you verbatim, mimicking your voice, tone, inflection, facial expression, body position, movement. Check him for accuracy, and if it

fits, say so. If it doesn't, produce your evidence. Be explicit; don't make
a guessing game out of this. Then reverse roles.

This exercise helps to focus on really listening to and really seeing
another person. Listening and looking require one's full attention. We pay
a heavy price for not seeing and not hearing accurately as we end up by
making assumptions and treating them as facts.

A person can look either with attention or without attention. Whoever
is being looked at may not know the difference and assume he's being
seen when he is not. And what a person thinks he sees is what he reports.
If that individual happens to be in a position of power—a parent, a
teacher, or an administrator—he can cause personal pain to another.

Let's consider words a moment. When someone is talking to you, do
his words make sense? Do you believe them? Are they strange, or do they
sound like nonsense? Do you have feelings about the other person and
yourself? Do you feel stupid because you don't understand? Puzzled
because you can't make sense? If so, can you say so and ask questions? If
you can't, do you just guess? Do you not ask questions for fear you'll be
thought stupid, and thus you remain stupid? What about the feeling of
having to be quiet?

If you concentrate on these kinds of questions, you stop listening. I
say it this way, "To the degree that you are involved with internal pot
dialogue, you stop listening."

As you literally try to hear the other person, you are, at the very
least, in a kind of three-ring circus. You are paying attention to the sound
of the other person's voice, experiencing past and future fears concerning
you both, becoming aware of your own freedom to say what you are
feeling, and finally concentrating on efforts to get the meaning from your
partner's words.

This is the complicated inner space activity each person has, out of
which communication develops and on which interaction between any two
people depends.

Let's go back to the exercises.

Could you begin to feel how it was to use yourself fully to get the other's
meaning? Do you know the difference between full listening and half
listening? When you were imitating did you find that your attention
wandered and you made more errors in seeing?

My hope is that you can learn to engage yourself fully when listening
and not make believe. If you don't want to or can't listen, don't pretend.
You'll make fewer mistakes that way. This is particularly true between
adults and children.

Now let's go to the next part of the meaning exercises.

Sit face-to-face with your partner as before. Now one of you make a
statement you believe to be true. The other responds with, "Do you

mean . . ." to indicate whether or not he has understood. Your aim is to get three yeses. For example:

"I think it's hot in here."

"Do you mean that you're uncomfortable?"

"Yes."

"Do you mean that I should be hot, too?"

"No."

"Do you mean that you want me to bring you a glass of water?"

"No."

"Do you mean that you want me to know that you're uncomfortable?"

"Yes."

"Do you mean that you want me to do something about it?"

"Yes."

At this juncture at least one has understood the other's meaning. If the partner were not able to get any yeses, then the other would simply have to tell what he meant.

Try this several times with the same statement, changing partners each time. Then try a question. Remember you are trying to get the meaning of the question, not to answer it. Do several rounds.

You are probably discovering how easy it is to misunderstand someone by making assumptions about what he meant. This can have serious results, as we've indicated, but they can also be funny.

I remember a young mother who was eager to clue into her young son's sexual questions. Her opportunity came one day when he asked her, "Mommy, how did I get here?" Believe me, she made the most of her opportunity. When she finished, her son, looking extremely puzzled, said, "I meant, did we come by train or by airplane?" (The family had moved some months previously.)

As you were doing the meaning exercises, were you able to become more fully aware of the trust and enjoyment that can come from engaging in a deliberate effort to understand?

Has this ever happened at your house? You and your spouse meet at the end of the day. One of you says, "So, how was your day?" The other answers, "Oh, nothing special."

What meanings are evident in this exchange? One woman who went through this fairly frequently said that this was her husband's way of turning her off. Her husband told me this was the way his wife showed him she didn't care.

"So, how was your day?" can mean, "I had a tough day, and I'm glad you're here. I hope it will go better now."

It can mean, "You're usually such a grouch. Are you still grouchy?"

It can mean, "I am interested in what happens to you. I would like to hear about anything exciting that happened to you."

"Oh, nothing special" can mean "Are you really interested? I'd like that."

It can mean "What are you trying to trap me in now? I'll watch my step."

How about some examples from your family?

There are a couple of very common communication traps based on the assumption so many people make that everyone else already knows everything about them.

There is that *hint method*, using one-word answers. Remember this old story that is illustrative of the point?

An inquiring reporter visited a rather plush old men's home. As the director proudly escorted him around, the reporter heard someone call out "31" from a nearby room. This was followed by great laughter. This procedure went on with several other numbers, all of which got the same response. Finally someone called out, "Number 11!" There was a dead silence. The reporter asked what was going on, and the director replied that these men had been there so long they knew all each other's jokes. To save energy they had give each joke a number. "I understand that," said the reporter. "But what about Number 11?" The director responded, "That poor guy never could tell a joke well."

The other communication trap is that so often people assume that no matter what they actually say, everyone else should understand them (the *mind-reading method*).

I am reminded of a young man whose mother was accusing him of violating an agreement to tell her when he was going out. He insisted he had told her. As evidence he said, "You saw me ironing a shirt that day, and you know I never iron a shirt for myself unless I am going out."

I think we've established at least so far that in human communication there is always mutual picture-taking, but that the people involved may not share their pictures, the meanings they give the pictures, nor the feelings the pictures arouse. The meanings are then guessed at, and the tragedy is that the guesses are then taken as facts.

At this point there can't be much doubt that our guesses about one another are anything but 100 percent accurate. I believe this guessing procedure is responsible for a great deal of unnecessary human estrangement.

Part of the problem is that we are such sloppy talkers! We use words such as *it, that,* and *this* without clarifying them. This is particularly difficult for the child because he has fewer clues from experience to help him. Anyone in this situation is in an impossible bind if his rules require that he act as though he understood.

Thousands of times I've heard one person say to another, "Stop that!" What is *that*? The second person may have no idea. Just because I see you doing something I want you to stop doesn't mean you know what I'm talking about. Many, many harmful pot reactions can be avoided simply by remembering to say to someone else what you are literally seeing and hearing.

This brings us to what I consider one of the most impossible hurdles in human relationships. That is the assumption that *you* always know what *I* mean. The premise appears to be that if we love each other, we also can and should read each other's minds.

The most frequent complaint I have heard people make about their family members is, "I don't know how he feels," which results in a feeling of being left out. This puts a tremendous strain on any relationship, particularly a family one. People tell me they feel in a kind of no-man's-land as they try to make some kind of a bridge to a family member who doesn't show or say what he feels.

It's important to point out, however, that many people who are accused of this are often feeling very strongly, but are unaware they aren't showing it. They believe themselves to be as transparent to others as they are to themselves.

I have a little experiment I use to help people in the problem of awareness. I ask two people to discuss something, and video tape it. Then I play back the tape and ask each to respond to what they see in comparison to what they remember feeling as it happened. Many people are astonished as they see things of which they were not even in the remotest way aware when the tape was being made.

I remember a terrible ruckus in a family because the father sent his son to the lumber yard for a longer board. The child was obedient, wanted to please his dad, and thought he knew what was expected. He dutifully went and came back with a board that was three feet too short. His father, disappointed, became angry and accused his son of being stupid and inattentive. The father knew how long a board he wanted, but it apparently had not occurred to him that his son wouldn't know also. He literally had never thought of this and did not see it until we discussed it in the session.

Here is another example. A sixteen-year-old son says at 5:30 P.M. on a Friday night, "What are you doing tonight, Dad?" Ted, his father, replies, "You can have it!" Tom, the son, answers, "I don't want it now." With irritation Ted snaps, "Why did you ask?" To which Tom responds angrily, "What's the use?"

What are they talking about? Tom wanted to find out if his father were planning to watch him play basketball that night. Tom didn't ask his father directly because he was afraid he might say no, so he used the hinting method.

Ted got the message that Tom was hinting, all right, but he thought it was a request for the family car that night. Tom thought his dad was putting him off. Ted then thought Tom was ungrateful. These interactions ended with both father and son being angry and each feeling the other didn't care. I believe these kinds of exchanges are all too frequent among people.

Sometimes people have become so used to saying certain things in certain situations that their responses become automatic. If a person feels bad and he's asked how he feels, he will answer, "Fine," because he's told himself so many times in the past that he *should* feel fine. Besides, he probably concludes, no one is really interested anyway, so why not pick the expected answer? He has programmed himself to have only one string on his violin, and with only one string he has to use it with everything, whether it applies or not.

People can process their mental pictures by *describing* what they see or hear—by using *descriptive* not judging language. Many people intend to describe, but their pictures are distorted because they use judgmental words. If I can tell you what meaning I make of a given picture, avoid being judgmental, and tell you what I feel about it, and you do the same with me, at least we are straight with each other. We might not like the meaning we discover, but at least we understand. For example my camera picture is that you have a dirt smudge on your face. If I say, "For the love of heaven, what a slob!" I am being judgmental. If I use descriptive words, I would say, "I see a dirt smudge on your face."

Two traps are implicit here: *I read you in my terms* and *I hang a label on you*. To me the label *is* you. For example, you are a man, and I see tears in your eyes. Since I think men should never cry because that shows weakness, I conclude that you are weak, and I treat you accordingly. (Personally I happen to feel just the opposite, but the above is a popular view.)

I think you are ready now to try the ultimate risk with your partner.

This time assign yourself the task of confronting him with three statements you believe to be true about him and three you believe to be true about yourself. You'll probably be aware that these are your truths as of now; they are not the real truths for all time. To keep focused on telling your now truths, try beginning with the following words, "At this point in time I believe such and such to be true about you." If you have a negative truth, see if you can put words to that. In my opinion no relationship can be a nurturing one unless all states and aspects can be openly and freely commented upon.

I used to tell my students that they had it made when they could say straight to someone that he had a bad smell about him, in such a way that he received the information as a gift. It is painful at the outset, but definitely useful in the long run. Many people have reported to me that contrary to their expectations, relationships stood on firmer and more nuturing and trusting ground when they found they could be straight with negative as well as positive content.

On the other hand many people never put words to expressing appreciation. They just assume the others know of it. This, coupled with the fact that most people aren't a bit shy about voicing objections, results in estrangment and resentment. Who doesn't like (and need!) a pat on the head from time to time?

I recommend that families have the same kind of confrontation as the exercise just described at least once a week if not daily. After all, the first and basic learning about communication comes in the family. Sharing your inner space activity with one another accomplishes two important things: becoming really acquainted with the other person and thus changing strangeness to something familiar, and also making it possible to use your communication to develop nurturing relationships—something we all continue to need.

You should now be more aware that every time two people are together, each has an experience that affects him in some way. The experience can serve to reinforce what was expected—either positively or negatively. It may create doubts about the other's worth and thus create distrust, or it may deepen and strengthen the worth of each, and the trust and closeness between them. Every interaction between two people has a powerful impact on the respective worth of each and what happens between them.

If encounters between a couple become doubt-producing, the individuals involved begin to feel low pot about themselves. They begin to look elsewhere—to work, to children, to other heterosexual partners. If a husband and wife begin to have sterile and lifeless encounters, they eventually become bored with one another. Boredom leads to indifference, which is probably one of the worst human feelings there is and, incidentally one of the real causes of divorce. I am convinced that anything exciting, even if it's dangerous, is preferable to boredom. Fighting is better than being bored. You might get killed from it, but at least you feel alive while it's going on.

If, on the other hand, communication between a couple produces something new and interesting, then aliveness and/or new life comes into being; there develops a deepening, fulfilling relationship, and each feels better about himself and the other.

I hope that now after the many exercises you have experienced, my earlier words about the communication process will have more meaning: *communication is the greatest single factor affecting a person's health and his relationship to others.*

FOR DISCUSSION

1. Satir says that "communication is the largest single factor determining what kinds of relationships he makes with others and what happens to him in the world about him." Do you find this to be true on the basis of your own experiences? In what specific ways does communication enter your interpersonal relationships?

2. Which of your communication patterns, habits, or tendencies would you like to change? How might you go about effecting such changes?

3. Satir illustrates the sensory message, the brain's interpretation of it, and the consequent feelings and feelings about the feelings. Illustrate this same sequence with an example from your own experience. What are some of the implications of this sequence of events?

4. Try one of the games or experiences which Satir discusses and explain the insights that such an experience may encourage. As an exercise for the entire class, break up into small groups or dyads and perform one of the exercises suggested by Satir. After completing the exercise each group should report to the entire class a description of the exercise performed, the difficulties (if any) experienced, and the insights derived as a result of participating in this exercise.

5. Explain the difference between descriptive and judgmental or evaluative language from a purely lingistic perspective and from an interpersonal communication perspective; that is, describe the differences between these two kinds of statements and explain the implications of these differences for interpersonal communication.

How to Communicate Effectively

J. S. Bois

1. Accept the other as one whom you have to take as he is, whether you like it or not. Take into account—as facts that you cannot change at the moment—his values, purposes, opinions, feelings, etc., inasmuch as you know them at the start, and inasmuch as you will understand them to remain rigid or fluctuate in the course of the encounter.

2. Expect and invite the other to express freely his feelings, purposes, values, fears, doubts, information, interpretations, etc., that are related to the situation in focus. Help him reveal himself as he reacts semantically, from moment to moment, within his space-time world of values.

3. Express your own semantic reactions* in a similar manner, using the pronoun 'I' as the subject of your statements, and making clear that all such statements are subject to elaborations and corrections in the light of whatever the encounter will develop to be.

4. Keep in a felt contact with each other, making the exchange of information and views a secondary activity, guided by a companionable feeling mood and couched in words that help enhance that friendly feeling mood.

5. Do not evaluate critically the other person's views against your

* By semantic reaction Bois refers to a total reaction of the entire person—body and mind, emotion and intellect.

J. S. Bois, *Communication as Creative Experience* (Los Angeles, CA.: Viewpoints Institute, 1968.), pp. 24.

own as the standard of truth and wisdom, but take his views as a tentative standard against which you re-examine and re-evaluate your own opinions and feelings. By doing so, each of you will enrich his own range of vision and add new dimensions to his own structuring of the situation.

6. See the whole process as a dynamic cooperative encounter, not so much for the purpose of discovering some elusive 'objective' solution to a well defined problem, but as a joint attempt to reach a higher level of wisdom, together and singly.

7. Let each of you measure the success of the experience, not in terms of a victory for the individual views you held prior to this encounter, but in terms of the increase in mutual trust and willingness to help each other you have achieved by working together in a difficult and/or touchy situation.

FOR DISCUSSION

1. Which of Bois' suggestions do you find most difficult to follow? Why?

2. What do you suppose communication would be like if Bois' recommendations were followed? More specifically, how would your communications differ with, for example, your peers, your parents, your teachers?

Communication Blocks

Tom Greening and Dick Hobson

Clear communication is essential to sustain satisfying and effective relationships in all areas of life—personal, business, and social. We need to be able to say what we mean in a way that gets results. But most of us sometimes have trouble getting across what we really want to say to other people. We may wish to give or request advice, information, or instructions, or share a feeling, offer sympathy, or express a need. But blocks get in the way. Sometimes people don't hear us the way we want to be heard. Sometimes we can't get through because we don't have effective communication skills for a particular situation. Business partners split up, employees get fired, husbands and wives divorce, children run away from home, doctors get sued for malpractice, and the waitress forgets to bring you coffee because communication breaks down.

Actually, you are always communicating *something*, but it may not be what you want to communicate. Or it may be received by the other person differently from the way you intended. Communication involves a sender and a receiver. However, all too often the message sent is not the same as the message received. For good communication, both people must be good senders and receivers. It takes two to tango. It takes two to argue. It takes two to keep an angry silence going. The point is, communication is a shared problem. Either person can take steps to improve it.

• Don't withdraw into discouragement or righteousness when you have communication blocks. You *can* do something. Blaming yourself or the other

Reprinted with permission of Seaview Books from *Instant Relief: The Encyclopedia of Self Help* by Tom Greening, Ph.D. and Dick Hobson. Copyright © 1979 by Tom Greening, Ph.D. and Dick Hobson.

person won't help, but taking a new approach may, even if you have to do all the work in the beginning. Good communication skills tend to bring out the best in other people. Your partner can learn from you, even when not aware of the change that is happening.

• Try being more specific and personal in what you say. Speak for yourself; don't use vague generalizations about people in general.

• Pay attention to what is happening in the present moment within yourself, in the other person, and between the two of you. Do this even if the topic concerns the past, the future, or other people. Pay special attention to *feelings*—when they are overridden they cause serious communication blocks.

• Be sparing in making moralistic or evaluative judgments. Use them only when you really want to and need to, because they can turn your partner off even if they aren't aimed at him or her. Everyone has insecurities and guilts, and no one needs more judges and critics. If you do have criticisms to make, remember that to be effective you first have to get yourself taken seriously as an expert or trusted friend, and that takes communication.

• People usually want support, approval, and agreement. Be as generous with these as you can. Even if a person is determined to be pessimistic and self-critical, he or she may at least want some agreement, rather than opposition in the form of a pep talk. Don't become a yes-man, but don't neglect to give affirmation whenever you honestly can. It will make people open up to you and be more receptive to what you have to say.

• Take time and effort to know what you want to communicate. "Do not operate mouth until brain is in gear." Spontaneous, unrehearsed communication is a natural, necessary, and enjoyable part of daily life. But there are also times when you will do better if you dig deeper into yourself in privacy to discover what you want to convey. Particularly if people don't seem to understand you or take you seriously, you might consider whether you are speaking with conviction in a way that commands interest and respect.

• Give your partner time and "space" in which to communicate. Don't interrupt or complete his or her sentences. Make it clear that your intention is to communicate, not to make a speech, conduct a monologue, or win a debate. That takes real listening.

• Remember that feelings are facts. Your partner may feel differently from you because he or she sees things differently. You won't get anywhere arguing that the feelings are wrong, because the person is directly experiencing the reality of those feelings. Let your partner know you hear the feelings being expressed. Then go on to explore the causes of your different views and reactions, and to look for areas of agreement or compromise.

• Face the fact that the message you think you are receiving is not always the message sent. Repeat your partner's message back to him or her in your own words and ask if you've heard it correctly. This will clear up distortions, show that you are really trying to hear, and keep you from tuning out in order to prepare your rebuttal before the other person has finished talking.

• Ask yourself if your goal is to communicate or to win. Are you willing to put yourself out there as clearly as you can, let the other people respond, and hear them nondefensively? Or do you want to control, dominate, and manipulate? There may be times when you prefer to do these things for noble or ignoble reasons, but at least don't confuse them with communication. True communication involves the capacity to be open and effectively expressive to your feelings, ideas, values, wants, intentions, and requirements, without the use of "managed news" or force to get your way. If people seem to resist you or to hold back from communicating, you might do well to explore whether they see you as trying to win at their expense.

• Look at what you might be trying to win. It isn't just the actions of others that we try to control. Often we try to win a virtue contest. The relationship becomes a courtroom complete with judge, jury, prosecutor, defense attorney, witnesses, and evidence. Confessions must be extracted, guilt must be proven, and self-worth must be weighed. Unfortunately, with this approach, if one person wins, the other loses, and the relationship fails.

• Watch out for anger and covert resentment as barriers to communication. Silence often occurs because a person is afraid to erupt into anger or to risk triggering it. Shouting and threats of physical violence can easily overload a relationship—avoid them if you can. But that doesn't mean you should suppress anger altogether. You may need to clear the air by venting some anger, or allowing some to be blasted at you. Overprotectiveness of yourself or your partner can dam up the flow of expression to the point where you also can't say positive things.

• When you are in the process of getting anger out in the open, in a quarrel or a blunt confrontation, remember that anger also conceals vulnerability, fear, and hurt. Try to listen for those feelings too, in yourself and in the other. Shift over to a compassionate concern for the feelings when the timing seems right. Think of a raging lion with a thorn in its foot and look for the thorn.

• If you feel courageous and can find people you trust enough to play rough with, try this method: Agree that for a specified period of time you are going to suspend the normal rules of politeness, tact, consideration, fairness, and even truth. Say whatever you want, no matter how exaggerated, distorted, unfair, insulting, or inflammatory. Let it all hang out. Do this only if you have confidence that you and whomever you do it with will be able to take it in the spirt of a constructive exercise, rather than carrying it on into "real life" with hurt feelings and grudges. This kind of experiment can open up issues that can later be explored more sanely.

• Own up to the secret payoffs you may be getting by not communicating clearly. Maybe you feel you have more to lose than to gain by opening up. "Better to keep one's mouth shut and be thought a fool than to open it and remove all doubt." Perhaps you remain distant and aloof to maintain a sense of your superiority. Perhaps you fear the consequences of getting close to someone.

• Don't give mixed messages, at least not if you expect to be understood. Contradictory messages can be confusing and even demoralizing to other people. Of course, we always communicate in several different ways at different levels. There is more going on than the literal meaning of our words. Along with the message, there a message about the message. The second message can be conveyed by tone of voice, facial expression, or body language. Usually this message fits, is congruent with the literal message. Other times it is incongruent—for example. "I am not angry," said with gritted teeth, or "Okay, have it your way," said sarcastically. These messages put the receiver in a conflict. To which message should you respond? What can you do? If you are getting a double message, point out both messages. If you are giving a message, make your implicit message explicit.

• Be clear about limits and requirements, and the consequences if they are not met. Don't work at being nice, nondirective, sympathetic, or tolerant when what you really need to do is set someone straight about your true feelings and intentions. It is not fair or effective to lull people into a false impression of you as a mouse and then suddenly roar at them like a lion. Parents sometimes have this trouble in disciplining children, and people raised in a strict religious environment sometimes also have difficulty being appropriately tough. You don't have to become a monster—just an honest person who bends only so far. Give people a fair warning of your limits, and be consistent about your requirements so they can learn what you are like.

• Take a course or a home-study program in communications skills. Join a group like Toastmasters where you will be able to practice public speaking in a supportive setting. The Dale Carnegie course has been popular for many years and has been continually updated with modern training methods. Find a congenial discussion group on a topic that interests you. Set aside time with someone close to you during which you agree to work conscientiously on deepening your communication and providing each other with feedback.

• Take a look at the "response modes" you use and the results they produce for you. Professor Gerald Goodman at UCLA has developed a way of looking at communication that focuses on six response modes, or what he calls various kinds of "helping-talk": question, advisement, spacing, reflection of feelings, interpretation, and self-disclosure. Become aware of what these ways of talking are, when you use them, and how they affect the conversation.

QUESTIONS

Closed-ended questions ("What time is it?") are useful for getting specific information. In helping communication, open-ended questions ("How was your day?") are usually more useful. Questions are often used to disguise a command or piece of advice ("Don't you think the door needs closing?" instead of "Please close the door"). If you are overusing questions and obscuring what you really mean, try sending more direct messages.

ADVISEMENT

When people ask for help, they usually expect advice. But advice is often rejected. Receiving advice makes some people feel put down. So be cautious if you do give advice. Make sure you really understand the other's concern. Reflect their feelings back to them. Ask yourself if you are really competent to give advice. If you give advice, give clear support for it and avoid focusing on the other's personality. Most people can choose their own solutions.

SPACING

Silence can be golden. Give your partner time to pause and think. Verbal crowding and interrupting are two of the worst causes of problems in communication. They are small behaviors that eventually produce big difficulties.

REFLECTION OF FEELINGS

This is the most underused but probably the most helpful aid to communication. Reflect feelings back by stating in your own words the essence of the feeling in the other's message. For example, someone might say to you, "I don't know what to do. Whichever way I go could be disastrous." You could day, "I guess you're feeling cornered." Reflections make people feel understood. Make your reflections crisp and concise. Sometimes people repeat their message over and over again, getting louder each time. This means that they don't feel their message is getting through to you. Reflect their feelings. They will feel understood and go on to say something new.

INTERPRETATION

This classifies or explains behavior. It is usually overused. Focus on understanding the other person, rather than giving explanations. Do not label or pigeonhole.

SELF-DISCLOSURE

Use "me-too" disclosures to convey empathy: "Hey, I had that feeling too when I . . ." Self-disclosures are about immediate here-and-now experiences; they are very useful for solving communication difficulties. If you are confused, for example, tell your partner. If what he or she says touches you deeply, share that.

Use this framework to see communication more clearly and give yourself more options to choose from.

FOR DISCUSSION

1. Recall a recent communication block from your own experience. Describe its development, the way it was maintained, and its effects. Using the suggestions of Greening and Hobson, what could you have done to improve the communication and the relationship?

2. Select one of your close relationships and analyze your own communication behavior for the six response modes discussed by Greening and Hobson. Write down these response modes and the specific ways in which you use them. After you have done this—in detail—ask your relationship partner to comment on your use of each response mode. (It would be best to have your partner read Greening and Hobson's discussion of these modes rather than for you to explain them.) Do you and your partner see your behavior differently? The same? In what ways might your communication behaviors be improved?

3. Which of the suggestions of Greening and Hobson do you find most difficult to deal with? Why?

4. Develop a plan for "communication improvement" based on the suggestions of Greening and Hobson. How are you going to implement this program? Be as specific as possible.

Communication
Motivations

James C. McCroskey and Lawrence R. Wheeless

Dave, Kellie, Mark, and Ruth are the planning committee for the dance that their coed dorm intends to sponsor during registration week for the second semester. Their meeting has already begun. Let's listen in for a bit.

Kellie: *Since we have so little money, we have to decide whether to spend most of it on the band or get a cheaper band and more refreshments.*

Mark: *I'm for a better band; we can bring our own "refreshments."*

Kellie: *What do you think, Ruth?*

Ruth: *I'm not sure.*

Kellie: *Maybe we should determine first how much bands cost. Dave, you were going to look into that. What did you find out?*

Dave: *I didn't get around to it.*

Mark: *How the hell are we going to make a decision when we don't know what everything costs? Man, we only asked you to do one thing, and you didn't even do that!*

Dave (to Mark)**:** *Why don't you bug off . . .*

Kellie: *Please, Dave. That won't help us make a decision. Mark, we know we can get some kind of band for about $150. Why don't we figure on using $150 to $200 on the band?*

Dave (aside to Ruth)**:** *We ought to tell them to stick that dance in their ear. Who wants to spend a whole evening with a bunch of dorm freaks anyhow?*

From James C. McCroskey and Lawrence Wheeless, *Introduction to Human Communication* (Boston: Allyn & Bacon, 1976), pp. 71–91.

> **Ruth:** *What time is it?*
>
> **Mark:** *I guess that would be okay, Kellie. But you had better check soon to see if we can get a good band for that money.*
>
> **Kellie:** *Is that our decision then?*
>
> **Dave:** *Okay by me. Who cares anyway?*
>
> **Mark:** *Yeah, that's okay.*
>
> **Ruth:** *(silence).*
>
> **Kellie:** *What do you think Ruth?*
>
> **Ruth:** *I don't know. Does anybody know what time I am supposed to register?*

Our dance committee has just engaged in "communication." The outcome may or may not be satisfactory to the other inhabitants of the dorm; that remains to be seen. The outcome, however, was probably not equally satisfactory to all of the members of the committee, because each was motivated in disparate ways and each communicated differently within the group. These problems can be attributed in large part to differences in motivations of the individuals.

To communicate or not to communicate is *not* the question. To be human is almost synonomous with "to communicate." But all human beings do not communicate to the same degree, as we saw in our committee meeting above. Some people are involved in communicating from the moment they get up in the morning until the moment they go to bed at night. Other people are involved in very few communication experiences in a given day. Communication is a constant for all human beings, but the *amount* of communicating that a person does is highly variable from one human being to another. In this chapter we will examine some of the variables that account for the amount of communication in which various people engage.

THE MOTIVATION TO COMMUNICATE

A sizable portion of our total communication experience in a given day is initiated by people other than ourselves. Frequently we have little choice about whether or not we communicate. Someone walks into our room or our office and asks us a question. We must communicate in return, even if all we do is ignore the other person. That behavior in itself will certainly communicate. Nevertheless, we do exert considerable control over the extent to which we communicate. In some instances we may choose to communicate and other instances we may choose not to. The question posed here is why we act in some cases while in others we do not.

Our choice of whether or not to communicate is normally based upon our projection of the outcome of communicating in the given instance. Generally, if we predict that the outcome will be to our advantage, we will choose to communicate. If our projection is negative, however, we will be more likely to avoid communication. The outcomes with which we are concerned are affinity, information or understanding, influence, decision, and confirmation.

Affinity

Affinity between two people is often a desired outcome of communication. If person A likes and respects person B, then person A has affinity for person B. Most of us have an inner need for warm relationships with other people. We do not want to be isolated from our fellow human beings. Consequently, we often seek to communicate with other people in order to establish such affinity relationships with them. Some people have less need for affinity than others, and they will probably seek less communication on a social level than will people with higher affinity needs. In our committee meeting Mark exhibited a fairly low affinity need when he snapped at Dave. Dave snapped back, but evidenced some need for affinity by turning to Ruth for support. Of course, he didn't get it. Some people have extremely high affinity needs, and they may try excessively hard to communicate with other people. Such excessive needs can result in overexuberance, the "trying too hard" syndrome, or the "yes man," communication pattern. It has been estimated that between 50 and 90 percent of all interpersonal communication exists primarily because of the participants' motivation to seek affinity with one another. Even when other outcomes may be the principle ones desired in a communication relationship, seldom is affinity completely irrelevant to the relationship. Even Walter Cronkite wants to be loved.

Information or Understanding

It has been said that "knowledge is power." In many cases this may be true. To know that the stock market will go up gives us the power to make money quickly. In other cases, whether knowledge is power or not, knowledge is necessary. Consequently, when we need information to understand something or to make a decision, this need is very likely to motivate us to communicate to obtain that information. Our committee chairwoman evidenced this need when she turned to Dave to ask about the cost of bands. Mark also indicated that he felt this need when he snapped at Dave because he couldn't provide the information requested. The need for information is a common motivator behind communication. Students come to class and/or read textbooks (at least in some instances), because they feel a need for information or understanding. We read the newspaper and watch television in order to find out about what is going on in the world. In short, we often talk to other people or read their works in order to obtain information, and other people may seek to talk with us or read our work in order to obtain information they feel they need.

Influence

As we have emphasized throughout this book, change is an important outcome of communication. We often wish to change the attitudes or behaviors of other people, or to *influence* them. Human beings can control their own environment to some extent, but they must depend upon other human beings for cooperation to exercise efficient control over the environment to maintain the society in which we live. Primitive human beings often found the need to work together for a common purpose, necessitating one individual's influencing another individual's behavior.

The outcome of influence should not be confused with the motivation to manipulate. Although we may manipulate people when we are influencing them, manipulation is not a necessary condition of influence. The outcome of influence merely means to change the attitude or behavior of another individual. That change may be in the interests of the other person, in the interest of ourselves, or in the mutual interests of both parties. It is an outcome that is essential in contemporary society.

In our committee meeting, Kellie appeared to have a strong need to influence. She took over the meeting right away and attempted to direct the group to a decision by making statements and asking for agreement. In the end, her decision was the one the group accepted. Earlier, however, Mark attempted to influence the group in a different way—toward an expensive band—but that influence attempt seemed to have little or no impact. Both Dave and Ruth gave little evidence of a need to influence in the meeting. Dave seemed not to care, and Ruth hardly participated at all.

Decision

Whenever we are confronted with a choice, we must make a decision. In some cases we simply wish to have information that other people can provide us and other opinions prior to making our own decision. In other cases, we engage in communication with people so that we may reach a decision jointly. This outcome is a very common goal of small-group communication. Such was the case in our committee meeting. The group existed to decide how to handle the proposed dance.

Confirmation

After we make a decision it is common for us to seek communication with other people to be certain that our decision was the correct one. We seek confirmation from the opinions of other people and the information they can provide. You will recall that our committee decided to spend $150 to $200 on the band, but left Kellie with the responsibility of confirming that decision as a wise one later. Since Mark wanted a more expensive band, it is likely that he will try to confirm that the decision reached will result in having a good band without spending the extra money. To do this he will probably try to talk to people who have heard the band that is selected before to see if they like it.

When we choose from a variety of alternatives (better band or more refreshments), particularly when more than one of those alternatives is attractive, we are often disturbed by having had to reject one desirable alternative to accept another. (I can't afford both to travel to Europe this summer and return to school in the fall.) To reduce this psychological stress, we often communicate with other people to confirm that they would have made a similar choice had they been in our position.

In summary, the normal motivations to communicate focus on five major outcomes of human communication. The normal person needs affinity and information, wants to influence, needs to make decisions, and desires confirmation for past decisions. We communicate to fulfill these needs.

THE MOTIVATION *NOT* TO COMMUNICATE

As we have indicated, there are many reasons for a person to seek communication with other human beings. Nevertheless, some people engage in much less communication than others. In some instances, this reduced level of communication is normal and in other instances it is abnormal. Let us consider both.

Normal Withdrawal from Communication

The normal person will avoid communication under some circumstances. There are two conditions that are particularly likely to result in a reduced level of communication. The first is a desire to be left alone. Almost all of us have experienced the feeling that we simply wish to withdraw from communication at times. This may be expressed by taking a vacation away from our job or community and going somewhere where we don't know many people and few people are likely to initiate communication with us. This feeling is also evidenced by people who simply take their telephone off the hook for an hour or so. These behaviors are not unusual, and most of us engage in them at one time or another. We may even build our homes in such a way as to make this withdrawal behavior more plausible. We may build a study in our home where we can go and be away from everyone else for a period of time and avoid communication. Or we may simply go to our bedroom and lock the door.

Another normal reason for not initiating communication is to avoid disclosing something about ourselves. . . . At this point we will note only two important points. First, people have a need to disclose their feelings, worries, concerns, and aspirations to someone else. Such disclosure is highly related to the development of affinity between people. However, second, people normally engage in this kind of behavior with only a relatively small number of other people. While self-disclosure can help to develop warm, friendly relationships, opposite effects are also possible.

As we have noted before, information often is power. In some instances we may not wish to let another individual know too much about ourselves. In order to avoid disclosing information about ourselves to the other individual, we may withdraw from communication contact. In both this instance and the one noted above, the avoiding behavior should be considered normal. It is a kind of behavior we would expect most human beings to engage in at one time or another. It is the many people who seek to avoid communication for other reasons whose behavior is abnormal.

Before going further, we wish to clarify our use of the term *normal*.

Normal is a very relative concept. If we meet someone on the street who is walking along with a finger placed firmly in his or her left ear, and we see the person engaging in the same behavior day after day, we would conclude that the person is not behaving "normally." However, if in our culture almost everyone were to walk around with their finger in their ear, then the person who did not do that would be abnormal. In reference to communication behavior, then, *normal* is related to what most people in our culture do. *Abnormal* is the term we use to describe behavior that deviates from what most people do. Abnormal does not necessarily mean there is something wrong, but as we use it here it does have that connotation.

Abnormal Withdrawal from Communication

There are two personality characteristics that have been found to result in abnormal withdrawal from communication. The first is called "anomie" or "alienation." Anomie is a state marked by a failure to understand or accept society's norms and values. A person with this type of personality is likely to be inordinately insecure, and in extreme cases may even be suicidal. The person frequently has feelings of meaninglessness, powerlessness, aloneness, and hopelessness. In general, he or she tends to reject accepted norms and retreats from society. Many young people in the 1960s were alienated from the social and political systems. Some dropped out of school and society and sought fulfillment in rural, remote areas.

The norms of society with reference to communication are reflected in specific motivations, and the alienated individual tends to reject those motivations and withdraw from communication. Since the goals to be achieved by communication are not desirable to such an individual, things that would motivate the normal person to communicate have little or no effect on the alienated person. Although some research has suggested that this syndrome is more characteristic of people in low socioeconomic status groups in our society, it is important to note that the syndrome is present in the spectrum of socioeconomic classes. The anomic tendency is a personality characteristic that is not directly related to communication, but one that has a major impact on the communication behavior of the affected person. Communication is only one of many normal behaviors within a society that are rejected by this individual. When such a person does communicate it can be expected that the type of communication in which he or she engages would be sharply different from the communication behavior of others. But the most important characteristic of this individual with relation to communication is simple withdrawal. The alienated person is not motivated to communicate by the same things that impel others. Consequently, there is little reason to seek interaction with other people.

Alienation may be either a general personality characteristic, as we have considered it above, or it may apply to only a given group in which the individual finds her or himself, or even only to a given task. In our committee meeting, Dave showed strong signs of alienation. He had little interest in the decision to be made and expressed strongly negative feelings about the other people who live with him in the dorm. We can not tell whether Dave has an alienated personality or is just alienated from his dorm mates without observing his communication in many other settings. Ruth also gave some indication of alienation; she withdrew almost completely from the discussion. However, the hostility that accompanies alienation was not present, so it is more likely that the second personality characteristic that leads to withdrawal would apply in her case.

The second characteristic that leads individuals to avoid and withdraw from communication is *communication apprehension*. This characteristic has also been referred to by a number of other labels such as "speech fright," "stage fright," "speech anxiety," and "reticence." All of these labels apply to at least part of the characteristic that we refer to here as communication apprehension. The individual suffering from communication apprehension is a person for whom apprehension about participating in communication outweighs any projection of gain from communicating in a given situation. Such people are motivated to communicate by the same elements that motivate any other human being, which we have discussed previously, but they are blocked from acting upon that motivation by an apprehension about the communication act itself. The communication apprehensive individual anticipates negative feelings and outcomes from communication, and thus either avoids communication, if possible, or suffers from a variety of anxiety related feelings while communicating. Because of the extent of this characteristic within our society and its major impact on human communication behavior, we will consider this characteristic in more detail below.

THE NATURE AND EFFECTS OF COMMUNICATION APPREHENSION

At the outset, let us make it clear that communication apprehension has only to do with apprehension about communicating, either orally or in writing. It should not be confused with a generally anxious personality. Generally, anxiety and communication apprehension are not highly related (the correlation is about .30 between them). Thus, a person can be very normal in all other respects, but be highly apprehensive about communication. On the other hand, a person could be highly neurotic, afraid of her or his own shadow, and still not be a communication apprehensive.

You may be asking yourself at this point, "Why should I know about communication apprehension? I'm not a communication apprehensive." To begin with, the chances are about one in five that your *are*. Extensive research has indicated that between 10 and 20 percent of all college students suffer from extreme communication apprehension, and that the percentages are about the same in groups all the way from junior high school students to senior citizens. But let us assume for the moment that you are not a communication apprehensive (chances are at least four out of five that our assumption is correct!). Why, then, should you be concerned?

Communication apprehension severely disrupts the communication of the person with the problem. It affects both source functions and receiver functions. Since the individual is disrupted, any communication system (dyad, small group, organization) of which the person is a part is also disrupted. Recall our committee meeting. Ruth gave every indication of being a communication apprehensive. What did she contribute to the group? Whatever good ideas she may have had were not shared with the group. The decision was not better as a result of her being in the group. She might as well have stayed in her room. Have you ever been in a group with a Ruth? Odds are that you have been in many. Ruth and other communication apprehensives may have as much to offer as anyone else in the group (there is no correlation between communication apprehension and intelligence), but they don't offer it. Thus, the product of our group with Ruth's input is not as good as it could be.

Communication apprehension leads to ineffective encoding by the individual when she or he is functioning as a source. Since the person is more concerned with the anxiety associated with communication than with the outcome of the communication, encoding choices may be made on the basis of avoiding anxiety rather than enhancing the probability of the desired outcome. The most common manifestation of this feeling is withdrawal, or noncommunication. Simply put, the person doesn't talk. Communication apprehension can also have a negative impact on the communicator as a receiver. If the individual is concerned about having to perform as a source, this may dominate the individual's thinking so that she or he cannot properly function as a receiver either.

Communication apprehension is a pervasive characteristic that has implications for all types of communication systems. It appears that it may be more severe in some settings than in others, but severely apprehensive individuals are affected by communication apprehension whenever they are involved in any kind of communication, particularly where they may have to serve as a source of communication. It should be stressed here that communication apprehension is characteristic of all human beings, but to varying degrees for individual human beings. Almost everyone feels some apprehension when confronted by a very formal communication demand, such as formal public speaking. The type of person that we label here a communication apprehensive will, however, feel much more apprehension in such settings than will the normal person, and even more importantly, will feel considerable apprehension even in very informal communication, such as an interview for a job, an interaction among a small group, or even talking with one or two friends.

We have already noted that the main behavioral outcome of communication apprehension is a withdrawal from communication. But we need to explain what is meant by "withdrawal." In some cases withdrawal is very obvious, such as the person who refuses to give a public speech, or, someone like Ruth, who won't talk in a small group. Other withdrawal symptoms are less obvious, and in some cases are almost unnoticed by the average person. For example, communication apprehensive individuals tend to select a different type of housing than will less apprehensive individuals. When given a free choice, the high apprehensive will choose housing that provides the least opportunity for people to impose communication demands on her or him. For example, in a dormitory setting the high apprehensive will usually choose to live at the end of a hallway, out of the mainstream of social interaction on the dorm floor, and away from stairwells that would cause people to have to pass by his or her room. Less apprehensive people, on the other hand, are prone to seek rooms where interaction is more likely—near an entrance, near a communal rest room or near the stairwell. Similarly, in a housing or apartment complex the highly apprehensive individual will prefer houses that are removed from social interaction points in the development, such as playgrounds or washing facilities, while less apprehensive individuals will seek such busy interaction as well as preferring backyards that connect with those of other people so that "talking over the fence" is easy.

As indicated in Figure 1, in a small group setting there are often seating positions where the apprehensive person will not have to engage in as much communication as he or she would in other seats. Notice where Ruth chose to sit. Her behavior was typical of the high apprehensive. Kellie's choice was typical of the low apprehensive, as was Mark's. The high apprehensive will also normally avoid seating positions where leadership would be expected, such as at the head or foot of the table, whereas less apprehensive people tend to gravitate to those seats.

The kind of behavior we have been describing in the last two paragraphs is probably unconsciously motivated for the most part. Neither the high nor the low apprehensive is likely to make low conflict choices with full awareness of the implications. Nevertheless, these choices are made and an environment is created that reduces the amount of communication the high apprehensive will be forced into.

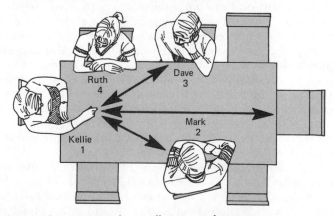

FIGURE 1. Interaction patterns in small groups. Arrows indicate most frequent interaction patterns for all seats. Numbers indicate the amount of leadership expected for the occupied seats.

No matter how hard the communication apprehensive individual tries, of course, she or he will have to engage in some communication in our modern society. Observation of such people in interaction settings, however, indicates that these individuals will still talk far less than will less apprehensive individuals. This pattern holds true whether we are talking about a dyadic relationship, a small-group communication relationship, or any other communication system. Further, when highly apprehensive individuals do communicate they evidence much more tension in their interaction than do less apprehensive individuals. In addition, the contributions made by highly apprehensive individuals tend to display less interest in the topic under discussion and to be less relevant to the subject being discussed than do the contributions of less apprehensive individuals. Recall Ruth's behavior in the meeting. When Dave tried to get her involved in a side interaction, she simply asked what time it was. When she was asked to concur with the group's decision, she expressed her concern for her registration schedule. Such reactions tend to discourage others from seeking further communication with the apprehensive, whereas directly relevant comments can result in responses of disagreement or questions that pressure the apprehensive to talk even more.

It has also been found that in dyads and small groups highly apprehensive individuals tend to take less risk in their communication with other people and to avoid disclosing information about themselves more than do less apprehensive individuals. Such people are harder to get to know, and, thus, are harder to communicate with than less apprehensive individuals. Consequently, the probability of ineffective communication is much higher with communication apprehensive individuals than with more normal people.

After having read the descriptions of how high apprehensives behave in communication, if you suspect that you may be a high apprehensive, or are simply curious about your own level of apprehension, we suggest that you fill out the following two questionnaires. The first is the "Personal Report of Communication Apprehension." The PRCA is designed to measure your level of apprehension about oral communication. The "Writing Apprehension Test" is designed to measure your level of apprehension about writing. Both the PRCA and the WAT have been extensively tested and used in numerous research studies. If you score (instructions for scoring are below) above 75 on the PRCA or above 60 on the WAT, this is an indication of some communication apprehension. But unless your score is above 88 on the PRCA or above 72 on the WAT, you are probably not a high communication apprehensive.

Should your score on either questionnaire suggest that you may be a high communication apprehensive, we suggest that you seek help to overcome this problem. If your English, Speech, or Communication department has a program for helping people with communication apprehension, you should seek help there first. If no such program is available, you should check with your school's counseling service. Most colleges and universities have people in their counseling service who are trained professionals who can provide systematic desensitization or whatever other treatment might be most appropriate. The decision to seek help, if you have this problem, may be the most important decision you ever make. Quite literally, it may change your whole life.

Scoring the PRCA and WAT

To compute your PRCA score, follow these 3 steps.

1. Add up your scores for items 1, 3, 5, 8, 9, 10, 12, 13, 15, 16, 19, 20, 22, and 24.

2. Add up your scores for items 2, 4, 6, 7, 11, 14, 17, 18, 21, 23, and 25.

3. Complete the following formula:
PRCA Score = 84 − (total from step 1) + (total from step 2)

To compute your WAT score, follow these 3 steps.

1. Add up your scores for items 1, 4, 5, 10, 13, 18, 19, and 20.

2. Add your scores for items 2, 3, 6, 7, 8, 9, 11, 12, 14, 15, 16, and 17.

3. Complete the following formula:
WAT Score = 48 − (total from step 1) + (total from step 2)

PRCA

DIRECTIONS: This instrument is composed of twenty-five statements concerning feelings about communicating with other people. Please indicate the degree to which each statement applies to you by marking whether you (1) Strongly Agree, (2) Agree, (3) Are Undecided, (4) Disagree, or (5) Strongly Disagree with each statement. There are no right or wrong answers. Work quickly, just record your first impression.

		SA	A	UN	D	SD
1.	While participating in a conversation with a new acquaintance I feel very nervous.	1	2	3	4	5
2.	I have no fear of facing an audience.	1	2	3	4	5
3.	I talk less because I'm shy.	1	2	3	4	5
4.	I look forward to expressing my opinions at meetings.	1	2	3	4	5
5.	I am afraid to express myself in a group.	1	2	3	4	5
6.	I look forward to an opportunity to speak in public.	1	2	3	4	5
7.	I find the prospect of speaking mildly pleasant.	1	2	3	4	5
8.	When communicating, my posture feels strained and unnatural.	1	2	3	4	5
9.	I am tense and nervous while participating in group discussion.	1	2	3	4	5
10.	Although I talk fluently with friends I am at a loss for words on the platform.	1	2	3	4	5
11.	I have no fear about expressing myself in a group.	1	2	3	4	5
12.	My hands tremble when I try to handle objects on the platform.	1	2	3	4	5
13.	I always avoid speaking in public if possible.	1	2	3	4	5
14.	I feel that I am more fluent when talking to people than most other people are.	1	2	3	4	5
15.	I am fearful and tense all the while I am speaking before a group of people.	1	2	3	4	5
16.	My thoughts become confused and jumbled when I speak before an audience.	1	2	3	4	5
17.	I like to get involved in group discussions.	1	2	3	4	5

18.	Although I am nervous just before getting up, I soon forget my fears and enjoy the experience.	1	2	3	4	5
19.	Conversing with people who hold positions of authority causes me to be fearful and tense.	1	2	3	4	5
20.	I dislike to use my body and voice expressively.	1	2	3	4	5
21.	I feel relaxed and comfortable while speaking.	1	2	3	4	5
22.	I feel self-conscious when I am called upon to answer a question or give an opinion in class.	1	2	3	4	5
23.	I face the prospect of making a speech with complete confidence.	1	2	3	4	5
24.	I'm afraid to speak up in conversations.	1	2	3	4	5
25.	I would enjoy presenting a speech on a local television show.	1	2	3	4	5

WAT[1]

Directions: Below are a series of statements about writing. There are no right or wrong answers to these statements. Please indicate the degree to which each statement applies to you by marking whether you (1) Strongly Agree, (2) Agree, (3) Are Uncertain, (4) Disagree, or (5) Strongly Disagree with the statement. While some of these statements may seem repetitious, take your time and try to be as honest as possible.

		SA	A	UN	D	SD
1.	I avoid writing.	1	2	3	4	5
2.	I have no fear of my writing being evaluated.	1	2	3	4	5
3.	I look forward to writing down my ideas.	1	2	3	4	5
4.	My mind seems to go blank when I start to work on a composition.	1	2	3	4	5
5.	Expressing ideas through writing seems to be a waste of time.	1	2	3	4	5
6.	I would enjoy submitting my writing to magazines for evaluation and publication.	1	2	3	4	5
7.	I like to write my ideas down.	1	2	3	4	5
8.	I feel confident in my ability to clearly express my ideas in writing.	1	2	3	4	5
9.	I like to have my friends read what I have written.	1	2	3	4	5
10.	I'm nervous about writing.	1	2	3	4	5
11.	People seem to enjoy what I write.	1	2	3	4	5
12.	I enjoy writing.	1	2	3	4	5
13.	I never seem to be able to clearly write down my ideas.	1	2	3	4	5
14.	Writing is a lot of fun.	1	2	3	4	5
15.	I like seeing my thoughts on paper.	1	2	3	4	5
16.	Discussing my writing with others is an enjoyable experience.	1	2	3	4	5
17.	It's easy for me to write good compositions.	1	2	3	4	5
18.	I don't think I write as well as most other people.	1	2	3	4	5
19.	I don't like my compositions to be evaluated.	1	2	3	4	5
20.	I'm no good at writing.	1	2	3	4	5

[1]The WAT was developed and validated by our former colleagues, John A. Daly and Michael D. Miller. We are grateful to them for allowing us to include this instrument in our book.

Since the communication apprehension phenomenon has a major impact on the communication behavior of individuals, it might be expected that this would have an impact on the way people are perceived as a result of their communication. Research has confirmed this expectation. Communication apprehensive people are much less likely to be perceived as leaders by their peers. They are viewed as less competent, less sociable, and less extroverted by their peers. They also are seen as less composed, less task-attractive, less socially attractive, and in some cases even less physically attractive. They are perceived as less desirable dates and potential marriage partners. In short, the highly communication apprehensive individual engages in less communication and as a result is perceived in a generally negative way by other individuals, whether these other people are communication apprehensives themselves or whether they are more normal.

> Can you distinguish between high and low communication apprehensives in terms of:
> the amount of communication attempted
> choice of housing
> choice of seat in a small group setting
> their interaction behaviors
> the ways they are perceived by others?

The causes of communication apprehension are not yet fully known; however, the characteristic has not been related to heredity. Rather, it is produced in the individual by the environment in which he or she grows and matures. The best explanation for the existence of the communication apprehension syndrome that has been advanced to date is one of "patterned conditioning." It is thought that communication apprehension is developed from early childhood by the process of reinforcement. If a child is not reinforced for communicating with his or her parents, peers, or teachers, it is likely that the child will develop communication apprehension. This development may in itself be reinforced by rewarding the child for not communicating. The home in which a child is told to be quiet and not talk at the dinner table is a good example. The talkative child may be likely to be punished rather than rewarded for attempting to initiate communication whereas the quiet child may be reinforced for that behavior. The quiet child in our culture is much more likely to be described as "well behaved." This is true both in the home and in the school.

Considerable research has been done in the area of communication apprehension to determine how extensive the problem is. The results of these investigations indicate that probably between 10 and 20 percent of the American population suffers from severe, debilitating communication apprehension; that is, the normal functioning and communicating of these individuals is severely restricted by their high apprehension about communication. Further, it is estimated that an additional 20 percent of the population suffers from communication apprehension to a degree substantial enough to interfere to some extent with their normal functioning.

In short, communication apprehension is probably the most common handicap that is suffered by people in contemporary American society. Unfortunately, this handicap is generally ignored in schools, both at lower levels and all the way through college. Relatively few attempts have been made to develop methods for overcoming the problem and freeing individuals from communication apprehension. The most commonly employed methods are used in speech and English classes. Unfortunately, the approach operates from the faulty assumption that people are anxious about speaking or writing situations because they do not have the knowledge or experience about communication that will permit them to relax and communicate normally. Thus the "treatment" commonly involves requiring the student to give a number of public speeches after instruction in speech making, or writing a number of compositions after instruction in composition. While this approach is very helpful to people who are not severely handicapped by communication apprehension, it is much more likely to make the problem more severe for the highly apprehensive individual. Since the apprehensive is most likely to communicate ineffectively in this demanding setting, it will simply be another unrewarding, failure experience which will further condition the individual to be apprehensive about communicating rather than easing the stress connected with communicating. An awareness of this flaw in speech and composition training has been increasing in higher education over the past decade, but is as yet generally unrecognized at secondary and elementary levels.

Alternative methods for helping people who suffer from severe communication apprehension have been explored more vigorously in recent years. Several methods have been found to be helpful, most notably a behavior therapy known as *systematic desensitization.* Research has indicated that between 80 and 90 percent of the people severely handicapped by communication apprehension can be helped to a major extent, or even cured, by this particular treatment. Of course, neither this nor any other single treatment method is a magical "sure-cure." Different people need to be helped in different ways. Unfortunately, few English, Speech, or Communication departments in higher education are equipped to provide the help with communication apprehension that their students need. Until such help is made readily available to all those who need and want it, a very large proportion of our population will continue to suffer from communication apprehension, and, as a result, they and we will suffer from the loss of effective communication with them.

When involved in almost any communication system, we must keep in mind that there are a large number of communication apprehensives around us, even if we are not highly apprehensive ourselves. While most people are motivated to seek communication with others to achieve certain desired outcomes (affinity, information or understanding, influence, decision making, confirmation), communication apprehensives are primarily motivated by their desire to avoid communication. In short, many of the people with whom we are motivated to communicate do not share our motivations. When we are trying to communicate with a person who is a high apprehensive, we must take care to avoid projecting our motivations on the other person. If we are to communicate successfully we must try to make our communication with the other person as nonthreatening as possible. To the extent that we can succeed in that attempt, we can create an atmosphere where a person can communicate without apprehension blocking those essential efforts.

FOR DISCUSSION

1. Do the reasons offered by McCroskey and Wheeless accounting for the motivation to communicate adequately and accurately describe your own communication motivations? Can you think of examples that would not be covered by affinity, information or understanding, influence, decision, and conformation?

2. Take both apprehension tests and analyze your scores. If you come out to be a high communication apprehensive discuss this with your instructor.

3. Analyze your own communication behavior in terms of apprehension. Can you detect any attempts to avoid communication along the lines suggested by McCroskey and Wheeless?

Defensive Communication

Jack R. Gibb

One way to understand communication is to view it as a people process rather than as a language process. If one is to make fundamental improvement in communication, he must make changes in interpersonal relationships. One possible type of alteration—and the one with which this paper is concerned—is that of reducing the degree of defensiveness.

DEFINITION AND SIGNIFICANCE

Defensive behavior is defined as that behavior which occurs when an individual perceives threat or anticipates threat in the group. The person who behaves defensively, even though he also gives some attention to the common task, devotes an appreciable portion of his energy to defending himself. Besides talking about the topic, he thinks about how he appears to others, how he may be seen more favorably, how he may win, dominate, impress, or escape punishment, and/or how he may avoid or mitigate a perceived or an anticipated attack.

Such inner feelings and outward acts tend to create similarly defensive postures in others; and, if unchecked, the ensuing circular response becomes increasingly destructive. Defensive behavior, in short, engenders defensive listening, and this in turn produces postural, facial, and verbal cues which raise the defense level of the original communicator.

Defense arousal prevents the listener from concentrating upon the message. Not only do defensive communicators send off multiple value, motive, and affect cues, but also defensive recipients distort what they

From *Journal of Communication*, (1961): 141–48. Reprinted by permission of the author and the International Communication Association.

receive. As a person becomes more and more defensive, he becomes less and less able to perceive accurately the motives, the values, and the emotions of the sender. The writer's analyses of tape recorded discussions revealed that increases in defensive behavior were correlated positively with losses in efficiency in communication.[1] Specifically, distortions became greater when defensive states existed in the groups.

The converse, moreover, also is true. The more "supportive" or defense reductive the climate the less the receiver reads into the communication distorted loadings which arise from projections of his own anxieties, motives, and concerns. As defenses are reduced, the receivers become better able to concentrate upon the structure, the content, and the cognitive meanings of the message.

CATEGORIES OF DEFENSIVE AND SUPPORTIVE COMMUNICATION

In working over an eight-year period with recordings of discussions occurring in varied settings, the writer developed the six pairs of defensive and supportive categories presented in Table 1. Behavior which a listener perceives as possessing any of the characteristics listed in the left-hand column arouses defensiveness, whereas that which he interprets as having any of the qualities designated as supportive reduces defensive feelings. The degree to which these reactions occur depends upon the personal level of defensiveness and upon the general climate in the group at the time.[2]

Evaluation and Description

Speech or other behavior which appears evaluative increases defensiveness. If by expression, manner of speech, tone of voice, or verbal content the sender seems to be evaluating or judging the listener, then the receiver goes on guard. Of course, other factors may inhibit the reaction. If the listener thought that the speaker regarded him as an equal and was being open and spontaneous, for example, the evaluativeness in a message would be neutralized and perhaps not even perceived. This same principle applies equally to the other five categories of potentially defense-producing climates. The six sets are interactive.

Because our attitudes toward other persons are frequently, and often necessarily, evaluative, expressions which the defensive person will regard as nonjudgmental are hard to frame. Even the simplest question usually conveys the answer that the sender wishes or implies the response that would fit into his value system. A mother, for example, immediately

[1] J. R. Gibb, "Defense Level and Influence Potential in Small Groups," in *Leadership and Interpersonal Behavior*, eds. L. Petrullo and B. M. Bass (New York: Holt, Rinehart and Winston, Inc., 1961), pp. 66–81.

[2] J. R. Gibb, "Sociopsychological Processes of Group Instruction," in *The Dynamics of Instructional Groups*, ed. N. B. Henry (Fifty-ninth Yearbook of the National Society for the Study of Education, Part II, 1960), pp. 115–35.

Table 1. Categories of behavior characteristic of supportive and defensive climates in small groups

Defensive climates	Supportive climates
1. Evaluation	1. Description
2. Control	2. Problem orientation
3. Strategy	3. Spontaneity
4. Neutrality	4. Empathy
5. Superiority	5. Equality
6. Certainty	6. Provisionalism

following an earth tremor that shook the house, sought for her small son with the question: "Bobby, where are you?" The timid and plaintive "Mommy, I didn't do it" indicated how Bobby's chronic mild defensiveness predisposed him to react with a projection of his own guilt and in the context of his chronic assumption that questions are full of accusation.

Anyone who has attempted to train professionals to use information-seeking speech with neutral affect appreciates how difficult it is to teach a person to say even the simple "who did that?" without being seen as accusing. Speech is so frequently judgmental that there is a reality base for the defensive interpretations which are so common.

When insecure, group members are particularly likely to place blame, to see others as fitting into categories of good or bad, to make moral judgments of their colleagues, and to question the value, motive, and affect loadings of the speech which they hear. Since value loadings imply a judgment of others, a belief that the standards of the speaker differ from his own causes the listener to become defensive.

Descriptive speech, in contrast to that which is evaluative, tends to arouse a minimum of uneasiness. Speech acts which the listener perceives as genuine requests for information or as material with neutral loadings is descriptive. Specifically, presentations of feelings, events, perceptions, or processes which do not ask or imply that the receiver change behavior or attitude are minimally defense producing. The difficulty in avoiding overtone is illustrated by the problems of news reporters in writing stories about unions, communists, Negroes, and religious activities without tipping off the "party" line of the newspaper. One can often tell from the opening words in a news article which side the newspaper's editorial policy favors.

Control and Problem Orientation

Speech which is used to control the listener evokes resistance. In most of our social intercourse someone is trying to do something to someone else—to change an attitude, to influence behavior, or to restrict the field of activity. The degree to which attempts to control produce defensiveness depends upon the openness of the effort, for a suspicion that hidden motives exist heightens resistance. For this reason attempts of nondirective therapists and progressive educators to refrain from imposing a set of values, a point of view, or a problem solution upon the receivers meet with many barriers. Since the norm is control, noncontrollers must earn the perceptions that their efforts have no hidden motives. A bombardment of persuasive "messages" in the fields of politics, education, special causes, advertising, religion, medicine, industrial relations, and guidance has bred cynical and paranoidal responses in listeners.

Implicit in all attempts to alter another person is the assumption by the change agent that the person to be altered is inadequate. That the speaker secretly views the listener as ignorant, unable to make his own decisions, uninformed, immature, unwise, or possessed of wrong or inadequate attitudes is a subconscious perception which gives the latter a valid base for defensive reactions.

Methods of control are many and varied. Legalistic insistence on detail, restrictive regulations and policies, conformity norms, and all laws are among the methods. Gestures, facial expressions, other forms of nonverbal communication, and even such simple acts as holding a door open in a particular manner are means of imposing one's will upon another and hence are potential sources of resistance.

Problem orientation, on the other hand, is the antithesis of persuasion. When the sender communicates a desire to collaborate in defining a mutual problem and in seeking its solution, he tends to create the same problem orientation in the listener; and, of greater importance, he implies that he has no predetermined solution, attitude, or method to impose. Such behavior is permissive in that it allows the receiver to set his own goals, make his own decisions, and evaluate his own progress—or to share with the sender in doing so. The exact methods of attaining permissiveness are not known, but they must involve a constellation of cues and they certainly go beyond mere verbal assurances that the communicator has no hidden desires to exercise control.

Strategy and Spontaneity

When the sender is perceived as engaged in a stratagem involving ambiguous and multiple motivations, the receiver becomes defensive. No one wishes to be a guinea pig, a role player, or an impressed actor, and no one likes to be the victim of some hidden motivation. That which is concealed, also, may appear larger than it really is with the degree of defensiveness of the listener determining the perceived size of the suppressed element. The intense reaction of the reading audience to the material in the *Hidden Persuaders* indicates the prevalence of defensive reactions to multiple motivations behind strategy. Group members who are seen as "taking a role," as feigning emotion, as toying with their colleagues, as withholding information, or as having special sources of data are especially resented. One participant once complained that another was "using a listening technique" on him!

A large part of the adverse reaction to much of the so-called human relations training is a feeling against what are perceived as gimmicks and tricks to fool or to "involve" people, to make a person think he is making his own decision, or to make the listener feel that the sender is genuinely interested in him as a person. Particularly violent reactions occur when it appears that someone is trying to make a stratagem appear spontaneous. One person has reported a boss who incurred resentment by habitually using the gimmick of "spontaneously" looking at his watch and saying, "My gosh, look at the time—I must run to an appointment." The belief was that the boss would create less irritation by honestly asking to be excused.

Similarly, the deliberate assumption of guilelessness and natural simplicity is especially resented. Monitoring the tapes of feedback and evaluation sessions in training groups indicates the surprising extent to which members perceive the strategies of their colleagues. This perceptual clarity may be quite shocking to the strategist, who usually feels that he has cleverly hidden the motivational aura around the "gimmick."

This aversion to deceit may account for one's resistance to politicians who are suspected of behind-the-scenes planning to get his vote, to psychologists whose listening apparently is motivated by more than the manifest or content-level interest in his behavior, or to the sophisticated, smooth, or clever person whose "oneupmanship" is marked with guile. In training groups the role-flexible person frequently is resented because his changes in behavior are perceived as strategic maneuvers.

In contrast, behavior which appears to be spontaneous and free of deception is defense reductive. If the communicator is seen as having a clean id, as having uncomplicated motivations, as being straightforward and honest, and as behaving spontaneously in response to the situation, he is likely to arouse minimal defense.

Neutrality and Empathy

When neutrality in speech appears to the listener to indicate a lack of concern for his welfare, he becomes defensive. Group members usually desire to be perceived as valued persons, as individuals of special worth, and as objects of concern and affection. The clinical, detached, person-is-an-object-of-study attitude on the part of many psychologist-trainers is resented by group members. Speech with low affect that communicates little warmth or caring is in such contrast with the affect-laden speech in social situations that it sometimes communicates rejection.

Communication that conveys empathy for the feelings and respect for the worth of the listener, however, is particularly supportive and defense reductive. Reassurance results when a message indicates that the speaker identifies himself with the listener's problems, shares his feelings, and accepts his emotional reactions at face value. Abortive efforts to deny the legitimacy of the receiver's emotions by assuring the receiver that he need not feel bad, that he should not feel rejected, or that he is overly anxious, though often intended as support giving, may impress the listener as lack of acceptance. The combination of understanding and empathizing with the other person's emotions with no accompanying effort to change him apparently is supportive at a high level.

The importance of gestural behavioral cues in communicating empathy should be mentioned. Apparently spontaneous facial and bodily evidences of concern are often interpreted as especially valid evidence of deep-level acceptance.

Superiority and Equality

When a person communicates to another that he feels superior in position, power, wealth, intellectual ability, physical characteristics, or other ways, he arouses defensiveness. Here, as with the other sources of disturbance, whatever arouses feelings of inadequacy causes the listener to center upon the affect loading of the statement rather than upon the cognitive elements. The receiver then reacts by not hearing the message, by forgetting it, by competing with the sender, or by becoming jealous of him.

The person who is perceived as feeling superior communicates that he is not willing to enter into a shared problem-solving relationship, that he probably does not desire feedback, that he does not require help, and/ or that he will be likely to try to reduce the power, the status, or the worth of the receiver.

Many ways exist for creating the atmosphere that the sender feels himself equal to the listener. Defenses are reduced when one perceives the sender as being willing to enter into participative planning with mutual trust and respect. Differences in talent, ability, worth, appearance, status, and power often exist, but the low defense communicator seems to attach little importance to these distinctions.

Certainty and Provisionalism

The effects of dogmatism in producing defensiveness are well known. Those who seem to know the answers, to require no additional data, and to regard themselves as teachers rather than as co-workers tend to put others on guard. Moreover, in the writer's experiment, listeners often perceived manifest expressions of certainty as connoting inward feelings of inferiority. They saw the dogmatic individual as needing to be right, as wanting to win an argument rather than solve a problem, and as seeing his ideas as truths to be defended. This kind of behavior often was associated with acts which others regarded as attempts to exercise control. People who were right seemed to have low tolerance for members who were "wrong"—i.e., who did not agree with the sender.

One reduces the defensiveness of the listener when he communicates that he is willing to experiment with his own behavior, attitudes, and ideas. The person who appears to be taking provisional attitudes, to be investigating issues rather than taking sides on them, to be problem solving rather than debating, and to be willing to experiment and explore tends to communicate that the listener may have some control over the shared quest or the investigation of the ideas. If a person is genuinely searching for information and data, he does not resent help or company along the way.

CONCLUSION

The implications of the above material for the parent, the teacher, the manager, the administrator, or the therapist are fairly obvious. Arousing defensiveness interferes with communication and thus makes it difficult—and sometimes impossible—for anyone to convey ideas clearly and to move effectively toward the solution of therapeutic, educational, or managerial problems.

FOR DISCUSSION

1. In listening or reading we often become defensive or resentful of the speaker or writer without being able to pinpoint the specific source of this defensive attitude. Examine your own recent listening and/or reading behavior for defensive reactions in terms of the six categories of behavior defined by Gibb. Can these categories effectively explain your defensive reactions? What other categories might be significant in explaining defensive communications?

2. Write two paragraphs or speeches on a real or fictional incident. Write one so that it is primarily or wholly defensive and one so that it is primarily or wholly supportive. First, describe the way in which the language used conveys the defensive and supportive climates. Second, ask one or more listeners to react to these communications. Do their reactions support Gibb's conclusions regarding defensive versus supportive listening?

3. Compare and contrast two persons (for example, teachers, friends, employers) who seem to represent extremes in terms of their tendency to arouse defensive and supportive climates. Specify, as concretely as possible, the communication behaviors of these persons that produce these different climates and relate these behaviors to Gibb's six categories. What specific advice would you give to the communicator prone to create a defensive climate? What factors do you think might account for his tendency toward defensive communication?

4. Draw up a list of "suggestions for persuasive communication" that might be derived from Gibb's discussion of defensive communication. Are these suggestions in agreement or in disagreement with those found in a representative text on persuasion or rhetoric?

VERBAL
MESSAGES

This section of readings is devoted to verbal messages—the part of communication that has perhaps been studied more than any other. The articles included here deal with some of the most significant dimensions of communication.

In the first article I provide a general overview of language and verbal messages, focusing on two basic questions: What is language? and How does language work? Throughout these two related discussions characteristics of language are identified and principles of verbal messages (or language in use) are explained. These characteristics and principles should provide you with a clear understanding of the nature of language and how it functions. This in turn should provide you with a foundation for exploring the more specialized dimensions of verbal messages focused on in the remaining articles.

In "The Power of a Name," Mary Marcus demonstrates that we have different meanings for first names. She shows how these names can influence our expectations, our friendships, the way in which we think of others, and even our opinions of ourselves.

Over the past several years a great deal has been written about the differences between male and female communication. In "Speaking Up: Communicating with Confidence" Barbara Westbrook Eakins and R. Gene Eakins advance some of their conclusions concerning male and female communications based on an exhaustive review of the research in both verbal and nonverbal dimensions. Here they cover such issues as how men and women are talked about as well as how men and women communicate. The authors also offer some suggestions for a nonsexist treatment of both women and men.

One of the ways in which we may state a preference or put forth a position is to ask it as a question, which is an admittedly indirect and somewhat strange way of going about communicating. For example, instead of saying "I'm tired" we might say "What time is it?" or instead of saying "I'd like to go out with you on

Saturday night" we might say "Would you like to go out Saturday?" or "Are you busy Saturday?" Jacques Lalanne, in his "Attack by Question," brings this tendency and its implications to consciousness and provides insight into the values of directness and how this might best be achieved.

Language and Verbal Messages

Joseph A. DeVito

In discussing language and verbal message systems there are two basic questions that need to be considered. The first question is "What is language?" (What are the major defining characteristics of language? Of what does language consist?) The second question is "How does language work?" (What are the characteristics of language-as-used? How does the verbal message system operate?) Each of these questions is considered in this essay. First, I focus on the nature of language and attempt to answer the question of what language is by identifying the six major characteristics that define language as a unique and human quality. Second, I focus on the principles of verbal interaction, the features that are present in all verbal interactions regardless of their specific purpose, their particular context, or their unique participants.

WHAT IS LANGUAGE?

Language is a specialized, productive system capable of displacement and composed of rapidly fading, arbitrary, culturally transmitted symbols and rules. Contained in this definition are six characteristics of human language: specialization, productivity, displacement, rapid fading, arbitrariness, and cultural transmission.

From Joseph A. DeVito, *The Interpersonal Communication Book,* 2nd ed. (New York: Harper & Row, 1980), pp. 171–179.

Specialization

A specialized communication system, according to Charles Hockett, is one whose "direct energetic consequences are biologically irrelevant." Human language serves only one major purpose—to communicate. It does not aid any biological functions. On the other hand, while a panting dog communicates information about its presence and perhaps about its internal state, the panting serves first and foremost the biological function of temperature regulation. The fact that communication accompanies or results from this behavior is only incidental.

Productivity

Human language evidences productivity—sometimes referred to as openness or creativity. That is, our verbal messages are novel utterances, each utterance is generated anew. There are exceptions to this general rule, but these seem few and trivial. For example, sentences such as "How are you?" "What's new?" "Good Luck," and similar expressions do not evidence productivity; they are not newly created each time they are uttered. Except for sentences such as these, all other verbal messages are created at the time of utterance. When you speak, you are not repeating memorized sentences but rather creating your own sentences. Similarly, your understanding of verbal messages evidences productivity in that you can understand new utterances as they are uttered. Your ability to comprehend verbal messages is not limited to previously heard and learned utterances.

The rules of grammar have imposed some restrictions on the way in which sentences may be generated, and so complete productivity, in regard to form at least, does not exist. For example, we do not utter such sentences as, "The rock thinks quietly," or "The tulip attacked the poor old turtle." Our language has built-in restrictions that, to stick with these examples, require that a "human" or "animal" noun (rather than an "inanimate" noun such as *rock* or *tulip*) serve as the subject of such verbs as *thinks* or *attacked*. The poet, of course, may and frequently does violate such rules.

Some animal systems also evidence productivity. For example, bees can communicate about new sources of food and new home sites, and so their stystem is productive in this sense. And yet it is a very limited productivity; it seems restricted to such topics as food, housing, and the general maintenance of the hive and colony. Human message systems, on the other hand, evidence an almost unlimited productivity, which enables us to talk about millions of topics in millions of different ways.

Another dimension of productivity is that human message systems allow the introduction of new words. When something is discovered or invented, we can create new words to describe it. When new ideas or new theoretical concepts are developed, we can create words to describe them. And it does not seem to matter whether we create the new word by joining together old words or parts of old words or create it from scratch. What does matter is that the language system is open to expansion—a feature that seems absent from just about all known animal communication systems.

Displacement

Human language can be used to talk about things that are remote in both time and space; one can talk about the past and the future as easily as the present. And one can talk about things that one has never and will never perceive—about mermaids and unicorns, about supernatural beings from other planets, about talking animals. One can talk about the unreal as well as the real, the imaginary as well as the actual. Displacement also refers to the fact that messages may have effects or consequences that are independent of their context. Thus, for example, statements uttered in one place today may have effects elsewhere tomorrow. That is, both the referents (what is talked about) and the effects of messages may be displaced.

Displacement is an important capability of human verbal-message systems because it is absent from most animal communication systems. For example, birds do not emit danger calls unless danger is actually present. Dogs do not bark or growl unless there is a disturbance in the immediate environment. These systems lack the ability for displacement references. On the other hand, bee language does evidence displacement. When forager bees locate a food supply, they return to the hive and perform an intricate dance that indicates how much food has been found, how far away the food is, and in which direction the bees must fly to reach the food. Similarly, when scout bees locate a new home site, they return and perform a dance that communicates its distance from available food supplies, its distance from other bee hives, the protection it affords from wind and rain, and similar issues relevant to the suitability of a new home. The bee communication system, then, evidences displacement, because its members may communicate about things that are not physically present in their immediate environment.

Displacement, together with productivity, also makes possible the ability to lie. Humans are able to lie because they are able to form new utterances (productivity) and because their utterances are not limited to what is in one's immediate environment (displacement). Thus, for example, we may say, "I found a sunken treasure off the coast of Manhattan, and for a mere $27.50 I'll give you a map that will make you a millionaire," without this sentence's ever having been uttered before and without any concern for what is or is not actually present in one's environment.

In other words, there are no linguistic limitations that restrict our utterances to accurate descriptions of reality. Although animal lovers are fond of telling stories about pets trying to fool them, it appears that lying is extremely rare, if not totally absent, in animal communication. Bees, for example, seem incapable of lying; at least there have been no reports of bees communicating false information concerning food supplies or home sites.

Rapid Fading

Speech sounds fade rapidly; they are evanescent. They must be received immediately after they are emitted or else they will not be received at all. Although mechanical devices now enable sound to be preserved much as writing is preserved, this is not a characteristic of human language. Rather, these are extralinguistic means of storing information and aiding memory. Of course all signals fade; written symbols and even symbols carved in rock are not permanent. In relative terms, however, speech signals are probably the least permanent of all communicative media.

Arbitrariness

Language signals are arbitrary; they do not possess any of the physical properties or characteristics of the things for which they stand. The word *wine* is no more tasty than the word *sand,* nor is the latter any less wet.

Opposed to arbitrariness is *iconicity.* Iconic signals do bear a resemblance to their referents. A line drawing of a person is iconic in representing the body parts in proper relation to each other. But it is arbitrary in representing the texture and thickness of the anatomical structures.

Both arbitrariness and iconicity are relative. For example, a line drawing is more arbitrary than a black-and-white photograph, which is more arbitrary than a color photograph. Paralinguistic features (volume, rate, rhythm) are more iconic than the features normally classified as belonging to language. Rate, for example, may vary directly with emotional arousal and hence would be iconic. But the sound of the word *fast* is not actually fast.

Cultural Transmission

The form of any particular human language is culturally or traditionally transmitted. The child raised by English speakers learns English as a native speaker, regardless of the language of his or her biological parents. The genetic endowment pertains to human language in general rather than to any specific human language.

One of the consequences of cultural transmission is that any human language can be learned by any normal being. All human languages— English, Chinese, Italian, Russian, Bantu, or any of the other approximately 3000 languages—are equally learnable; no one language should present any greater difficulty for a child than any other language. It should be added, however, that this ability to learn any language is true only at particular times in the life of the individual. One generally cannot learn to speak a language as fluently as a native after passing a certain age, usually around puberty.

These six features do not, of course, exhaust the characteristics of language. Taken together, however, they should serve to clarify how human language is made up and some of its dimensions and should enable you to better distinguish human language from all other communication systems—whether these be animal systems, such as the language of the bee, or invented languages, such as the language of semaphore or mathematics.

HOW DOES LANGUAGE WORK?

The six principles described below are applicable to any and all verbal interactions. Principles such as these are significant for two major reasons. First, they provide a convenient summary of essential qualities of verbal interaction. In effect, they define what constitutes a verbal interaction—its nature and its essential aspects. Second, these principles are useful for analyzing verbal interactions that are primarily or even partially linguistic. These principles provide us with a set of questions to ask about any verbal interaction.

These principles are taken from one of the most interesting research studies done on language. Three researchers—Robert Pittenger, Charles Hockett, and John Danehy—pooled their talents to analyze in depth the first five minutes of a psychiatric interview. Each word, phrase, and sentence, each intonation, pause, and cough, were subjected to an incredibly detailed analysis. At the conclusion of this research the authors proposed the following findings or principles, which they felt would be of value to future students and researchers attempting to understand and analyze verbal interactions.

The Principle of Immanent Reference

Human beings have the ability to use what Leonard Bloomfield calls "displaced speech" and what Charles Hockett labels "displacement"; that is, human language may make reference to the past as well as to the future; humans can talk about what is not here and what is not now. Nevertheless, all verbalization makes some reference to the present, to the specific context, to the speaker, and to the hearer(s). All verbal interactions, in other words, contain immanent references.

In attempting to understand verbal interaction, then, it is always legitimate to ask such questions as, "To what extent does this communication refer to this particular situation?" "To what extent does this communication refer to the speaker?" "In what ways is the speaker commenting on the hearer(s)?"

The answers to such questions may not be obvious. In many instances the answers may never be found. Yet these questions are potentially answerable and thus always worth asking.

The Principle of Determinism

All verbalizations are to some extent determined; all verbalization is to some extent purposeful. Whenever something is said, there is a reason. Similarly, when nothing is said in an interactional situation, there is a reason. Words, of course, communicate, and there are reasons why the words used are used; but silence also communicates, and there are reasons why silence is used. Watzlawick, Jackson, and Beavin, in *Pragmatics of Human Communication,* put it this way: one cannot *not* communicate. Whenever we are in an interactional situation, regardless of what we do or say or don't do or say, we communicate. Words and silence alike have message value; they communicate something to other people who in turn cannot *not* respond and are therefore also communicating.

Consequently, it is always legitimate in analyzing interactions to ask the reasons for the words as well as the reasons for the silences. Each communicates and each is governed by some reason or reasons; all messages are determined.

The Principle of Recurrence

In our interactions individuals will tell us—not once but many times and not in one way but in many ways—about themselves—who they are, how they perceive themselves, what they like, what they dislike, what they want, what they avoid and so on.

Whatever is perceived as important or significant to an individual will recur in that person's verbal interactions; he or she will tell us in many different ways and on many different occasions what these things are. Of course, these things will rarely be communicated in an obvious manner. People who find themselves in need of approval do not directly ask others for approval. Rather, they go about obtaining approval responses in more subtle ways, perhaps by asking how others like their new outfit, perhaps by talking about their grades on an examination, perhaps by talking about how they never betray a confidence, and so on.

The Principle of Relativity of Signal and Noise

What constitutes a signal and what constitutes noise in any given communication is relative rather than absolute. If we are interested in hearing a particular story and the speaker, in narrating it, breaks it up by coughing, we might become annoyed because the coughing (noise) is disturbing our reception of the story (signal). But suppose this individual seeks some form of medication and in his or her interactions with the doctor coughs in a similar way. To the doctor this coughing might be the signal; the coughing might communicate an important message to the doctor. Similarly, when listening to a stutterer tell a story, we may focus on the story, which would be the signal. The stuttering would be the noise interfering with our reception of the signal. But to the speech pathologist the stuttering is the signal to which he or she attends, and the story might be the noise.

The point is simply this: What is signal to one person and in one context might be noise to another person in another context.

The Principle of Reinforcement/Packaging

In most interactions messages are transmitted simultaneously through a number of different channels. We utter sounds with our vocal mechanism, but we also utilize our body posture and our spatial relationships at the same time to reinforce our message. We say "no" and at the same time pound our fist on the table. One channel reinforces the other; the message is presented as a "package."

The extent to which simultaneous messages reinforce each other or contradict each other, then, is extremely important in understanding human communication. A verbal message when accompanied by different nonverbal messages is not the same message and cannot be responded to in the same way.

The Principle of Adjustment

Communication may take place only to the extent that the parties communicating share the same system of signals. This is obvious when dealing with speakers of two different languages; one will not be able to communicate with the other to the extent that their language systems differ.

This principle takes on particular relevance, however, when we realize that no two persons share identical signal systems. Parents and children, for example, not only have different vocabularies to a very great extent but, even more importantly, have different denotative and especially different connotative meanings for the terms they have in common. Different cultures and subcultures, even when they share a common language, often have greatly differing nonverbal communication systems. To the extent that these systems differ, communication will not take place.

The characteristics discussed in this essay are universals of the human language system and hence are in no way restricted to any one form of communication. They are as applicable to intrapersonal as to interpersonal communication. Thus, for example, our intrapersonal communications evidence displacement in our fantasies and day dreams as well as in our plans for tommorrow and in our criticism or praise of ourselves for yesterday's failures or successes.

The discussions of the features of specialization, rapid fading, arbitrariness, productivity, and cultural transmission as universal characteristics of verbal messages are applicable in toto to intrapersonal communication and so need not be singled out here.

The principles of verbal messages, like the characteristics, are applicable to all verbal messages and hence are as relevant to intrapersonal communication as they are to interpersonal communication. Like interpersonal messages, intrapersonal messages are determined. Our fantasies, our creative spurts, and our lapses of attention are all determined; all occur for some reason(s). When we talk with ourselves or with others, what we say and how we say it have purposes and are determined. Recurrence is an easily detected feature of intrapersonal communication. The frequent intrapersonal messages are likely to be the most important messages, just as they are in interpersonal communication. Signal and noise are relative concepts in intrapersonal communication as well as in interpersonal communication. In normal persons the principle of adjustment seems always to operate in intrapersonal communication for maximal efficiency. Lastly, we should note that it is helpful to become aware of the packaged nature of intrapersonal messages. The lack of correspondence among message channels often signals self-doubts, sources of indecision, or a lack of self-confidence and conviction. To the extent that we become aware of these feelings, we will be in a better position to do something about them. Thus, if an inconsistency signals self-doubt, we should examine the possible reasons for this self-doubt and make corrections— perhaps alter the intended course of behavior, perhaps obtain more information, perhaps delay the action.

SOURCE NOTE

For the characteristics of language I relied on the work of Charles F. Hockett, particularly "The Problem of Universals in Language," in J. H. Greenberg, ed., *Universals of Language* (Cambridge, Mass.: M.I.T. Press, 1963), and "The Origin of Speech," *Scientific American* 203(1960):89–96. The concepts of language universals are thoroughly surveyed in Greenberg's *Universals of Language*. Most of the material, however, presumes a rather thorough knowledge of linguistics.

On language universals, see also Jean Aitchison, *The Articulate Mammal* (New York: McGraw-Hill, 1977). The six principles of verbal interaction were based on Robert E. Pittenger, Charles F. Hockett, and John J. Danehy, *The First Five Minutes: A Sample of Microscopic Interview Analysis* (Ithaca, N.Y.: Paul Martineau, 1960). Also in this area, see Eric H. Lenneberg, "Review of *The First Five Minutes*," *Language* 38(1962):69–73. For additional material on expressive language, see Robert E. Pittenger and Henry Lee Smith, Jr., "A Basis for Some Contributions of Linguistics to Psychiatry," *Psychiatry* 20(1957):61–78, and Norman A. McQuown, "Linguistic Transcription and Specification of Psychiatric Interview Material," *Psychiatry* 20(1957):79–86.

On these universals and the ways in which human communication differs from animal communication, see A. Akmajian, R. A. Demers, and R. M. Harnish, *Linguistics: An Introduction to Language and Communication* (Cambridge, Mass.: MIT Press, 1979).

FOR DISCUSSION

1. Another characteristic of language often mentioned is that of prevarication— the ability to lie. On what other characteristics does prevarication depend? Do animal communication systems possess prevarication? How can you be sure of your response?

2. Think back to your previous interactions with one of your close friends. In what ways did your friend's communications evidence immanent reference? Determinism? Recurrence? (Be as specific as possible.)

3. In what specific ways do your own communications evidence immanent reference? Determinism? Recurrence?

4. How do your fantasies and daydreams differ from your interpersonal interactions in terms of the principles of verbal messages?

5. What other characteristics or principles of verbal messages might you identify? Why do you think these are useful additions to those presented in this essay?

How to Win at Wordsmanship

Newsweek, May 6, 1968

After years of hacking through etymological thickets at the U.S. Public Health Service, a 63-year-old official named Philip Broughton hit upon a sure-fire method for converting frustration into fulfillment (jargonwise). Euphemistically called the Systematic Buzz Phrase Projector, Broughton's system employs a lexicon of 30 carefully chosen "buzzwords":

Column 1	Column 2	Column 3
0. integrated	0. management	0. options
1. total	1. organizational	1. flexibility
2. systematized	2. monitored	2. capability
3. parallel	3. reciprocal	3. mobility
4. functional	4. digital	4. programming
5. responsive	5. logistical	5. concept
6. optional	6. transitional	6. time-phase
7. synchronized	7. incremental	7. projection
8. compatible	8. third-generation	8. hardware
9. balanced	9. policy	9. contingency

The procedure is simple. Think of any three-digit number, then select the corresponding buzzword from each column. For instance, number 257 produces "systematized logistical projection," a phrase that can be dropped into virtually any report with that ring of decisive, knowledgeable authority. "No one will have the remotest idea of what you're talking about," says Broughton, "but the important thing is that they're not about to admit it."

The Power
of a Name

The man on the TV screen throws his hands in the air, a silly grin on his face, watching as the family washing machine overflows. As he's standing in soapy water up to his ankles, his wife bounds in, takes charge, and tells him that with Brand A, he needs only a quarter cup of detergent to get the family wash sparkling white. More likely than not, the sheepish, bumbling husband is named Harvey.

In 1965, to protest such advertisements, New Yorker Harvey Edwards organized a group of 150 Harveys and besieged the ad agencies. The Harveys won their fight, and three sponsors retired their offending commercials. To counter the media's portrayals of men named Harvey as weak and bumbling, the group set up an award for the best positive portrayal of a Harvey. The first winner: Columbia Pictures' Harvey Middleman, Fireman.

Harveys and other people with unusual names often do suffer. Psychologists and educators have found that while names cannot guarantee fame or insure neurosis, they can help or hinder the development of a good self-image, friendships, and even affect success in school and on the job.

As Humpty-Dumpty told Alice in Through the Looking Glass, certain names imply that their owners have specific characteristics. Alice asked, "*Must* a name mean something?" Humpty-Dumpty replied, "Of course it must . . . *My* name means the shape I am . . . With a name like yours, you might be any shape, almost."

Trustworthy John. Whenever researchers ask people to describe the owners of specific names, they find wide agreement. In 1963, a British

From *Psychology Today* (October 1976), 75–76, 108. Reprinted from *Psychology Today*. Copyright © 1976 Ziff-Davis Publishing Company.

psychologist asked a group of citizens to rank names as to their age, trustworthiness, attractiveness, sociability, kindness, and lack of aggression. He found that Johns are seen to be trustworthy and kind; Robins are young; Tonys, sociable; Agneses, old; Agneses and Matildas, unattractive; and Anns, nonaggressive.

In the United States, psychologists Barbara Buchanan and James Bruning got college students at Penn State and Ohio Universities to rate 1,060 names. The students reported how much they liked or disliked them, whether the names were active or passive, and how masculine or feminine they seemed. The students had no difficulty agreeing that they especially liked active Michael, James, and Wendy, and that Michael and James were extremely masculine while Wendy was quite feminine. They disliked passive Alfreda, Percival, and Isadore, and felt that Percival's and Isadore's masculinity was in doubt. So was Alfreda's femininity. Feeling about most names was less intense.

In another study, psychologist E. D. Lawson asked a group of students to rank men's names. Ten of the 20 names (David, Gary, James, John, Joseph, Michael, Paul, Richard, Robert, and Thomas) were those most common on the campus. The other 10 (Andrew, Bernard, Dale, Edmond, Gerd, Ivan, Lawrence, Raymond, Stanley, and Matthew) were selected at random from the total enrollment. Both men and women held stereotypes about the 20 names; they saw common names as better, stronger, and more active than unusual ones.

Even children share stereotypes about names. In one experiment, kindergarteners, third- and sixth-graders judged a list of 10 uncommon names. The children matched the names with such descriptions as: "Who runs?" "Who sits?" Apparently stereotypes are learned, because while third- and sixth-graders confirmed the adults' stereotypes, kindergarten children did not. Five of the names (Sargent, Baxter, Otto, Shepard, and Bruno) were those rated by adults as active; the other five (Aldwin, Winthrop, Alfred, Milton, and Wendell) were rated as passive. Either the older children had already met people whose names fit the stereotypes, or they had picked up the stereotypes from parents, teachers, friends, or the media.

Psychologists have also found that names affect the way in which people think of themselves. New Zealanders who like their names are likely to have high self-esteem, and Americans who dislike their names do not feel as good about themselves as people who like theirs.

Strange Names and Psychosis.   Uncommon names seem more of a handicap for men than for women. In the 1940s, B. M. Savage and F. L. Wells found that students with unusual names were more likely than their classmates to flunk out of Harvard. They were also more likely to be neurotic. Chicago researchers A. Arthur Hartman, Robert Nicolay, and Jesse Hurley looked for evidence of psychosis in a group of men who had been referred for psychiatric evaluation. Half the men were burdened with strange names (Oder, Lethal, Vere, and so on), and the other half had common names. The researchers found more psychosis among the Oders and Lethals and the others with odd names.

Women with unusual names appear to be no more disturbed than those with common names; at least researchers find that those with uncommon names are not especially neurotic. The difference may have something to do with differing attitudes toward names between the sexes. Researchers have studied the attitudes of each sex toward names and found that men are likely to have common names; they also prefer them. Women more often have unusual names and prefer unusual names for themselves and others.

People don't live in a vacuum; the impact of a person's name on his or her self-esteem and mental health is determined largely by how others react to a person with that name. Psychologists John McDavid and Herbert Harari asked members of four youth groups to rate how much they liked each of 75 names. Forty-nine of the names belonged to the fourth- and fifth-graders in the study. A month later, the students named three people they liked in their group and three they didn't like. The boys and girls with names that were very popular on the list of 75 names turned up again and again among the most popular children on the second list. Those with unpopular names were often among the unpopular children. Since not all the children knew each other, McDavid and Harari were able to separate the views of children who knew a child with a particular name from those of children who did not. The relationship between ratings and popularity stayed strong, indicating that a person's name alone is a powerful influence on his popularity.

Intellectual Bloomers. Stereotypes also affect school achievement. The characteristics we attach to a stereotype describe the way we expect others to behave. Psychologists have found that expectations can become

---

Changing fashions in names

1898:	Mary, Catherine, Margaret, Annie, Rose, Marie, Esther, Sarah, Frances, Ida
	John, William, Charles, George, Joseph, Edward, James, Louis, Francis, Samuel
1928:	Mary, Marie, Annie, Margaret, Catherine, Gloria, Helen, Teresa, Jean, Barbara
	John, William, Joseph, James, Richard, Edward, Robert, Thomas, George, Louis
1948:	Linda, Mary, Barbara, Patricia, Susan, Kathleen, Carol, Nancy, Margaret, Diane
	Robert, John, James, Michael, William, Richard, Joseph, Thomas, Stephen, David
1964:	Lisa, Deborah, Mary, Susan, Maria, Elizabeth, Donna, Barbara, Patricia, Ann (e), Theresa (Ann & Theresa are tied)
	Michael, John, Robert, David, Steven, Anthony, William, Joseph, Thomas, Christopher, Richard
1972:	Jennifer, Michelle, Lisa, Elizabeth, Christine, Maria, Nicole, Kimberly, Denise, Amy
	Michael, David, Christopher, John, Jarnes, Joseph, Robert, Anthony, Richard, Brian
1975:	Jennifer, Michele, Christine, Lisa, Maria, Melisa, Nicole, Elizabeth, Jessica, Erica
	Michael, John, Robert, David, Christopher, Anthony, Joseph, Jason, José

NEW YORK CITY FASHIONS. People with popular names are a step ahead on the path to success. In New York City, fashions in names have changed over the years, and this list of popular names reflects custom and immigration patterns. While it is as good to be "John" today as it was in the 19th century, "Mary" has long since given way to "Maria."

self-fulfilling prophecies, and that people often do behave as we expect them to. Harvard psychologist Robert Rosenthal calls this the Pygmalion effect. In his now classic study, Rosenthal randomly selected 20 percent of the children in 18 elementary-school classrooms and labeled them "intellectual bloomers." He told their teachers that these children would show gains in intellectual achievement during the upcoming year. At the end of the year, these children did, in fact, show gains as compared with the children who were not labeled "bloomers."

Harari and McDavid tried to find out if the Pygmalion effect would also work with name preferences. The researchers had a group of teachers grade essays written by fifth-grade students. The names used to identify the authors of the essays were either desirable or undesirable. The desirable names were Karen, Lisa, David, and Michael. The undesirable names were Elmer, Adelle, Bertha, and Hubert.

Surprisingly, essays supposedly written by students named Adelle received the highest grades, with those written by Lisas and Davids close behind. As expected, the essays labeled with unpopular names generally did receive the lowest grades. Harari and McDavid explain the triumph of the unpopular Adelle by speculating that teachers consider the name to be more "scholarly," and awarded grades accordingly.

A recent study by S. Gray Garwood of Tulane also shows the impact of expectations on behavior. Garwood compared sixth-grade children with desirable names (Jonathan, James, John, Patrick, Craig, Thomas, Gregory, Richard, and Jeffery) with children with undesirable names (Bernard, Curtis, Darrell, Donald, Gerald, Horace, Maurice, Jerome, Roderick, and Samuel). He found that the children who had names that teachers liked were better adjusted, had higher expectations for academic success, and scored higher on achievement tests than children with names that teachers disliked.

Teachers probably convey their expectations by tone of voice, smiling, creating a warmer learning environment, by giving students information about their performance, or by actually devoting more teaching time to the students he or she prefers. Providing more information and teaching time can lead to the differences in academic achievement that Garwood found. The quality of the learning environment can lead students to believe in the teacher's expectations and lower or raise their own expectations for success.

Wednesday's Child. This cycle of self-fulfilling prophecies is not limited to the classroom. The Ashanti of Ghana name their children in accordance with the day of the week on which the child is born. Monday's child is given the name Kwadwo, and is thought to be quiet, peaceful, and retiring. Wednesday's child, Kwaku, is believed to be quick-tempered and aggressive. In 1954, psychologist Gustav Jahoda read juvenile-court records to verify a rumor that a majority of crimes were committed by children named Kwaku. The records showed that a significantly greater number of crimes against persons were committed by people named Kwaku than those named Kwadwo. It's unlikely that children are born with dramatically different temperaments, so the difference in the crime rate is probably due to different expectations of the parents and different upbringing based on these expectations.

All of the studies mentioned above stress the disadvantages of uncommon names. However, all is not lost for people with unusual names. An uncommon name may actually be an advantage in particular occupations. An informal study by William Gaffney of names and jobs revealed that Army officers from West Point tend to have unusual names, as do college professors. Edwin Newman notes in his book, Strictly Speaking, that college presidents and heads of foundations have more than their share of uncommon names, and that many have first names which could easily be last names. Examples: Kingman Brewster, President of Yale University and McGeorge Bundy, President of the Ford Foundation. Sam Goldwyn probably had an inkling about the advantage of an uncommon name. In one of his classic malapropisms, Goldwyn chastised an acquaintance for the name he gave his son. "Now why did you name him John? Every Tom, Dick, and Harry is named John."

FOR DISCUSSION

1. Do you respond to names as Marcus claims people in general do? How do you account for your response to people on the basis of their first names?

2. Do you think your name has influenced the way people respond to you? In what specific ways?

3. If you were to select a name for yourself at this time in your life what would it be? Why?

4. How do your expectations about people—based on their names or on other data—affect your communications with them? Be as specific as possible.

How to Speak Educatorese

Mike Royko

Until now, only professional educators knew how to speak educatorese, that mysterious language with which they befuddle the rest of us.

But now, for the first time, anyone can learn to speak it.

All you need is the new guide: "How To Speak Like an Educator Without Being Educated."

And as a public service, the guide is being printed in its entirety below.

In a moment, I'll provide instructions on its use. But first, a word of credit to its creators.

The guide is the work of two rhetoric and speech teachers at Danville (Ill.) Junior College, Barbara Stover and Ilya Walker. They compiled it after years of wading through Administrative circulars. They did it for fun, but some of their students have found that the phrases are useful in preparing papers for sociology classes.

The guide is simple to use.

Take one word from each of the five columns. It doesn't matter which word. Take them in any order, or in no order.

For instance, if you take the second word of column "A", the fourth word from column "B," the sixth word from column "C," and the eighth and tenth words from the last two columns, you will have:

Flexible ontological productivity implement control group and experimental group.

That doesn't make sense, does it? But now add a few connecting words, and we have:

Flexible and ontological productivity will implement the control group and experimental group.

That still doesn't make any sense. But it sounds like it does. Which means it is perfect educatorese.

You can do it with any combination of the words. As an example, use the first five digits of my officephone: 321-21,etc . . .

This works out to:

Adaptable reciprocal nucleii terminate total modular exchange.

Add a few little words and you have a splendid sentence, worthy of at least an assistant superintendent:

"Adaptable and reciprocal nucleii will terminate in total modular exchange." And you can quote me on that.

Go to it. With this guide you say things like:

"The interdisciplinary or supportive input will encapsulate vertical team structure."

Or: "Optimal ethnic accountability should facilitate post-secondary education enrichment."

Try it yourself. Once you get the hang of it—who knows?—you might wind up with the superintendent's job.

-A-
comprehensive
flexible
adaptable
culturally
perceptual
evaluative
innovative
interdisciplinary
conceptual
ideological
optimal
minimal
categorically
unequivocally
intrapersonal
interpersonal

-B-
cognitive
reciprocal
stylistic
ontological
prime
supportive
workable
resultant
behavioral
judgmental
ethnic
attitudinal
multicultural

encounter
counterproductive
generative
cognate

-C-
nucleii
interaction
focus
balance
chain of command
productivity
conformance
panacea
rationale
input
throughput
accountability
feedback
objective
resources
perspective
curricula
priorities
diversity
environment
overview
strategies
posture
introversion
posits
concept

-D-
indicates
terminate
geared
compile
articulate
verbalize
facilitate
implement
incur
sensitize
synthesize
integrate
fragment
maximize
minimize
energize
individualize
encapsulate
orientate

-E-
total modular exchange
in-depth discussion
multipurpose framework and goals
serial communication
serial transmission of applicable cable
tools and instrumentation
post-secondary education enrichment
changing needs of society
motivational serial communications
high potential for assessing failure
control group and experimental group
student-faculty relationships
identifiable decision-making process
sophisticated resource systems analyses
vertical team structure
translation in depth
classroom context
individual horizons

Speaking Up

Communicating with Confidence

Barbara Westbrook Eakins and R. Gene Eakins

In this . . . chapter, the temptation is almost irresistible to impose upon the reader's consciousness layer after layer of communication prescriptions. Certainly, the investigation of the subject of women's and men's communication has left both authors with a set of conclusions, some shared and some held individually, about how to improve discourse between the sexes. As a result of our research, one assumption that we initially held as a tentative and tenuous hypothesis has crystallized into a clear belief—that arbitrary role assignments in a sexist society are barriers to communication between all people; women, men, and children. So-called sex-role socialization has created and has perpetuated attitudes and behaviors that are injurious to all.

We recognize that many women and men are content with the old order and have no wish to alter or to radicalize their modes of communication. It would be simplistic and naive to state that they should feel perfectly free to continue in these accustomed ways. The point is that communication involves everyone in society. Generally, we are not free to pick and choose those with whom we communicate. To the degree that one person communicates in a style that demeans and subordinates another; to that degree is human dignity eroded. Since we cannot choose to live and communicate in a vacuum, we must recognize that we all share the burden of freeing our discourse from sex-role power wielding.

In attempting to collect and organize our suggestions for improving female-male communication, we must confess to experiencing a certain degree of frustration and apprehension. So much consideration needs to

From Barbara Westbrook Eakins and R. Gene Eakins, *Sex Differences in Human Communication* (Boston: Houghton Mifflin, 1978), pp. 180–191.

be given to a variety of issues. To this end, we offer the following suggestions distilled from our research and conclusions. To arrange these suggestions into some meaningful form for consideration by the reader, we have divided the material into verbal and nonverbal categories.

VERBAL BEHAVIOR

It seems obvious that the improvement of communication between the sexes requires attitudinal and behavioral changes. Certainly attitude and behavior are interdependent, and any alteration of one will mean consequential change for the other. Just where to interrupt the existing chain from thought to deed is debatable. It seems to us that the most positive change ought to begin with altering attitudes. In recent times we have seen much lip service paid to the concept of equal rights in the form of token behavioral modification, but little real progress toward human equality has been effected. The consistent theme running through this [chapter] is that an asymmetric relationship exists between women and men in society. The research in all areas of human communication consistently underscores the dominant power status of males and the dominated, subordinated status of females. One of the most compelling appeals for human equality in communicating is made by J. B. Priestley:

> I am convinced that good talk cannot flourish where there is a wide gulf between the sexes, where the men are altogether too masculine, too hearty and bluff and booming, where the women are too feminine, at once both too arch and too anxious. Where men are leavened by a feminine element, where women are not without some tempering by the masculine spirit, there is a chance of good talk.[1]

One of the ways to alter the asymmetric power relationship is to expose myths and stereotypes about female-male communication. The common belief that women talk more than men is not supported by research. If this very obvious stereotype is false, then how many other popular notions about female-male communication can stand the test of powerful inquiry? We need a massive program of on-going empirical study about our traditional beliefs concerning talk between and within the sexes.

In business the attitudes of women and men about women need to change. Right now the business organization fits the male experience. Nancy Conklin, talking about discourse in the organizational setting, notes the difference between women's and men's talk. Women's talk is often characterized as gossiping, an activity of low value. If they try to elevate themselves above gossiping—that is, to be like men—women are said to be

---

[1]J. B. Priestley, "Journey down the Rainbow," *Saturday Review,* 18 August 1956, p. 35, cited by Carolyn G. Heilbrun, *Toward a Recognition of Androgyny* (New York: Alfred A. Knopf, 1973).

carrying on conversation, which is still regarded as a form of entertainment. Men, in contrast, are said to have discussions in conferences and meetings, and they talk "straight from the shoulder" in "a businesslike way." Conklin urges women to develop strategies for dealing with the new interactional situations presented by board-room and locker-room talk. Women should either acquire the style of speaking accepted for these occasions or establish their credentials as group members with their own forms of communication. Women must "recognize, legitimize, and creatively develop their own speech genres. Clearly the back-slapping joke will never be a female vehicle."[2]

The point has been made that technology is having a homogenizing effect on women and men. The mystique of the great fighting male and the earth-mother female is one of the casualties of modern change. This iconoclasm ought to be accelerated and encouraged. Especially in the world of work a spirit of androgeny should be encouraged. Women and men ought to be encouraged to accept whatever business position or to enter any profession they prefer without any social stigma attached to their selection of these roles.

In small-group communication men are expected to "pro-act." They analyze, clarify, evaluate, and control the flow of conversation. Women are expected to react. They stroke, positively reinforce, listen, reduce tension, and restore unity. There is no evidence that men or women are more biologically suited to pro-act or react. Nor is either role superior to the other. Courses in effective group communication should stress listening as a passive skill for men to acquire and using humor as an active skill for more women to acquire.

Also, women need to take another look at their existing communication skills. Instead of deprecating them and wishing to be more like their male counterparts, they need to expand these skills, as well as to acquire so-called male techniques.

Conklin argues that women have "acute sociolinguistic sensitivity," whereby they become attuned to the behavior of others, relying on external norms. As a result, women may allow themselves to be defined by standards that are not necessarily their own. They may become estranged from their own culture and from other women. But women's sensitivity to the behavior of others can be turned into a powerful advantage for them. There are strengths in their skills in manipulating language, in their repertoire of stylistic devices, in their attentiveness to others' communication. "Both in dealing with the power structure, and in dealing with other women, an awareness of the ebb and flow below the surface of the interaction is a useful tool and also a valuable weapon."[3]

---

[2]Nancy Faires Conklin, "Toward a Feminist Analysis of Linguistic Behavior," *The University of Michigan Papers in Women's Studies* 1 (1974): 51–73.

[3]Ibid., pp. 51–73.

It is easier to identify biases in language than to remedy or eliminate them. To change male-oriented language, some writers suggest replacing the traditional generic *man, he,* or *himself* with inclusionary language or sex-blind substitutes. The following are possibilities:[4]

1. Words such as *people, human beings, humanity, the human race, citizens,* or *inhabitants* can substitute for *man* or *mankind.*)

2. Occupational, activity, or other kinds of terms ending in *-man* can be replaced by words that can include persons of either or both sexes. For example, "insurance man" can be replaced by "insurance agent," "cameraman" by "camera operator," "mailman" by "mail carrier," "foreman" by "supervisor," "workman" by "worker," "cleaning woman" by "office cleaner," and so on.

3. Terms such as *one, you,* "she and he," or "he and she" can be substituted for the masculine pronoun *he.* For example, "As for the new employee, *she or he* can . . . ," or *"one* can . . . ," or *"you* can. . . ."

4. The sentence can be recast in the plural. Use "Students can program their studies themselves," rather than "Each student can program his study himself."

Some writers favor creating new forms. They find "he or she" or "he/she" awkward, the use of "they" or plural construction ungrammatical or inconvenient at times, and exlusionary tactics absurd in some instances. Several have suggested some new generic personal pronouns. Miller and Swift and Densmore, for example, have suggested sets of personal pronouns to replace the old male-oriented ones.[5] They are shown in Table 1.

Other authorities, however, hold the opinion that it is unrealistic to expect to get rid of generic masculine terms and that it makes more sense to adjust to them. While suggesting that we try to avoid misleading use of the word *man,* Nilsen advocates concentrating efforts on educating people to the way language is.[6] She feels that special efforts should be directed toward using illustrations that include both females and males whenever a generic masculine term such as *man* or *he* is used, to emphasize its use as an all-inclusive term.

Of course, new word usage seems awkward at first. But as Paul Gray commented in *Time,* the words that survive over time are generally those

---

[4]Elizabeth Burr, Susan Dunn, and Norma Farquhar, "Women and the Language of Inequality," *Social Education* 36 (1972): 842; "Guidelines for Equal Treatment of the Sexes in McGraw-Hill Book Company Publications" (New York: McGraw-Hill Book Company, n.d.)

[5]Casey Miller and Kate Swift, "One Small Step for Genkind," *New York Times Magazine,* 16 April 1972, p. 36 (reprinted from *New York* Magazine, December 20, 1971); Dana Densmore, "Speech is the Form of Thought (KNOW, Inc., P.O. Box 86031, Pittsburgh, Pa. 15221, March 1970).

[6]Alleen Pace Nilsen, "The Correlation between Gender and Other Semantic Features in American English" (Paper presented at Linguistic Society of America, December 1973).

Table 1 Inclusive pronouns

	Miller and Swift	Densmore
Nominative replacement for "she or he"	Tey "Each should do as tey pleases."	She (which includes in one word "she and he") "Each should do as she pleases."
Objective replacement for "her and him"	Tem "Each will get what is coming to tem."	Herm (includes her and him) "Each will get what is coming to herm."
Possessive replacement for "his and her"	Ter(s) "One should make ter own way." "One should normally claim only what is rightfully heris."	

that are useful, "and the useful ones sound better as the years go by."[7] Certainly we are all aware of the vigorous campaigns waged over the past few years to eliminate sexist terms from our speaking. We recall the awkward early attempts to use the term *chairperson* in place of the familiar *chairman,* and we note that the word falls rather easily from the tongue and on the ear today. It is probably not too difficult to adjust to new, nonsexist words.

One of the authors willingly admits that the experience of writing this book has made him extremely conscious of the inequities imposed upon women by our language. There is a tendency to dismiss the importance of eliminating sexist references from our communication primarily because the overall massive effect of biased language usage is missed when one considers only one or two specific examples of linguistic prejudice. To insist on eliminating the generic *man* from *chairman* appears to be nitpicking until one realizes the impact on behaviors and attitudes of thousands of such references in our language.

We have seen at least some of the ways that language is used in relation to the sexes. Although language is regarded as a monolith that is not readily shifted or remolded, some suggestions have been offered for chipping away the rough spots in regard to some of the presumed inequities in naming and describing women and men:

1. More gender balance should be obtained in language usage. More examples featuring females could be added in our discourse and some of the active, courageous, assertive, and confident traits tradition-

[7]Paul Gray, "The Father Tongue," *Time,* 9 August 1976, p. 72.

ally reserved for males could be attributed to females as well. Conversely, some of the sensitive, caring, amenable traits generally ascribed to females could be portrayed in males.

Graham writes of a "new archetypal woman" that took form when she was involved in composing a wordbook for children.[8] This new woman appeared in many of the examples used to clarify word definitions. The new type of woman had brains and courage. From the *A* page, where for the word *abridge* she quoted the Nineteenth Amendment, to the *Z* page where "she zipped down the hill on her sled," she exhibited active and participative characteristics in addition to being gentle, kind, and understanding: "When she 'plunged into her work, her mind began to percolate' (not her coffee). . . . 'She prided herself on her eloquence' (not on the sheen of her freshly waxed floors)."

Along with the "new liberated woman" to be depicted in our communication, writers have suggested a new liberated man. Such a man could be described with more than the one-sided tradition-bound male characteristics of being active, courageous, and ready to compete. Like his female counterpart, he too could be vulnerable. Like the examples contained in the wordbook for children, he could be portrayed variously with human traits: "striving to attain mastery over his emotions"; "his resolve began to waver"; or "tears welled up in his eyes." His career options can be expanded, as in "He studies typing at night," or "He teaches kindergarten."

2. Another suggestion is to guard against language that treats either sex as objects or things in a dehumanizing manner. Women should be described in terms other than their physical or sexual attributes, especially in contexts where men are described by their skills, professional positions, or mental attributes.

3. Language that treats women as possessions or extensions of men or solely in terms of their relationship to men should be avoided.

4. Some publishers' guidelines have been formulated to help writers to utilize language that provides fair and balanced treatment for the sexes and to avoid language that can reinforce sexist attitudes and assumptions. These quidelines, of course, are helpful in oral communication as well. The adoption of many of the feminists' suggestions in leading publishers' guidelines has lent support to the feminist position on language. We have summarized one such set of guidelines, which seems to be quite broad in scope, issued by McGraw-Hill. See "Nonsexist Treatment of Men and Women," pages 186–187.

[8] Alma Graham, "The Making of a Nonsexist Dictionary," *Ms.* 2 (December 1973): 13.

An ideal system of human communication ought to stress the following values:

1. cooperation
2. interpersonal discovery
3. self-realization
4. self-expression

However, until such a utopia emerges, women need to recognize the predominant male value system that governs communication. This system includes

1. promoting individual supremacy
2. getting the competitive edge
3. generating and directing personal action to wrest success and reward from the world

Such a value acquisition will require a special, ultrasophisticated form of assertiveness training for females who wish to acquire the concomitant communication skills. Many behavioral forms will need to be changed.

Stylistically, women will be perceived as more authoritative and sure of themselves as they learn to use fewer tag questions. These expressions give the impression that a woman is not sure of herself or hesitates to express an opinion. Though their use may indicate politeness, it can be a sign and a statement of weakness. The same holds true for qualifiers and disclaimers. They indicate a willingness to be disputed and also convey the speaker's wish not to be held accountable for the statement and willingness to accept other views.

With regard to their speaking voices, women need to recognize that male intonation patterns are currently associated with authority. Many women will need to develop authoritative vocal patterns. Especially they should strive to avoid using the intonation of a question when making a declarative statement, since this connotes uncertainty.

NONSEXIST TREATMENT OF WOMEN AND MEN

1. Avoid typecasting in careers and activities.
    a. Avoid typecasting women in traditional roles.
    b. Avoid showing men as subject to the "masculine mystique" in interests, attitudes, and careers.
    c. Attempt to break job stereotypes for women and men.
    d. Show married women who work outside the home and emphasize the point that women have choices about their marital status.
    e. Address course materials to students of both sexes.
    f. Portray women and girls as active participants the same as men and boys, and not only in connection with cooking, sewing, shopping.

2. Represent members of both sexes as whole human beings.
   a. Represent women and men with human (not just feminine or masculine) strengths and weaknesses. Characteristics praised in males should also be praised in females.
   b. As in portraying men and boys, show women and girls also as active, logical, accomplishing.
   c. Sometimes show men as quiet and passive, fearful and indecisive, just as women are sometimes portrayed.

3. Accord women and men the same respect and avoid either trivializing women or describing them by physical attributes when men are described by mental attributes.
   a. Avoid: (1) girl-watching tone and sexual innuendoes; (2) focusing on physical appearance; (3) using female-gender word forms, such as "poetess"; (4) treating women as sex objects or as weak and helpless; (5) making women figures of fun or scorn (not "the weaker sex" but "women"; not "libber" but "feminist").
   b. Avoid references to general ineptness of males in the home or dependence on women for meals.
   c. Treat women as part of the rule, not the exception (not "woman doctor," but "doctor"). Avoid gee-whiz attitude toward women who perform competently.
   d. Represent women as participants in the action, not as possessions of men. (Not, "Pioneers moved West, taking their wives and children," but "Pioneer women and men moved West, taking their children.")
   e. Avoid portraying women as needing male permission to act.

4. Recognize women for their own achievements.

5. In references to humanity at large, use inclusive language.
   a. Avoid the generic word *man,* since it is often not interpreted broadly. (Not "mankind" but "humanity"; not "manmade" but "artificial"; not "primitive man" but "primitive peoples."
   b. Avoid the generic pronouns he, him, his in reference to a hypothetical person or humanity in general.
      1. Reword sentence. (Not "The average American drinks his coffee black," but "The average American drinks black coffee.")
      2. Recast into plural. ("Most Americans drink their coffee black.")
      3. Replace the pronoun with "one," "you," "he or she," and so forth.
      4. Alternate male and female expressions and examples: "I've often heard supervisors say, 'She's not the right person for the job,' or 'He lacks the qualifications.' "
      5. If the generic *he* is used, explain in the preface and in the text that the reference is to both females and males.
   c. Replace occupational terms ending in *-man* by inclusive terms. (Not "businessman," but "business manager"; not "fireman," but "fire fighter.")

   d. Avoid language that assumes all readers are male. (Not "you and your wife," but "you and your spouse.")

6. Use language that designates and describes the sexes equally.
   a. Use parallel language for women and men. (Not "man and wife," but "husband and wife" or "man and woman." Not "Billie Jean and Riggs," but "King and Riggs" or "Billie Jean and Bobby.")
   b. Identify women by their own names, not in terms of their roles as wife, mother, and so forth. (Not "Nehru's daughter," but "Indira Gandhi.") Avoid unnecessary reference to marital status.
   c. Use terms that include both sexes; avoid unnecessary references to gender.
   d. Use nonsexist job titles. (Not "maid" and "house boy" but "house-" or "office cleaner.")
   e. Avoid linking certain pronouns with certain work or occupations. Pluralize or else "he or she" or "she and he." (Not "the shopper . . . she," but "shoppers . . . they"; not "the breadwinner . . . his earnings," but "the breadwinner . . . her or his earnings."
   f. Do not always mention males first. Alternate the order: "women and men," "gentlemen and ladies," "she or he."

In terms of language, women need to expand their semantic space. Any labels that mark women as secondary beings should be vigorously expunged. Such innocuous-sounding words as "poetess," "songstress," and "authoress" denote the feminine referent and connote a reduction of potency. They innocently and insidiously mark the special female example, which does not belong to the general masculine order and is, consequently, inferior by implication.

Women are recognizing that too often their identity depends on a male. She is "John's wife" or "Mrs. James Smith" or "Harry's widow." Even the contemporary practice by feminists of hyphenating their maiden name with their husband's name seems less than satisfactory to some. They are just adding another male-derived name—that is, their father's surname— to their husband's name.

The Buckley law has guaranteed everyone freedom of access to personal letters of recommendation and dossiers. One can anticipate that letters describing men only in terms of their work capabilities and women in terms of their social graces will be discarded in favor of descriptions that stress performance capabilities equally.

These are some of the techniques of verbal behavior that women need to acquire. Now let us turn to a consideration of nonverbal behavior.

NONVERBAL BEHAVIOR

What kinds of correctives can we apply to our nonverbal behaviors? It has been suggested that it is easier to change nonverbal interaction patterns than it is to alter speech patterns. Some possible suggestions for women include the following:

1. Examine your own style of nonverbal behavior for sex-stereotyped patterns and particularly for self-defeating and destructive patterns. Try to recognize when you are intimidated. If you do respond with submissive behaviors, perhaps then it will be because you have made the conscious decision that this is appropriate behavior, and it will not be an automatic or reflexive response on your part.

2. Monitor yourself for the ever-present nervous grinning and uneasy smiling that is often cued by dominance behavior from another. Smile when you are happy, when you feel good. Phony smiling may weaken your position because your smile will be relatively meaningless.

3. When someone looks at you, don't drop your eyes. Look back. Stare someone in the eye, if appropriate.

4. Touch others when you feel it is appropriate and be aware of who is touching you. Refuse to accept tactual assertion of authority. Do not submit to another's will because of the subtle implication of that person's touch. Remove your hands from the grasp of persons who hold them too long and remove another's hands from your person when such a touch or grasp is unsolicited and unwanted.

5. Be more relaxed in demeanor and assume an open posture. Do not be afraid to claim moving-around space for yourself.

6. Do not be too quick to make way for the other person as you approach one another. Expect some "give" from the other as well. Establishing eye contact or looking at the other, rather than averting the eyes, is useful in such a situation.

7. Free your gestures to express your feelings. Avoid histrionics but do not hesitate to point, clench your fist, or use other forceful gestures if they convey your ideas well.

8. Be aware of small gestures, such as the head tilt, that can do you a disservice when you are looking directly at another. Tilting your head can mitigate the directness of your gaze by giving it an air of submissiveness.

9. Remember you have some responsibility for socializing the next generation. Be aware of what you are nonverbally teaching children, in terms of submissiveness and acquiescence to power and privilege, through nonverbal communication.[9]

Possible suggestions for males include the following:

1. Begin to develop an awareness of what you are signaling and signifying nonverbally.

2. Restrain your invasions of others' personal space if it is not by mutual consent.

[9]Many of these suggestions were taken from the following: Nancy Henley and Barrie Thorne, "Womanspeak and Manspeak: Sex Differences and Sexism in Communication, Verbal and Nonverbal," *Beyond Sex Roles*, ed. Alice Sargent (St. Paul, Minn.: West Publishing Company, 1977), p. 216; Nancy Henley, "Nonverbal Interaction and Personal Growth," *Siscom '75: Women's (and Men's) Communication*, ed. Barbara Eakins, Gene Eakins, and Barbara Lieb-Brilhart (Falls Church, Va.: Speech Communication Association, 1976), pp. 144–145; Nancy Henley, "Sounds of Silence," *Womankind* Television Series, Program 6, KAET-TV Channel 8, Arizona State University, 17 March 1976).

3. Avoid touch when it may be unsolicited, is not likely to be reciprocated, and seems to be used as an assertion of status or authority.

4. Keep in mind you may sometimes benefit by "losing your cool" and feeling free to express your emotions.

5. Monitor your reactions to being touched by women.

6. Remember you have some responsibility for socializing the next generation. Be aware of what you are nonverbally teaching children in terms of dominance, power, and privilege through nonverbal communication.

Because of women's apparent disadvantageous position in society, many writers feel women should develop supportive gestures with other women. Positive ways for women, and people in general, to give attention and support nonverbally to other women during communication interaction include the following:

1. Look at women what they speak.

2. Respond and react.

3. Do not interrupt.

4. Do not distract with noises or gestures while they are talking.

5. Develop gestures of mutual support, such as these behaviors: eye contact, leaning forward, nodding (where appropriate and genuine), and smiling (where appropriate and genuine), open posture.[10]

FOR DISCUSSION

1. Do you agree that language is "male-oriented?" Do you agree with the recommendations made by Eakins and Eakins and by others for eliminating this sex bias?

2. Examine your own language behavior. Is it male-oriented or sexist in any way? How? What might be done to change these language patterns?

3. Eakins and Eakins offer six major suggestions for "chipping away the rough spots in regard to some of the presumed inequities in naming and describing men and women." Which do you find the most useful? Which (if any) do you disagree with? What other suggestions might you offer?

4. Does your nonverbal behavior reflect a sex bias? In what way? How might this be altered? Are the suggestions of Eakins and Eakins useful to you in your everyday interpersonal interactions?

[10]Henley, "Nonverbal Interaction and Personal Growth," pp. 144–145.

Pointing the Finger at Sign Language

Elaine S. Polin

The battles being waged to eliminate sexism from spoken and written English are slowly being won. Now efforts are being made to eliminate sexism from sign language as well. "NABCOT," the newsletter of the Nassau County (New York) Board of Cooperative Educational Services, reports on efforts to modernize sign language. Ameslan, the American Sign Language, indicates male pronouns by a combination of hand gestures and reference to the brain area. The female pronouns are formed by referring to the lower facial areas.

A teacher at the Cleary Deaf Child Center in Ronkonkoma, Long Island, interviewed on the question of sexism in sign language, felt that students do not pick up sexist messages from these signs. She explained that the sign for "man" originated from the gesture of the man's tipping his hat and the sign for "woman" from the tying of the bonnet. Signs for "boy," "girl," and related pronouns are therefore extensions of these graphic gestures.

But then, all sign language is not the same. If Ameslan contains sexist implications, Italian sign language is more explicit. The sign for "woman" is the cupping of the hands above and below the breasts; the sign for "man" is the twirling of an imaginary mustache!

From *Ms.* (May 1979), p. 24.

A Dictionary of Jobs Abolishes Sexism in 20,000 Listings

The New York Times, *December 18, 1977*

Once a busboy was a busboy and a stewardess was a stewardess. Now a busboy is a dining room attendant and a stewardess is an airline flight attendant. And a governess is a children's tutor and a repairman is a repairer.

It is all there, page upon page, in the fourth edition of the Labor Department's Dictionary of Occupational Titles.

A dozen years in the making, weighing in at over five pounds, running more than 1,300 pages, the dictionary is a codified compilation of jobs ordinary and unusual.

Each job classification, developed after painstaking research and analysis, has a nine-digit code of its own. This report, for example, is the work of a 131.267-018.

In any listing of 20,000 job definitions a few odd ones will appear such as dog bather and bomb loader in this reference work for 30,000 state employment office workers.

"It's not something that is just an oddball thing. This is the fourth edition of this dictionary," said Arden Nelsen, a 166.067-010 at the Labor Department. That is occupational analyst in dictionary code.

The third edition, published in 1965, sold more than 100,000 volumes in a dozen years. The 1977 edition, a one-volume edition for the first time, is expected to be in demand as well, even though the Government Printing Office is asking $12 a copy.

The dictionary "eliminates sex and age references—both in job definitions and job titles—which were contained in more than 3,000 occupations in the previous edition," the Labor Department said in a statement.

It once was that a batboy was someone who made sure that baseball sluggers had the proper wood in their hands. Now that someone is a bat handler.

The old dictionary had separate listings for waiter and waitress. That presented a problem to the editors of the new dictionary, since they wanted to eliminate the ageism and sexism from their work. They struck a compromise: waiter-waitress.

A governess became a children's tutor, but Mr. Nelson said, "We're not very happy about having to give that classification. That's not a very original title."

The problem of what to do with busboy was particularly nasty, since the word contains elements that might be offensive to both women and older people.

"We decided to call them dining room attendants," Mr. Nelson said.

He added, "Where we had jobs that were repairmen or servicemen we just took the 'man' off and put the 'er' ending on it." So repairmen became repairer.

And some occupations have become obsolete. Stencil cutters, for example, have been dropped from the new edition, victims of the mushrooming photocopying industry.

Attack by Question

Jacques Lalanne

Questions have their place. Anyone who has seen a skillful lawyer break down a carefully constructed lie knows the value of effective questions, or cross-questions, as weapons.

But in everyday conversation, questions are usually a poor substitute for more direct communication. Questions are incomplete, indirect, veiled, impersonal and consequently ineffective messages that often breed defensive reactions and resistance. They are rarely simple requests for information, but an indirect means of attaining an end, a way of manipulating the person being questioned.

Where did you go?
Out.
What did you do?
Nothing.

This classic parent/child exchange illustrates in 10 words how ineffective questions may be. The parent isn't really asking for information, but making a charge. What comes across is: "You know you're not supposed to cross the street," or, "I told you not to go anywhere after eight o'clock," or, "You got your dress dirty again."

The child's answers, brief as they are, are just as devious. He's learned the hard way that a straightforward answer is likely to lead to trouble. So he uses evasion—"Out," or a half truth—"Nothing."

From *Psychology Today*, 9 (November 1975), p. 134. Reprinted from Psychology Today. Copyright © 1976 Ziff-Davis Publishing Company.

"When Did You Get Home?"   It's no surprise that questions make most of us feel uneasy. They remind us of times we'd rather forget. As children, before we learned the small skills of excuse and evasion, questions were often a prelude to accusations, advice, blame, orders, etc. At home we'd be asked what we did, or what we didn't do, and one seemed as bad as the other. At school, most questions seemed designed to ferret out what we didn't know rather than what we did.

When we become adults, the questions keep coming. As spouses, salespeople, bosses, even friends, we all use questions to manipulate in some way, convince of some truth, or convict of some error.

"Have you spoken to him about it?" often means, "You should speak to him, and soon." "When did you get home last night?" usually means, "You should have called me as you promised."

A person asking questions may feel in control of a conversation, but that type of conversation isn't very nourishing for the questioner, either, because he's not really involved. Instead of examining our own feelings, as questioners we focus attention on the other person. We replace what is going on inside us with what is happening outside; facts take on more importance than feelings.

For example, instead of saying, "I'm disappointed," we often ask, "When did you decide?" Joy and gratitude remain veiled behind "How did you prepare all that?" and instead of showing that we are worried, we ask, "Where were you, for heaven's sake?"

"I Was Afraid . . ."   It's easy to fall into the question-answer conversational trap, and we'd be better off consciously avoiding it. When we feel a question coming on, we could start listening to ourselves, identify our real feelings and express them, rather than hiding them in a question.

Instead of asking coolly, "Are you going out tomorrow afternoon?," we can become involved by revealing, "I'd appreciate it if you took me downtown tomorrow." The question, "What were you doing there so late?," does not express our real feelings as much as, "I was afraid you'd been in an accident."

Personal disclosures of this kind involve risk. By showing our real feelings, we chance direct refusal or rejection. But we also create a warm climate for direct, fruitful contact with the other person—something the tepid questioning approach rarely accomplishes.

When a questioner has us in his clutches, we can break the spell by paying careful attention to the speaker's tone of voice, gestures, and other hints to see what the real message is, and then respond to that deeper meaning. Feedback establishes communication and lets it circulate.

It could work like this. "Where were you so late last night?" might be answered, "You seem quite worried about it," a response which opens the door for a discussion of what is really bothering the questioner. In answer to "Are you going out Friday night?," words such as "Maybe we can make plans for the night" get at the real message in considerably less time.

BEYOND THE QUESTION MARK

Here are some everyday questions that work better as honest statements:

What time is it? *I'm tired. I'd like to go home now.*

Is it far? *I don't feel up to a long trip this weekend.*

Do you love me? *I wish you'd spend more time with me. You work every day and read in the evenings.*

How much did you pay? *I hope we have some money left for the rest of the week.*

Is it good? *I need to know if you like my soup. I made it the way you prefer.*

FOR DISCUSSION

1. Do parental questions, such as those suggested by Lalanne, make you uneasy? Why? What types of questions do you find particularly difficult and unsettling? Why?

2. Do you use questions instead of direct statements of feelings and thoughts? Why?

3. Rework the following questions into more direct honest statements. What are the advantages and disadvantages of each type of phrasing?

  a. Why did you do that?

  b. Is something wrong?

  c. Was the class interesting?

  d. Do I look O.K.?

  e. Do you feel like going for coffee?

4. Will your "attack by question" behavior change in any way as a result of reading this article? Explain.

NONVERBAL
MESSAGES

At one time in the history of communication, the role of nonverbal messages would have at best been considered minor. Verbal messages would have been accorded perhaps 90 percent of the emphasis and some brief notes would have been added attesting to the fact that some messages are communicated through nonverbal means. Today we realize that nonverbal messages are not footnotes to verbal messages; rather, they are complex and sophisticated communication systems which in many instances communicate even more meaning than do the verbal messages. Consequently, in this reader verbal and nonverbal messages are given approximately equal weight. This will not please every instructor nor every student, but it seems a fair representation of communication as it exists in its various forms and types.

George Miller's "Nonverbal Communication" provides an excellent overview of the nature of nonverbal communication and identifies the various types of nonverbal messages, such as gestures, the treatment of space, vocal volume and rate, touching, physical appearance, and the like. Miller also succeeds in clarifying the place of nonverbal messages within the total communication act.

The remaining articles in this section may be seen as attempts to expand and elaborate on the more significant nonverbal communication systems. Rowland Cuthill's "How to Read the Other Guy's Silent Signals" focuses on the role of body gestures, facial expressions, and body posture. It also covers the ways in which we present ourselves to others nonverbally and the ways in which we receive such messages from others.

Dale Leathers, in his "Paravocal Communication," covers the area of the vocal but nonverbal dimension of communication—the variations in volume, rate, pausing and the like—and the meanings that these aspects of our talk communicate.

In the last article J. Vernon Jensen discusses "Communicative Functions of Silence" and explains the numerous messages that we may communicate by remaining silent. Silence—like words and gestures—also communicates, sometimes even more clearly than eloquently phrased sentences.

All these articles should heighten your awareness of the varied types of nonverbal messages that may be and are constantly being employed by ourselves and by others. The varied meanings that these messages may have should become apparent.

Nonverbal Communication

George A. Miller

When the German philosopher Nietzsche said that "success is the greatest liar," he meant that a successful person seems especially worthy to us even when his success is due to nothing more than good luck. But Nietzsche's observation can be interpreted more broadly.

People communicate in many different ways. One of the most important ways, of course, is through language. Moreover, when language is written it can be completely isolated from the context in which it occurs; it can be treated as if it were an independent and self-contained process. We have been so successful in using and describing and analyzing this special kind of communication that we sometimes act as if language were the *only* kind of communication that can occur between people. When we act that way, of course, we have been deceived by success, the greatest liar of them all.

Like all animals, people communicate by their actions as well as by the noises they make. It is a sort of biological anomaly of man—something like the giraffe's neck, or the pelican's beak—that our vocal noises have so far outgrown in importance and frequency all our other methods of signaling to one another. Language is obviously essential for human beings, but it is not the whole story of human communication. Not by a long shot.

Consider the following familiar fact. When leaders in one of the less well developed countries decide that they are ready to introduce some technology that is already highly advanced in another country, they do not simply buy all the books that have been written about that technology

Communication, Language, and Meaning: Psychological Perspectives (New York: Basic Books, 1973).

and have their students read them. The books may exist and they may be very good, but just reading about the technology is not enough. The students must be sent to study in a country where the technology is already flourishing, where they can see it first hand. Once they have been exposed to it in person and experienced it as part of their own lives, they are ready to understand and put to use the information that is in the books. But the verbal message, without the personal experience to back it up, is of little value.

Now what is it that the students learn by participating in a technology that they can not learn by just reading about it? It seems obvious that they are learning something important, and that whatever it is they are learning is something that we don't know how to put into our verbal descriptions. There is a kind of nonverbal communication that occurs when students are personally involved in the technology and when they interact with people who are using and developing it.

Pictures are one kind of nonverbal communication, of course, and moving pictures can communicate some of the information that is difficult to capture in words. Pictures also have many of the properties that make language so useful—they can be taken in one situation at one time and viewed in an entirely different situation at any later time. Now that we have television satellites, pictures can be transmitted instantaneously all over the world, just as our words can be transmitted by radio. Perhaps the students who are trying to learn how to create a new technology in their own country could supplement their reading by watching moving pictures of people at work in the developed industry. Certainly the pictures would be a help, but they would be very expensive. And we don't really know whether words and pictures together would capture everything the students would be able to learn by going to a more advanced country and participating directly in the technology.

Let me take another familiar example. There are many different cultures in the world, and in each of them the children must learn a great many things that are expected of everyone who participates effectively in that culture. These things are taken for granted by everyone who shares the culture. When I say they are taken for granted, I mean that nobody needs to describe them or write them down or try self-consciously to teach them to children. Indeed, the children begin to learn them before their linguistic skills are far enough developed to understand a verbal description of what they are learning. This kind of learning has sometimes been called "imitation," but that is much too simple an explanation for the complex processes that go on when a child learns what is normal and expected in his own community. Most of the norms are communicated to the child nonverbally, and he internalizes them as if no other possibilities existed. They are as much a part of him as his own body; he would no more question them than he would question the fact that he has two hands and two feet, but only one head.

These cultural norms can be described verbally, of course. Anthropologists who are interested in describing the differences among the many cultures of the world have developed a special sensitivity to cultural norms and have described them at length in their scholarly books. But if a child had to read those books in order to learn what was expected of him, he would never become an effective member of his own community.

What is an example of the sort of thing that children learn nonverbally? One of the simplest examples to observe and analyze and discuss is the way people use clothing and bodily ornamentation to communicate. At any particular time in any particular culture there is an accepted and normal way to dress and to arrange the hair and to paint the face and to wear one's jewelry. By adopting those conventions for dressing himself, a person communicates to the world that he wants to be treated according to the standards of the culture for which they are appropriate. When a black person in America rejects the normal American dress and puts on African clothing, he is communicating to the world that he wants to be treated as an Afro-American. When a white man lets his hair and beard grow, wears very informal clothing, and puts beads around his neck, he is communicating to the world that he rejects many of the traditional values of Western culture. On the surface, dressing up in unusual costumes would seem to be one of the more innocent forms of dissent that a person could express, but in fact it is deeply resented by many people who still feel bound by the traditional conventions of their culture and who become fearful or angry when those norms are violated. The nonverbal message that such a costume communicates is "I reject your culture and your values," and those who resent this message can be violent in their response.

The use of clothing as an avenue of communication is relatively obvious, of course. A somewhat subtler kind of communication occurs in the way people use their eyes. We are remarkably accurate in judging the direction of another person's gaze; psychologists have done experiments that have measured just how accurate such judgments are. From an observation of where a person is looking we can infer what he is looking at, and from knowing what he is looking at we can guess what he is interested in, and from what he is interested in and the general situation we can usually make a fairly good guess about what he is going to do. Thus eye movements can be a rich and important channel of nonverbal communication.

Most personal interaction is initiated by a short period during which two people look directly at one another. Direct eye contact is a signal that each has the other's attention, and that some further form of interaction can follow. In Western cultures, to look directly into another person's eyes is equivalent to saying, "I am open to you—let the action begin." Everyone knows how much lovers can communicate by their eyes, but aggressive eye contact can also be extremely informative.

In large cities, where people are crowded in together with others they neither know nor care about, many people develop a deliberate strategy of avoiding eye contacts. They want to mind their own business, they don't have time to interact with everyone they pass, and they communicate this fact by refusing to look at other people's faces. It is one of the things that make newcomers to the city feel that it is a hostile and unfriendly place.

Eye contact also has an important role in regulating conversational interactions. In America, a typical pattern is for the listener to signal that he is paying attention by looking at the talker's mouth or eyes. Since direct eye contact is often too intimate, the talker may let his eyes wander elsewhere. As the moment arrives for the talker to become a listener, and for his partner to begin talking, there will often be a preliminary eye signal. The talker will often look toward the listener, and the listener will signal that he is ready to talk by glancing away.

Such eye signals will vary, of course, depending on what the people are talking about and what the personal relation is between them. But whatever the pattern of eye signals that two people are using, they use them unconsciously. If you try to become aware of your own eye movements while you are talking to someone, you will find it extremely frustrating. As soon as you try to think self-consciously about your own eye movements, you do not know where you should be looking. If you want to study how the eyes communicate, therefore, you should do it by observing other people, not yourself. But if you watch other people too intently, of course, you may disturb them or make them angry. So be careful!

Even the pupils of your eyes communicate. When a person becomes excited or interested in something, the pupils of his eyes increase in size. In order to test whether we are sensitive to these changes in pupil size, a psychologist showed people two pictures of the face of a pretty girl. The two pictures were completely identical except that in one picture the girl's pupil was constricted, whereas in the other picture her pupil was dilated. The people were asked to say which picture they liked better, and they voted in favor of the picture with the large pupil. Many of the judges did not even realize consciously what the difference was, but apparently they were sensitive to the difference and preferred the eyes that communicated excitement and interest.

Eye communication seems to be particularly important for Americans. It is part of the American culture that people should be kept at a distance, and that contact with another person's body should be avoided in all but the most intimate situations. Because of this social convention of dealing with others at a distance, Americans have to place much reliance on their distance receptors, their eyes and ears, for personal communication. In other cultures, however, people normally come closer together and bodily contact between conversational partners is as normal as eye contact is in America. In the Eastern Mediterranean cultures, for example, both the touch and the smell of the other person are expected.

The anthropologist Edward T. Hall has studied the spatial relations that seem appropriate to various kinds of interactions. They vary with intimacy, they depend on the possibility of eye contact, and they are different in different cultures. In America, for example, two strangers will converse impersonally at a distance of about four feet. If one moves closer, the other will back away. In a waiting room, strangers will keep apart, but friends will sit together, and members of a family may actually touch one another.

Other cultures have different spatial norms. In Latin America, for example, impersonal discussion normally occurs at a distance of two or three feet, which is the distance that is appropriate for personal discussion in North America. Consequently, it is impossible for a North and a South American both to be comfortable when they talk to one another unless one can adopt the zones that are normal for the other. If the South American advances to a distance that is comfortable for him, it will be too close for the North American, and he will withdraw, and one can chase the other all around the room unless something intervenes to end the conversation. The North American seems aloof and unfriendly to the South American. The South American seems hostile or oversexed to the North American. Hall mentions that North Americans sometimes cope with this difference by barricading themselves behind desks or tables, and that South Americans have been known literally to climb over these barriers in order to attain a comfortable distance at which to talk.

Within one's own culture these spatial signals are perfectly understood. If two North Americans are talking at a distance of one foot or less, you know that what they are saying is highly confidential. At a distance of two to three feet it will be some personal subject matter. At four or five feet it is impersonal, and if they are conversing at a distance of seven or eight feet, we know that they expect others to be listening to what they are saying. When talking to a group, a distance of ten to twenty feet is normal, and at greater distances only greetings are exchanged. These conventions are unconscious but highly reliable. For example, if you are having a personal conversation with a North American at a distance of two feet, you can shift it to an impersonal conversation by the simple procedure of moving back to a distance of four or five feet. If he can't follow you, he will find it quite impossible to maintain a personal discussion at that distance.

These examples should be enough to convince you—if you needed convincing—that we communicate a great deal of information that is not expressed in the words we utter. And I have not even mentioned yet the interesting kind of communication that occurs by means of gestures. A gesture is an expressive motion or action, usually made with the hands and arms, but also with the head or even the whole body. Gestures can occur with or without speech. As a part of the speech act, they usually emphasize what the person is saying, but they may occur without any speech at all. Some gestures are spontaneous, some are highly ritualized and have very specific meanings. And they differ enormously from one culture to another.

Misunderstanding of nonverbal communication is one of the most distressing and unnecessary sources of international friction. For example, few Americans understand how much the Chinese hate to be touched, or slapped on the back, or even to shake hands. How easy it would be for an American to avoid giving offense simply by avoiding these particular gestures that, to him, signify intimacy and friendliness. Or, to take another example, when Khrushchev placed his hands together over his head and shook them, most Americans interpreted it as an arrogant gesture of triumph, the sort of gesture a victorious prize fighter would make, even though Khrushchev seems to have intended it as a friendly gesture of international brotherhood. Sticking out the tongue and quickly drawing it back can be a gesture of self-castigation in one culture, an admission of a social mistake, but someone from another culture might interpret it as a gesture of ridicule or contempt, and in the Eskimo culture it would not be a gesture at all, but the conventional way of directing a current of air when blowing out a candle. Just a little better communication on the nonverbal level might go a long way toward improving international relations.

Ritualized gestures—the bow, the shrug, the smile, the wink, the military salute, the pointed finger, the thumbed nose, sticking out the tongue, and so on—are not really nonverbal communication, because such gestures are just a substitute for the verbal meanings that are associated with them. There are, however, many spontaneous gestures and actions that are unconscious, but communicate a great deal. If you take a moving picture of someone who is deeply engrossed in a conversation, and later show it to him, he will be quite surprised to see many of the gestures he used and the subtle effects they produced. Sometimes what a person is saying unconsciously by his actions may directly contradict what he is saying consciously with his words. Anthropologists have tried to develop a way to write down a description of these nonverbal actions, something like the notation that choreographers use to record the movements of a ballet dancer, but it is difficult to know exactly what the significance of these actions really is, or what the important features are that should be recorded. We can record them photographically, of course, but we still are not agreed on how the photographic record should be analyzed.

Finally, there is a whole spectrum of communication that is vocal, but not really verbal. The most obvious examples are spontaneous gasps of surprise or cries of pain. I suspect this kind of vocal communication is very similar for both man and animal. But our use of vocal signals goes far beyond such grunts and groans. It is a commonplace observation that the way you say something is as important as what you say, and often more important for telling the listener what your real intentions are. Exactly the same words may convey directly opposite messages according to the way they are said. For example, I can say, "Oh, isn't that wonderful" so that I sound enthusiastic, or I can say, "Oh isn't THAT wonderful" in a sarcastic tone so that you know I don't think it is wonderful at all. Because the actual words uttered are often misleading, lawyers and judges in the courtroom have learned that it is sometimes important to have an actual recording and not just a written transcript of what a person is supposed to have said.

Rapid and highly inflected speech usually communicates excitement, extremely distinct speech usually communicates anger, very loud speech usually communicates pomposity, and a slow monotone usually communicates boredom. The emotional clues that are provided by the way a person talks are extremely subtle, and accomplished actors must practice for many years to bring them under conscious control.

A person's pronunciation also tells a great deal about him. If he has a foreign accent, a sensitive listener can generally tell where he was born. If he speaks with a local dialect, we can often guess what his social origins were and how much education he has had. Often a person will have several different styles of speaking, and will use them to communicate which social role he happens to be playing at the moment. This is such a rich source of social and psychological information, in fact, that a whole new field has recently developed to study it, a field called "sociology of language."

One of the most significant signals that is vocal but nonverbal is the ungrammatical pause. In careful speech most of our pauses are grammatical. That is to say, our pauses occur at the boundaries of grammatical segments, and serve as a kind of audible punctuation. By calling them "grammatical pauses" we imply that they are a normal part of the verbal message. An ungrammatical pause, however, is not a part of the verbal message. For example, when I ... uh ... pause within a ... uh ... grammatical unit, you cannot regard the pause as part of my verbal message. These ungrammatical pauses are better regarded as the places where the speaker is thinking, is searching for words, and is planning how to continue his utterance. For a linguist, of course, the grammatical pause is most interesting, since it reveals something about the structure of the verbal message. For a psychologist, however, the ungrammatical pause is more interesting, because it reveals something about the thought processes of the speaker.

When a skilled person reads a prepared text, there are few ungrammatical pauses. But spontaneous speech is a highly fragmented and discontinuous activity. Indeed, ungrammatical pausing is a reliable signal of spontaneity in speech. The pauses tend to occur at choice points in the message, and particularly before words that are rare or unusual and words that are chosen with particular care. An actor who wanted to make his rehearsed speech sound spontaneous would deliberately introduce ungrammatical pauses at these critical points.

Verbal communication uses only one of the many kinds of signals that people can exchange; for a balanced view of the communication process we should always keep in mind the great variety of other signals that can reinforce or contradict the verbal message. These subtleties are especially important in psychotherapy, where a patient tries to communicate his emotional troubles to a doctor, but may find it difficult or impossible to express in words the real source of his distress. Under such circumstances, a good therapist learns to listen for more than words, and to rely on nonverbal signals to help him interpret the verbal signals. For this reason, many psychologists have been persistently interested in nonverbal communication, and have perhaps been less likely than linguists to fall into the mistaken belief that language is the only way we can communicate.

The price of opening up one's attention to this wider range of events, however, is a certain vagueness about the kind of communication that is occurring—about what it means and how to study it. We have no dictionaries or grammars to help us analyze nonverbal communication, and there is much work that will have to be done in many cultures before we can formulate and test any interesting scientific theories about nonverbal communication. Nevertheless, the obvious fact that so much communication does occur nonverbally should persuade us not to give up, and not to be misled by our success in analyzing verbal messages.

Recognizing the great variety of communication channels that are available is probably only the first step toward a broader conception of communication as a psychological process. Not only must we study what a person says and how he says it, but we must try to understand why he says it. If we concentrate primarily on the words that people say, we are likely to think that the only purpose of language is to exchange information. That is one of its purposes, of course, but certainly not the only one. People exchange many things. Not only do they exchange information, but they also exchange money, goods, services, love, and status. In any particular interaction, a person may give one of these social commodities in exchange for another. He may give information in exchange for money, or give services in exchange for status or love. Perhaps we should first characterize communication acts in terms of what people are trying to give and gain in their social interactions. Then, within that broader frame of reference, we might see better that verbal messages are more appropriate for some exchanges and nonverbal messages for others, and that both have their natural and complementary roles to play in the vast tapestry we call human society.

FOR DISCUSSION

1. Describe your own kinesic behavior in an interpersonal interaction with a close friend. How would this behavior differ when interacting with, say, the president of your college? With an individual to whom you have just been introduced and to whom you are romantically attracted? How would you describe this behavior when in a public speaking situation? Is this kinesic behavior effective? Ineffective?

2. Describe your own physical characteristics as specifically as you can. How satisfied are you with your body build? Your general attractiveness? Your height? Your hair? Your skin color and tone? What would you change? Why? How do you communicate your relative satisfaction—dissatisfaction?

3. How do you respond to interpersonal touching? Do you touch a great deal? Whom do you touch? Where do you generally touch them? Where do you avoid touching? Why? Do others touch you a great deal? How do you respond to such touching?

4. How do you treat space? Are you possessive of certain territories? Explain.

How to Read the Other Guy's Silent Signals

Rowland Cuthill

It's the most important meeting of your career. Let's say you're an architect, and you're at the final stage of negotiating your first million-dollar project. You've been through all the preliminaries and now you're meeting with Mr. Big—the man who'll decide if you get the job.

You make your presentation, and you know you're in top form. But suddenly you get a sinking feeling. Something, somewhere, isn't right. By the time the meeting's over, you're in a cold sweat. You're convinced you've blown it—but *how?*

You know your presentation was good. Suddenly, it dawns on you. You'd noticed—almost subconsciously—that halfway through the meeting the client had crossed his legs. Slowly he'd started tracing circles with his foot. When he spoke, his speech had suddenly become rapid, his questions staccato.

Sure enough, you lose out on the job. But long before you get the formal notice, you know it's hopeless. The give-away: the silent, nonverbal signals that the client sent you while you were pitching him.

Most of us—most of the time—take too narrow a view of communication. We think of it merely as an exchange of "facts" either spoken or written. We rarely realize that attitudes—including all-important emotions—are frequently communicated without words. Facial expressions, gestures with arms and legs—every move a person makes—often tell us more, and more honestly, than what a person says.

People working in certain professions are very much aware of their increased persuasiveness when they deliberately use these gestures and

From *Quest* (May 1977): 46–51. Reprinted by permission of *Quest Magazine*.

expressions—actors, professional gamblers, confidence men and politicians, for example.

An experienced practitioner makes a conscious attempt to impress with easy, slow, wide gestures; a relatively smooth brow; occasional head-on glances; slow, regular, and complete respiratory cycles; a resonant, inflective voice with optimistic timbre; a slightly uptilted chin; and composed hands.

If your persuadee responds with a forward-leaning posture, a generally rosy face, rapid breathing, barely masked excitement in face and voice, quick biting of the lip, and simultaneous eye-smile, then you can be fairly certain your opponent is buying your message.

Of course, your opponent can be as experienced at nonverbal communication as you are. In that case, two accomplished pros confront one another across an expanse of rosewood desk, all communication channels busily engaged, the various nonverbal signals constantly being given and interpreted. Little of what is transmitted, at any level, escapes either party; all such information is analyzed instinctively, and neither party questions his impressions and reactions (experience has taught each of them to trust cues). Both would be hard put to explain how they know what they know.

At first glance, the number of instruments required for nonverbal communication appears overwhelming. In fact, they are few, and they can be estimated fairly precisely. The voice has melody, timbre, stress and volume. Expression—facial or through body movement—can be analyzed into muscle sets and body parts, plus posture and gait.

A basic sign of attitude is a person's seated posture. A slightly forward lean indicates relaxed interest; a stiffly erect pose shows wariness; a backward sprawl, disrespect.

Social scientists advise individuals practising this form of "silent signals" interpretation to decide first whether their opponent's posture is habitual, or whether it is a specific response to *them*. To help in this, you are advised to note his body position when you begin the conversation, and be alert for changes in it during the exchange.

While some people are experienced enough in the use of words and expressions to make it difficult for you to know their feelings, there are always clues to follow:

1. When an individual's eyes are downcast, are covered by eyelids; when the face is turned away; when the smile is thin-lipped, restricted to the mouth, with nostrils not flared and eye creases not deepened—*you are being shut out.*

2. When an individual's mouth is relaxed, without the mechanical smile; chin is forward; eyes are still averted, but visible—*he is considering your presentation.*

3. When his eyes engage yours for several seconds at a time; a slight, one-sided smile, extending at least to nose level, is formed; brows are drawn together—*he is weighing your argument.*

4. When his head is shifted to the same level as yours; when his smile is

relaxed, and includes the mouth, nostrils, and eyes; when the eyes are fully visible, and when brows are clear or have slight horizontal lines—*he is enthusiastic,* and *you have made your point.*

Social scientists say the face and figure of your opponent may suggest approaches to use. For the timid or fearful persuadee (tense posture, peaked brows, hunched shoulders, pulled-in chin, wide eyes), a reassuring presence is indicated. If the individual seems depressed (lethargic manner, deep folds from mouth to chin, drooping eyes, saucer brows), light humor and quiet enthusiasm may put him in a receptive mood.

For the irritable individual (tense, jerky movements, brows drawn together and raised at the corners, pursed or tightly smiling mouth, numerous fine undereye lines), crisp efficiency and seriousness will probably prove the best course. The officious or disdainful individual (peaked brows, lifted chin, folded arms) is likely to respond to calm confidence mixed with deference.

A man who makes a good living teaching life-insurance salesmen how to read people's faces to increase sales, says understanding people isn't as difficult as it may seem. "But you must look carefully before you can understand them," say Robert Whiteside, author of the book called *Face Language.*

He says the size of a person's nose, the distance between the eyes, the fullness of the lips, and some 97 other characteristics of a person's face, indicate what kind of personality he has.

In essence, face language is the science of looking into people by studying their facial features; of understanding them by reading the messages ingrained on eyes, nose, mouth, lips and wrinkles. Whiteside has been studying and teaching face language since 1950, when he founded the "College of Personology."

Whiteside claims that people who use face language "definitely" increase their ability to persuade. He offers a success story: "An insurance salesman was about to have lunch with a very important client. He had not seen the man before, but as soon as he saw him, the salesman noticed that the man had small, beady eyes. Using that as a tip-off, he didn't talk to him about children, old times or sentimental things. He got right into talking about rates and service—all business. They had a good, solid session and achieved an awful lot, but they never once talked about their personal lives. They just got down to cases. Had he asked the customer, 'Oh, did your baby get over his cold?' or something like that, the man would have given him a fishy look, a kind of funny stare, and would have been thinking that it was none of his business. It would have irritated him that he was asked that question by a stranger."

Whiteside's sessions follow a lecture-type format. He first explains just what face language is, the reasoning behind it. etc. He then points out the most common facial indicators to look for, using large blow-up photographs of people's faces. He estimates that he has taught face language to some 2,000 salesmen.

After the lecture, Whiteside sometimes has individual sessions with members of the audience. "A big part of face language is that people apply it to *themselves* as they're on the firing line."

When he coaches individual salesmen, it's so they'll know how people tend to look at them. He converts their facial indicators into percentile points so they will know how they stand on different traits, such as stubbornness, sense of humor and so forth.

"Most people don't realize how they appear to others, although they certainly realize how the other guy appears to them," says Whiteside. "For instance, I might read a man's face and tell him that, according to the indicators, he pays too much attention to detail. After thinking about it, he'll agree. In other cases, we can determine whether he's too cold-blooded and businesslike and should be more warm, or whether he's too sentimental and should get down to cases."

As if having to worry about your facial expressions is not enough, now comes a sharp-eyed observer to suggest that the odd things you do with your eyeglasses are signals designed to impress or intimidate people.

Alfred P. Poll, a New York optician whose clientèle includes such jet-setters as Nancy Kissinger, Dustin Hoffman, and Leonard Bernstein, says that every little eyeglass movement can have a meaning all its own.

Says Poll: "The executive who suddenly removes his glasses and folds them into his case may be sending out the unspoken message that the meeting is over. And there is no sharper rebuke than hurling one's glasses across the desk as a show of displeasure. But the boss who wags his spectacles instead of his finger at an errant subordinate, is symbolically delivering a softer, more civilized reprimand.

"The person who compulsively folds and unfolds his specs, for instance, may be indicating boredom; the one who bends his temple bar may be revealing inner agitation; and someone who touches both temple tips together may be expressing intense concentration. And chewing on the temple tip is common among people who are tense, nervous or under great stress."

Poll, who designed the monocle worn by Charles Laughton in *Witness for the Prosecution,* argues that the way in which glasses are positioned on the face is also significant. The individual who props his glasses on his brow and regards his visitor with the naked eye may be demonstrating honesty and openness. By contrast, sliding the spectacles to the end of the nose and peering over the frames is the optical way of saying, "You're putting me on."

Hands and arms are expressive instruments, and can be used effectively in support of words and language, appearance and facial expression. "Take the handshake. We are able to find out—instantly—a great deal about the person who belongs to the hand we have just touched," says psychologist Mortimer R. Feinberg.

We have all had the faintly sickening shock of the "dead fish" handshake—usually accompanied by the person not looking at us directly. According to Feinberg, an analysis of the fish handshaker goes like this: he is ill at ease, he isn't used to shaking hands, and he probably detests being touched. He's probably arrogant—most arrogant people shy away from human contact, because they never know through which physical gesture their arrogance will reveal itself.

Then there's the "fingers-only" handshake—when the palm and back of the hand are rigorously retained. This person is bad news. If you are acquainted with someone resembling this individual, you might as well admit early on that he dislikes you. The fingers-only handshake is a declaration of war, directed at you personally.

Social scientists tell us that limbs reveal something about what others are thinking. *Beware folded arms and legs!* If, for example, you sit across a conference table from someone who does this, he could be sending you an urgent message. It may be a signal that he is turning you off, or cutting you out. This is frequently a position of defensiveness, in which an individual feels that you might be invading his territory, or that you've said something that makes him uneasy.

When this happens, say the experts, try to say something that will draw him out. Invite him to become part of the discussion again. A question or a request for an opinion will, on occasion, bring him back. "What do you think about . . . ?" is provocative, and could very well put him back on track.

Professional speakers are well aware of the power of persuasion through the use of silent signals. They give this piece of advice: outstretched hands with palms down create a feeling of calm, tranquility and peace. The same outstretched hands, palms up, invite participation, understanding—as well as suggesting that the speaker is giving himself over to his audience.

Forming shapes with the fingers—square, round and rectangle—or illustrating an all-encompassing point of view with widely spread hands, helps your audience grasp the point visually. Watch a good TV commercial to see how the professionals communicate.

Consider a one-to-one conversation with your boss, in which you decide to test the waters for reaction. For example, you find it necessary to refer to your unsatisfactory performance on the job, and you don't know how he will react. Dr. Alexander Lowen, a San Francisco psychologist who knows a lot about nonverbal communications, says, "If the boss retracts his shoulders, this might suggest suppressed anger." Other shoulder signals: raised shoulders imply fear; squared shoulders mean the person is shouldering his responsibility; and bowed shoulders tell us that the individual is carrying a heavy burden.

According to Dr. Lowen, the back, too, reveals some interesting characteristics. A straight back might indicate a strong ego, but also limited flexibility. An individual with a swayback might be extremely flexible, but the posture suggests a poorly defined ego.

How much does this tell about a person? Dr. Lowen says, "Obviously, it will take considerably more persuasion to move the inflexible person to your point of view. At the other extreme, it's quite likely that the person with the poorly defined ego, as demonstrated by his posture, would be hard pressed to convince a listener, but would probably be submissive or responsive to your point of view, even if it disagreed with his.

And what about the head? What does it tell about the character and personality of others? Held high in the air and tilted back, the head presents the picture of someone who is haughty and perhaps overly impressed with his own importance. But if it's tilted forward, sunken and resting on the chest, it may suggest that the person is suffering from defeat or depression. Inquisitive tilting of the head to one side implies that you might have to clarify an issue for your listener.

"And don't be misled by what appears to be the nod of consent," warns Robert R. Max, a communications consultant. "It could very well be a sign of agreement. However, it could also be the mesmeric state resulting from a dynamic presentation."

In some societies—in India for example—people move their heads up and down to mean *no*, and from side to side to mean *yes*. It's up to you to look for other signals that tell whether that up-and-down bobbing is genuine approval or not.

Physical props, such as a cup and saucer, can silently reveal a great deal about your personality. The intricate ballet of coffee-drinking and cup-handling is a fertile field for the observant. The person who holds the cup itself in his hand, keeps the saucer close, and maintains the cup rim close to the mouth, is protective, cautious, and unsure.

On the other hand, the person who hooks the handle with one finger, keeps the saucer at a distance, and puts the cup down firmly between sips, is apt to be dynamic, sure of himself, possibly vain and grandiose. Social scientists say that similar behavior patterns can be derived from how an individual lights a cigarette, and how he smokes it, and from whether—and what—he doodles.

A person can also create beneficial or dangerous emotional environments through body movements and tones of voice. To prove it, Ernst G. Beier, professor of psychology at the University of Utah in Salt Lake City, and his associate, Daniel P. Sternberg, conducted an experiment with 50 newlywed couples in an attempt to learn if they used body language to communicate cues indicating marital conflict or harmony.

Reporting their findings in *Psychology Today,* the social scientists were looking specifically for how the newlyweds, all between the ages of 18 and 24, responded to eye contact, laughing, talking, touching (of the self or of the spouse), and also for the way they held their arms and legs, open or closed.

"It became clear when we analyzed the data that nonverbal cues express a person's feelings very accurately," says Dr. Beier. The happy couples would sit closer together, look more frequently into each other's eyes, would touch each other more often than themselves, and would talk more to their spouses. The happier couples, in short, were able to create for each other a more comfortable and supportive bodily environment.

Meanwhile, the couples who were experiencing the most conflict sent out more distant vibrations. They tended to cross their arms and legs, had less eye contact, and touched themselves more frequently than they touched each other.

Why, despite the vast amount of research into nonverbal communication, does so much misunderstanding between people persist? Beier has an explanation: "We may say, for example, that we want another person to like us, and we absolutely believe what we say, yet we send out information through facial expressions, posture, tone of voice, and many other signals, that we don't like that person.

"Perhaps we made an error in communications, or perhaps the other person misinterpreted our meaning. A simpler explanation, particularly if such discordant behavior persists, is that we really wanted to communicate two different feelings at the same time. And we compromised. We maintained the self-image of a person who wants to show liking, but at the same time we managed to communicate *dis*like, without feeling responsible. It's a way of having our cake and eating it, too."

Although much has been written about various aspects of the voice, gestures, and expressions, no hard and fast rules exist for interpreting all nonverbal language. Actually, it's up to all of us to sharpen these skills through informal practice. A suggestion: watch television with the sound turned off, or observe the interactions of people in restaurants who are seated too far away for you to hear their conversations. Make a prediction about the eventual outcome, then follow the action all the way through to its conclusion.

And when you play the game for keeps by watching your real-life opponents for the truth behind the words they speak, remember that they may also be watching you.

FOR DISCUSSION

1. Cuthill suggests four clues to follow in reading silent signals, for example, when the individual's eyes are downcast, you are being shut out. Can you think of exceptions to these perhaps unrealistically clear-cut readings?

2. Do you make judgments of others on the basis of face language? What specific features do you focus on? Are you generally justified in your conclusions?

3. How do people read your face language? Ask some friends to share with you what they read in your face.

4. Do you agree with the observations of Alfred Poll, cited by Cuthill, on the meanings communicated by the handling of one's eyeglasses?

Paravocal Communication

Dale Leathers

So far we have been examining the effects of vocalic communication while excluding the effects of verbal communication. A significant portion of our communication can neither be clearly defined as vocal nor verbal in nature, however. Speech habits like "you know" and "sort of" appear to be clearly verbal or linguistic in form but they are not recognized as units of language. Consequently, they are listed as paralinguistic or extralinguistic phenomena. In the same manner belching, coughing, and laughing are essentially different sounds but they too have been identified as extralinguistic phenomena.

Since most of the researchers dealing with such phenomena are linguists or psycholinguists it is not surprising that they would try to place all identifiable behavior within a linguistic framework, and that those phenomena that do not conform to the rules or definitions of language would be placed in the all-inclusive category labeled paralinguistic or extralinguistic. Mahl and Schulze have made perhaps the most thorough and precise attempt to distinguish between linguistic and what they term extralinguistic factors in communication. Linguistic variations include the choice of the language (French or English, for example), variation in dialect, the use of simple or complex sentences, active or passive voice, present or past tense, and extensive or restricted vocabulary. Extralinguistic factors include variation in rate of speech, general loudness, general pitch level, throat clearing, belching, and a wide variety of body move-

From Dale G. Leathers, *Nonverbal Communication Systems* (Boston: Allyn and Bacon, 1976), pp. 133–136.

ments.[1] In their detailed classification of extralinguistic phenomena the vast majority of the variables they classify would be perceived by this author as vocal and not linguistic. Voice quality, rhythm, continuity of sound, and speech rate are just a few examples of phenomena that are vocal and not linguistic in nature.

Since virtually all of the variables we will discuss in this section are strictly vocal in nature, or closely related in nature to one of the nine attributes of sound previously identified in this chapter, these variables will be referred to as paravocal, rather than paralinguistic or extralinguistic variables.

While there are a large number of factors that might be fairly classified as part of paravocal communication, four of the most significant factors will be examined in this section: (1) rate of utterance, (2) rhythm, (3) hesitations, and (4) nonfluencies. Ideally, *we should be able to assess the effect of these four paravocal factors on communication.* Unfortunately, *we can do so only by inference since most studies attempt to determine what variables affect rate of utterance, rhythm, hesitations and nonfluencies rather than studying the effects of these factors on interpersonal communication.* As two authorities aptly note, one of the most striking revelations of an exhaustive survey of studies covering paravocal communication *"is the absence of systematic study of how the extralinguistic phenomena affect the listener's spontaneous, communicative behavior or his underlying psychological states and processes."*[2]

From a paravocal perspective, rate of utterance as perceived by listeners is not defined primarily in terms of how fast an individual is talking or uttering sounds. Rate of articulation is determined by the number of halts and pauses which interrupt the flow of utterance. A high rate of utterance has been found to be disruptive in interpersonal communication. High rates of utterance indicate an increase in the use of prepared and well-learned sequences or words, of cut and dried phrases and clichés, of trite and vernacular speech, and of commonplace utterance or professional jargon. As Goldman-Eisler so perceptively concludes, high rate of utterance

> indicates that there is less creative activity and that time serves no function other than that of sound transmission. While the mood which goes with speech that is being organized while being uttered seems to tend towards an arrest of time, that which accompanies speech requiring no further activity beyond the vocalization of learned connections travels through time at a pace dictated, at the best, only by external requirements such as intelligibility. Such speech will more easily become subject to corruption in the form of slurring, gabbling, etc., and the reason why we find these characteristics in pathological speech or speech produced under abnormal conditions may be due to the fact that such speech consists mainly of established speech habits.[3]

[1]G. F. Mahl and G. Schulze, "Psychological Research in the Extralinguistic Area," in *Approaches to Semiotics,* ed. T. A. Sebeok, A. S. Hayes, and M. C. Bateson (The Hague: Mouton, 1964), p. 59.

[2]Ibid., p. 78.

[3]F. Goldman-Eisler, "The Significance of Changes in the Rate of Articulation," *Language and Speech,* 4 (1961), 174.

The most consistent finding is that rate of utterance is a valid and accurate indicator of a speaker's psychological state. While this finding applies to both normal and abnormal speakers, emotional disturbance must still be regarded as directly related to variations in speech rate. By inference we can certainly conclude that a communicator using excessive rate is losing or apt to lose self-control, may become highly defensive, and, as cited above, is less capable of modifying his message to meet the demands of the situation.

The rhythm which characterizes a communicator's utterances is of great potential importance and its nature and effects are just beginning to be examined.[4] Dittmann notes that "the aspect of speech we have been working on is its rhythmical characteristic, its prosodic nature." To date, he has found a significant but not very close relationship between speech rhythm and body movements.[5] Goldman-Eisler has offered the provocative hypothesis that rhythmical utterances are directly related to cognitive rhythm in the communicator's thought processes. To paraphrase her findings: cognitive rhythm may result in periods of fluency characterized by rhythmicity in utterance. The only necessary, though not sufficient, condition for the appearance of temporal rhythm is that at least 30 percent of utterance be pausing time.[6]

Pauses or hesitations have a great impact in disrupting or facilitating the transmission of meaning in interpersonal communication. Pauses are defined as nonphonations of 200 milliseconds or more, measured on an oscillographic record of the speech.[7] Pauses or hesitation correspond to the highest point of uncertainty for the communicator which is typically the beginning of a unit of encoding or the beginning of the attempt to communicate a new idea.[8] This finding held up whether the pauses were filled or unfilled.[9] The duration of hesitation pauses was shown to be a

[4] A. Henderson, F. Goldman-Eisler, and F. A. Starbek, "Temporal Patterns of Cognitive Activity and Breath-Control in Speech," *Language and Speech,* 9 (1966), 216.

[5] A. T. Dittmann, "The Body Movement–Speech Rhythm Relationship as a Cue to Speech Encoding," in *Studies in Dyadic Communication,* ed. A. W. Siegman and B. Pope (New York: Pergamon Press, 1972), pp. 136–41.

[6] F. Goldman-Eisler, "Sequential Temporal Patterns and Cognitive Processes in Speech," *Language and Speech,* 10 (1967), 123–26.

[7] Dittmann, "The Body Movement–Speech Rhythm Relationship," p. 138.

[8] F. G. Lounsbury, "Pausal, Juncture, and Hesitation Phenomena," *Journal of Abnormal Social Psychology,* 49 (1954), 99.

[9] D. S. Boomer, "Hesitation and Grammatical Encoding," *Language and Speech,* 8 (1965), 152–62. In F. Goldman-Eisler, "A Comparative Study of Two Hesitation Phenomena," *Language and Speech,* 4 (1961), 18–26, the author makes the point that "filled pauses" are comprised of sounds such as α, ε, Æ , r, ə , m while silent hesitations are "unfilled pauses."

highly variable phenomenon, symptomatic of individual differences, sensitive to the pressures of social interaction, and to the requirements of verbal tasks. What is experienced as an increase of speed in talking proved to be variation in amount of pausing. *If you eliminate pauses, the perceived rate of articulation for a given communicator remains virtually constant.*[10]

Finally, perhaps the most studied factors which comprise paravocal communication are the eight types of nonfluencies identified by Mahl. Mahl identifies the eight types of nonfluencies as: (1) *"ah"*(Well . . . ah when I first came home.); (2) *sentence change* (Well she's . . . already she's lonesome.); (3) *repetition* (Cause they . . . they get along pretty well together.); (4) *stutter* (It sort of well I . . . I . . . leaves a memory); (5) *omission* (She mour . . . was in mourning for two years before.); (6) *sentence incompletion* (Well I'm sorry I couldn't get here last week so I could . . . ah . . . I was getting a child ready for camp and finishing up swimming lessons.); (7) *tongue slips* (includes neologisms and the substitution of an unintended for an intended word); (8) *intruding incoherent sound* (If I see a girl I'd like to take out I just . . . dh . . . ask her.)[11] While Mahl designed his speech disturbance categories as a measure of anxiety, they have two more important uses for the purposes of this chapter. In the first place they represent one definition of *disruptive paravocal communication* since each of the eight types of speech disturbance will tend to distort or prevent the exchange of meaning by vocal means. Second, and perhaps more importantly, they can serve to record the impact of such variables as interpersonal trust, confidence, and sincerity on the quality of paravocal communication. For example, one would expect the paravocal communication of an individual whose trust was being destroyed to be characterized by many more nonfluencies than an individual whose trust was being built. In fact this is precisely what Prentice found in a detailed study which examined the impact of this destruction on a communicator's fluency.[12]

In brief, paravocal communication can reveal much about the emotions a communicator is experiencing. More importantly, paravocal communication can be a major factor in determining the accuracy and efficiency with which meanings may be exchanged. It may serve as a reliable indicator that the vocalic communication system is not functioning as desired.

[10]F. Goldman-Eisler, *Psycholinguistics: Experiments in Spontaneous Speech* (New York: Academic Press, 1968).

[11]G. F. Mahl, "The Lexical and Linguistic Levels in the Expression of the Emotions," in *Expression of the Emotions in Man,* ed. P. Knapp (New York: International Universities Press, 1963), p. 81.

[12]D. S. Prentice, "The Process Effects of Trust-Destroying Behavior on the Quality of Communication in the Small Group," Ph.D. dissertation, University of California at Los Angeles, 1972.

FOR DISCUSSION

1. Describe your own paravocal communication. Write out this description in detail and show it to a few persons who know you well and ask them to comment on what they hear and what you have written. Remember that you hear yourself through both air and bone conduction; others hear you only through air conduction. Consequently, we can never hear ourselves as others do.

2. Listen to a television personality and analyze his or her paravocal communication. Describe this in detail. Compare your findings and conclusions with others.

3. Throughout the article Leathers advances a number of hypotheses concerning the relationship between paravocal communication and interpersonal communication. For example, the interpersonal communications of a person whose trust was being destroyed would be characterized by many nonfluencies. What other hypothesis might you advance? On what basis did you formulate this/these hypothesis(es)?

Communicative Functions of Silence

J. Vernon Jensen

*For everything there is a season, and a time for every purpose under heaven . . . a
time to keep silence, and a time to speak.*

Ecclesiastes 3:1, 7

Over the centuries man has revealed his superiority over the beasts of the
field, the fish of the sea, and the birds of the air, by gradually constructing
an intricate arbitrary system of sound symbols with which to communicate,
thus refining gestural efforts. By further inventing systems of orthographic
symbols, man has been able to preserve his message for succeeding
generations who are able to build upon it and hence progress to more
complex, and presumably higher, levels of existence. While aware of this
gift of communicating via sound and visual symbols, few of us are fully
sensitive to the reality that absence of sound—that is, silence—can also
perform a number of highly significant communicative functions. Helping
silence to function, of course, there are usually many reinforcing nonverbal
cues, such as a shrug of the shoulders, a frown, a tensed mouth, a glare,
a clenched fist, or a nod of the head, but silence is still a—if not *the*—
paramount factor in many communicative situations. Numerous factors of
context and also cultural influences will of course also play a role in the
various functioning of silence, so we must ascribe functions with caution.
Nevertheless we can look upon silence as performing (a) a linkage function,
(b) an affecting function, (c) a revelational function, (d) a judgmental
function, and (e) an activating function.

From J. Vernon Jensen, "Communicative Functions of Silence," *ETC: A Review of General
Semantics*, Vol. 30 (September, 1973), pp. 249–257, by permission of the International Society
for General Semantics.

First, silence can serve a *linkage* function, and in both a positive or a negative sense. That is, it can bind together people or it can sever relationships. Most of us certainly realize the truth of the statement by Thomas Mann, which appears so prominently in public-speaking textbooks and periodicals and in other literature, that "Speech is civilization itself. The word, even the most contradictious word, preserves contact—it is silence which isolates [p.518]."[9] We fully realize that silence separates us, isolates us, from our fellow human beings. Thus most alert humans seek to improve their ability to speak well—and the speech profession convinces itself of its own importance! Sometimes, of course, we purposely isolate ourselves by silence, in fact, protect ourselves by a wall of silence. For instance, in an urban setting or in other crowded situations, we do not talk too much to neighbors or those around us lest we be flooded with their presence.

We ought not, however, overlook the equally significant fact that silence also binds people together. Donald K. Smith has phrased a paradox, "Speech, the instrument of community, can destroy community [p.91],"[15] which we can turn around: "Silence, the instrument of isolation, can create community." Words frequently are intruding, unnecessary interlopers between lovers, whose mutual affection is warmly and clearly communicated by hours of silence in each other's presence. Love shared between husband and wife, mutual affection and trust between parents and children, and feelings of oneness between friends also permit a firm bond to be created and maintained without words being uttered. As one writer has phrased it, friends "can stalk along mile after mile together without a word but in perfect communication—each glad for the other's presence, each glad the other is alive, each grateful to be his friend, each feeling understood, each cherishing the other [p.59]."[16] Alexander Kendrick wrote of Edward R. Murrow and the latter's friend Bob Dixon: "They hunted . . . together, . . . and 'communicated in long silences' [p.307]."[8] Robert T. Oliver has written of the importance of friends.

> . . . someone with whom we can just sit, for a kind of comradeship in which talk is superfluous, in which a flow of quiet sympathy and mutual understanding is more eloquent than words . . . It is not through speech or acts but through silence that the deepest bonds are cemented. One sure fruit of this communion of silence is that it invites the deepest and most intimate of confidential sharing [p.153].[12]

Not only does silence link us with those near to us but also with those removed in distance, time, or point of view. In silence we think of and feel linked with an absent sweetheart, friend, parent, child, or spouse. In moments of silence we sense a bond with generations gone before us, and many organizations and nations institutionalize such formal moments of silence to commemorate a past event and forge bonds between the present and past generations. The Netherlands, for instance, in the evening of May 4th each year, stops for a moment of silence in memory of those who died in World War II.[7] People holding sharply differing religious or political views can tolerate each other in silence, and interfaith worship services rely heavily on silent moments.

Furthermore, religiously oriented individuals have throughout history insisted that silence is frequently a, if not *the,* communicative vehicle for linking man and his God (or whatever terms are employed to denote the creative power behind life). Bernhard Christensen, contemporary Protestant educator and theologian, has written: "Sometimes the deepest communion of all is wordless, even between earthly friends, and much more so between the soul and God [p.122]."[3] The Catholic monk, Thomas Merton, writes that "The monastic community exists . . . that all may more easily attain to their common end, which is union with God in solitude [p.43]."[11] Quakers have always had a central emphasis on silence, and most religious groups utilize at least brief periods of silent prayer. As James Pike stated: "In the . . . prayer of silence we give God the opportunity to speak directly to us in judgment on the past and in guidance for the future [p.178]."[13] The Buddhist monk in his disciplined silence feels at one with the external Power behind all of life, and finds "joy in being one with those waves of creation and destruction [p.50]"[1] inherent in life. Commenting on his months of aloneness at the Antarctic, Admiral Byrd wrote:

> I paused to listen to the silence. . . . The day was dying, the night being born—but with great peace. Here were the imponderable processes and forces of the cosmos, harmonious and soundless. Harmony, that was it! That was what came out of the silence—a gentle rhythm, momentarily to be myself a part of it. In that instant I could feel no doubt of man's oneness with the universe [p.85].[2]

Second, silence fulfills an *affecting* function. That is, silence has the power to affect us and those around us, and for both good or ill. Silence can heal and it can wound. We realize that by holding our tongue during an aggravated moment, keeping things unspoken, can be extremely important preventive medicine. Silence, then, can often increase the likelihood that two people will not wound each other. Also, after harsh words have been spoken, silence (and the passage of time) may help to heal any wounds inflicted, whereas additional words would merely increase the ill will.

But silence between two individuals can also wound, can cut as deeply as words. We are all aware of the pain involved when someone is given the "silent treatment." Silence can also communicate indifference—which can be as agonizing to the recipient as outright animosity. Silence may permit each person involved to exaggerate and distort to an incredible degree the supposed wrong committed by the other person; the proverbial mountain might indeed be constructed out of a prairie dog's hill. Also, the sore and ragged wound caused by silence may be as difficult to heal as any wound caused by words. Dag Hammarskjold put it incisively if somewhat pessimistically: "What happens during the unspoken dialogue between two people can never be put right by anything they say—not even if, with mutual insight into what has occurred, they should make a joint attempt at reparation [p.78]."[6]

Silence can communicate scorn, hostility, coldness, defiance, sternness, and hate; but it can also communicate respect, kindness, and acceptance. Potentially both balm and irritant, silence definitely *affects* us. Silence shatters a person in solitary confinement, but to a harried young mother, silence soothes.

Silence affects those involved by solidifying or melting existing relationships. It can harden ill will through absence of new facts and moods that might be offered by words; and the involved persons remain angry with each other until the silence is broken. The so-called "cooling off" period actually becomes a freezing period! Likewise silence can solidify existing good will by the nonappearance of any communication that might reduce the pleasant rapport.

Silence can also melt *status quo* relationships, for it sometimes permits tempers to subside and ushers in balanced judgment to replace harsh and exaggerated and warped attitudes and assertions. Often, then, silence makes the heart, if not grow fonder, at least grow more pliable, more flexible. Sometimes silence—and the passage of time—can also melt away existing good will, as when one becomes aware that he has been taken in by a fast-talking salesman, an eloquent orator, or a conniving colleague. One may discover upon silent reflection that what he at first took to be a favorable remark about himself by another individual was in reality a subtle unkindness.

Third, silence performs a *revelational* function in communication; that is, it can facilitate making something known but also can hide something. Certainly it is plain that the absence of words keeps from the auditor whatever might be on the mind of the would-be communicator. If a child says nothing about the happenings in school, the parent has difficulty knowing what transpired. If a person refuses to say anything about his problems to his colleague, the latter may never know what is troubling his companion. When a person in a small group is silent, it often communicates that he does not possess knowledge on the subject being discussed. When a student remains silent when asked a question, the teacher interprets it to mean that the student does not know the information requested.

On the other hand, silence also reveals much information. It may reveal much about our inner self, both to ourselves and to others. As the poet Kahlil Gibran has phrased it, "The silence of aloneness reveals to [your] eyes [your] naked [self] [p.68]."[4] Hammarskjold put it this way: "Silence shatters to pieces the mind's armor, leaving it naked before autumn's clear eye [p.167]."[6] Silence has a way of revealing one's "true" inner being, of stripping away the outer veneer, the pretensions built around oneself. Afraid of silence, many people fill their day with a host of "scheduled" activities so they do not have to be alone with their thoughts and themselves. Silence can be important in revealing the extremes of personality fulfillment, that is, of complete serenity and of complete derangement. Self-composure, peace, and calmness mark the "whole" person, the "adjusted" individual. Poets and religious mystics have always reminded us that to realize the true fulfillment of self, one must be able to immerse himself in silence. Thomas Merton has expressed it well:

> The world of men has forgotten the joys of silence, the peace of solitude which is necessary, to some extent, for the fullness of human living. . . . All men need enough silence and solitude in their lives to enable the deep inner voice of their own true selves to be heard at least occasionally. . . . If man is constantly exiled from his own home, locked out of his own spiritual solitude, he ceases to be a true person [p.143].[11]

In fact, some mystics such as Gibran would even chide: "You talk when you cease to be at peace with your thoughts; And when you can no longer dwell in the solitude of your heart you live in your lips, and sound is a diversion and a pastime [p.68]."[4] The Hindu yogi, the Buddhist monk, and the Trappist and Carthusian monks would heartily agree.

But if man talks to escape himself, certainly an equally strong case is evident that he occasionally reveals through silence an attempt to escape from himself, from reality around him. Clearly, excessive morbid silence reveals a lack of wholeness or adjustment. Mental hospitals are filled with sullen neurotics, deranged people sick with silence. In less severe forms, the silent moody person struggles with his lonesomeness in home, apartment or at work.

Silence can inform about other persons, events, or things also. When describing another person we frequently say much by what we omit, by those traits about which we are silent. The psychotherapist learns much about his patient by the latter's silence. The expression "Silence speaks louder than words" tells us of the revelational function of silence. In a courtroom or in other situations, negative evidence—that is, the absence of evidence, the testimony of silence—can be a highly significant admission. "If it were not true, he would have said so," can be quite decisive in the mind of a juryman. Silence can suggest guilt. Also, if we are silent, other people may assume we are being secretive about something, and our good faith may be questioned. Just as words often may hide much more than they reveal in certain situations, so can silence actually reveal more than it hides. To say nothing can reveal a host of assertions, but this leads us into a fourth major function.

Silence performs not only informational, affective, and linkage functions, but also *judgmental* functions. Silence is employed to register assent or dissent, favor or disfavor. Perhaps the most frequent judgment announced by silence is assent—agreement with what has been said, with what exists, with the *status quo*. Silence on the part of the auditor is frequently taken to mean agreement with the speaker. Since one is usually led to speak when something is wrong, that is, reacts to a problem, silence suggests that one sees nothing wrong, that he gives assent to what exists. Passive silence in the presence of political and social evils, in the face of the bigot's remark, in the presence of injustices and unsportsmanship, cloaks such *status quo* undesirables with an aura of acceptance. Hammarskjold has put it eloquently:

> The madman shouted in the market place. No one stopped to answer him. Thus it was confirmed that his thesis was incontrovertible [p.161].[6]

The sin of silence, giving assent where assent ought not to be given, is a troublesome burden carried at some time by virtually all conscientious people.

Silence can also register dissent with some *status quo* situation. Dissent through noble silence, though tortured by rack, fire, or dungeon, has highlighted many pages of history. More common and perhaps less dramatic episodes have been experienced by most people when they keep silent in a group that is being extremely unkind to some other person, or when some off-color joke is expressed. Silence can indeed make it clear that you disagree with the communicator. Civil rights silent sit-ins eloquently proclaimed dissent to existing segregated situations, despite taunts or bodily harm. Silence can defy a whole national regime, as the French Underground did to the German occupiers in World War II,[14,17] or as many do in Communist lands.[18]

Silence communicates not only the judgment of dissent but that of displeasure, of scorn, hostility, or anger. Silence chastises, for instance, when a teacher says nothing to the student who utters a nonsensical answer to a question, or when a parent keeps haughty silence when a child does something deemed foolish. John Howard Griffin, author of *Black Like Me*, reported on his experience with a white man who made improper advances: "The silence rattled between us and I felt sorry for the reprimand that grew from me to him in the silence [pp. 88–89]."[5]

Finally, silence performs an *activating* function in the communicative process. Silence, for instance, communicates an attitude of thoughtfulness. The public speaker who pauses before choosing certain words may give the impression of thoughtfulness, the carefulness of a reflective mind searching for the precise phrasing. The silent person is thinking, the talking person is not—so we often seem to assume. It is even asserted by some poets and mystics that speech is a barrier to thinking whereas silence perfects the thinking process. Gibran, for example, asserts:

> In much of your talking, thinking is half murdered. For thought is a bird of space, that in a cage of words may indeed unfold its wings but cannot fly [p.68].[4]

St Augustine wrote that in silence "the mind is in immediate contact with reality [p.187]."[10] On the other hand, silence is associated with the absence of mental activity. For instance, a day-dreaming child is reprimanded by parent or teacher for not giving thought to the subject at hand, for not thinking, "not doing anything," when in reality the silence of the youngster may very well be actively used thoughtfully.

Silence, when not accompanied by some physical activity, communicates the impression that the person is doing nothing, is not meaningfully engaged in some task, that no "activity" is taking place. A small child, for instance, understands that a parent is working, is "doing" something, if physical labor such as sweeping the floor, is involved; but if the parent sits in silence or reads a book, the child immediately assumes that "nothing" is being "done," and hence the parent is fair game to be disturbed. In less hurried cultures, just sitting *is* doing something, and they look at the rushing Westerner and say, "Don't just do something, sit there!"

Our talkative culture needs to realize more fully the value and communicative functions of silence. We need to view it not as periods in which there is an absence of communication but rather as an active agent, an important vehicle for significant communication. It is not necessarily an enemy, which "civilized" man is supposed to subdue, but rather a neutral component, potentially fostering or hindering healthy communication. More often than not, it should be viewed as a friendly variable that we need to embrace rather than destroy. Its eloquence needs to be more fully impressed upon us. We know the effectiveness of the command of silence—pauses—by the story-teller, actor, radio announcer, public speaker, and salesman; but we need also to recognize the importance of silence in all of life's interpersonal communicative situations. Silence has been associated throughout history with a sense of awe, reverence, respect, and mystery; we keep silence at funerals, at beautiful scenes, at some startling accomplishment, and during religious services. The prayerful assertion-exhortation of the ancient Hebrew, "The Lord is in his holy temple, Let all the earth keep silence," carries significant meaning to many still. The deaf have silence thrust upon them, the monk seeks it out, the distraught mother and overwhelmed executive desperately yearn for it. Many people scurry frantically to avoid it. Few of us could cope with the incredibly absolute silence of the desert, but we could cope with and profit by more moments and periods of silence than we probably at present experience. As communicologists, we need to understand more fully that silence performs many functions, which might be categorized as linkage, affecting, revelational, judgmental, and activating functions.

REFERENCES

1. BYLES, MARIE B. *Journey Into Burmese Silence.* London: George Allen & Unwin, 1962.

2. BYRD, RICHARD E. *Alone.* New York: G.P. Putnam's Sons, 1938.

3. CHRISTENSEN, BERNHARD. *He Who Has No Sword.* Minneapolis: T. A. Denison, 1964.

4. GIBRAN, KAHLIL. *The Prophet.* New York: Alfred A. Knopf, 1923.

5. GRIFFIN, JOHN HOWARD. *Black Like Me.* Boston: Houghton Mifflin, 1961.

6. HAMMARSKJOLD, DAG. *Markings.* Trans. Leif Sjoberg & W. H. Auden. New York: Alfred A. Knopf, 1964.

7. JANSSEN, PIERRE. *A Moment of Silence.* Trans. William R. Tyler. New York: Atheneum, 1970.

8. KENDRICK, ALEXANDER. *Prime Time: The Life of Edward R. Murrow.* Boston: Little Brown, 1969.

9. Mann, Thomas. *The Magic Mountain.* Trans. H. T. Lowe-Porter. New York: The Modern Library, 1927.

10. Mazzeo, Joseph A. St. Augustine's rhetoric of silence. *Journal of the History of Ideas,* 1962, *23* (2), 175–196.

11. Merton, Thomas. *The Silent Life.* New York: Farrar, Straus & Cudahy, 1959.

12. Oliver, Robert T. & Barbara, Dominick A. *The Healthy Mind in Communion and Communication.* Springfield, Ill.: Charles C Thomas, 1962.

13. Pike, James A. *Doing the Truth.* (2nd ed.) London: Victor Gollanz, 1966.

14. Sartre, Jean-Paul. The republic of silence. In C. Shrodes, C. Josephson, and J. R. Wilson (eds.), *Reading for Rhetoric.* (2nd ed.) New York: Macmillan, 1967.

15. Smith, Donald K. Teaching speech to facilitate understanding. *The Speech Teacher,* 1962, *11* (2), 91–100.

16. Steere, Douglas. *Dimensions of Prayer.* New York: Board of Missions, The Methodist Church, 1962.

17. Vercors (Jean Bruller). *The Battle of Silence.* London: Collins, 1968.

18. Wechsberg, Joseph. *Journey Through the Land of Eloquent Silence: East Germany Revisited.* Boston: Little Brown, 1964.

FOR DISCUSSION

1. Here are some of the emotions, feelings, and attitudes which Jensen observes silence can communicate. From your own experience, try to recall instances in which silence communicated these psychological states: love, indifference, hostility, coldness, defiance, hate, kindness, respect, acceptance, agreement, disagreement, thoughtfulness, awe, reverence, respect.

2. What functions other than those noted by Jensen might silence perform?

3. Watch a movie and keep a record of all the meanings silence communicated. Note also what nonverbal movements accompanied the silences. (If possible the entire class might watch the same movie and later compare records.)

4. Administer the following scale (or some similar one) to a few people to measure their attitudes toward silence. Perhaps you could test people from different age groups, or from different backgrounds, or from different national groups. Interpret your results. (Note: to the inevitable question your subjects will ask, "Silence? when? where? with whom?" merely answer that you want their impressions of silence in general. Scale positions may be interpreted roughly as follows: extremely, quite, fairly, neutral, fairly, quite, extremely.)

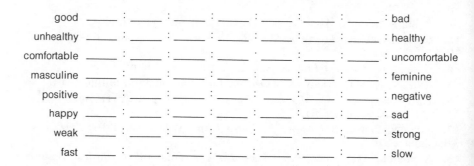

INTRAPERSONAL AND INTERPERSONAL COMMUNICATION

The readings in this section focus on intrapersonal and interpersonal communication—on communication with oneself and with one or two other people. These forms of communication are perhaps the most important; they are the most frequently used and have the most personal consequences, whether satisfying or dissatisfying.

In "Relationships within the Self," Ronald B. Levy discusses a number of significant dimensions of the self—what self is, structures of the self, self-concept, the ideal self, types of conflict, and the behavioral mechanisms used in dealing with frustration. Among the important concepts covered by Levy is that of the Johari window, a device that illustrates the significant aspects of the self and of others and reveals to whom these aspects are known. In reading this article (and in fact all the articles in this book) personalize it; see yourself as *the self* that Levy talks about.

In one of the finest articles on listening, Carl R. Rogers and Richard E. Farson discuss what they call "active listening." Working in an organizational framework and drawing examples from employee-employer interaction (this situation is applicable to all forms of communication), Rogers and Farson explain what listening at its best should be and how we might go about developing our active listening abilities. The suggestions are insightful, practical, and thoroughly worth trying.

An essential part of the art of communication is the feedback that we get from ourselves and from others. In "Feedback," Larry L. Barker considers the nature of feedback, its types, functions, and effects and some of the guidelines that might be followed in giving this feedback to others.

In "Overcoming Barriers: Coping with Conflict," Richard L. Weaver II considers one of the most important relationships existing between and among people, namely conflict. He focuses on the ways in which conflict is viewed and some of the ways in which we might deal with conflict in interpersonal communication. The task is not to eliminate the conflict but to manage it so that it exerts as little negative effect as possible. It might even lead to some positive effects.

All of these articles contain what I consider to be just the right amount of theory and practical advice. They are all grounded in the results of scientific research but they all have very practical goals in mind. You should derive, then, two major benefits from these articles: A clearer understanding of the theory and research in intrapersonal and interpersonal communication and greater insight into how you might improve your own intrapersonal and interpersonal communication behaviors as senders and as receivers.

WHAT IS THE SELF?

Structure and Operation of the Self

Each person is unique, and yet people have many things in common with each other. That aspect of us which determines our uniqueness as individuals is called our *self,* our personality, but we all share in common the fact that each of us is a unique self. No one of us is, or can be, just like someone else. Hence the self is both a distinguishing factor—a factor which helps us to be uniquely identified—and a unifying factor—one which unites us with every other individual.

But in order to understand the self, we must be aware of certain important ideas. In the first place, no one can completely know himself. This may be illustrated by the accompanying diagram (Figure 1).

Section 1, *KIO,* represents those things which the individual knows about himself which are also known, or could be known, to anyone who associates with him. These are the things which the individual has shared with others and which others have shared with him. Such shared items might include his name, educational background, parentage, place and date of birth, as well as favorable feelings and reactions which he and his associates have towards each other. Section 2, *KI,* represents those things which the individual, only, knows about himself. This is the secret area of the self. It contains things which the individual will want to hide or at least not share with others. Examples of such items might be sexual feelings

Ronald B. Levy, *Self-Relation Through Relationships,* (c) 1972. Reprinted by permission of Prentice-Hall, Inc., Englewood Cliffs, N.J.

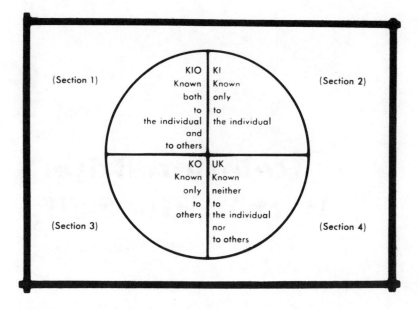

(Section 1)

KIO
Known
both
to
the individual
and
to others

KI
Known
only
to
the individual

(Section 2)

KO
Known
only
to
others

UK
Known
neither
to
the individual
nor
to others

(Section 3)

(Section 4)

and experiences, or negative feelings and attitudes which the individual has towards close associates or members of his family. Section 3, *KO,* represents those things which others, only, know and do not want to share with the individual—perhaps to shield him from pain or insult. Examples of this kind of item might include objectionable personal or physical characteristics of the individual: an objectionable voice; bad breath; nervous habits, such as nail-biting or throat-clearing; or a generally sour disposition. Section 4, *UK,* contains things which are consciously known neither by the individual nor by his associates. This section includes forgotten experiences in the past as well as material which is repressed and deals with private areas of experience. The total self is composed of all four of these sections, some consciously known, and some unknown to the individual. He can never know all of his self at one time.

The Structure of the Self

The second idea of which we must be aware is that the self is not rigidly determined or structured. It can be changed. Items which are contained in one of the four sections may, through psychotherapy, become known to a psychiatrist and eventually known to the individual himself, thus moving from *UK* to *KIO.* Also, the individual may feel guilty about some items in *KIO* and may repress them, thereby pushing them into *UK.* The four sections of the self are therefore not fixed in content, size, or importance, and the divisions between the sections are permeable; that is, items may be transferred through these divisions from one section to another.

The Self-Concept

If now we combine *KIO* and *KI,* we have all those aspects of the self of which the individual is aware; we call this combination the *self-concept.* The way the self-concept operates is the third important idea in this discussion.

The self-concept is not the total self, but it is an important aspect of the self for the behavior of individuals is based almost entirely on their perception of things. Therefore, an individual's behavior toward himself is based on how he perceives himself and how he organizes these perceptions—and it is these self perceptions, and his organization of them, which are his self-concept. If he considers himself to be ugly, unworthy, and bad, he may be likely to hide, to be self-effacing, and to avoid public attention or self-evaluation. However, he may also try to camouflage his supposed worthlessness with an air of bravado and extroversion. In either case it is his self-concept—the way he perceives himself—which directs his behavior. The differences in the type of behavior are not so much due to differences in self-concept as to the style of mechanisms which the individual uses to adjust to the frustration implicit in seeing himself in negative ways. He may have learned early in life that he could more skillfully use one style of adjustment mechanisms than another, and therefore, he unconsciously selects this style for his acting out. Hence the two different behaviors— hiding and bravado—may stem from the same low self-concept.

The Effect of Feelings and Values About Oneself

It is obvious from the preceding discussion, that the components of the self-concept—the items of *KIO* and *KI* of the diagram—are not just factual material. This brings us to the fourth important idea about the self: Not only are facts closely associated with feelings and values, these feelings and values are the most important factor in determining how we act and behave. It is really not so important, as far as influencing my behavior is concerned, whether I am, in reality, tall or short, thin or fat, old or young, college graduate or non-college graduate, married or single, homosexual or heterosexual, black or white, Protestant or Catholic. What is important is the value I give to having any one of these characteristics as opposed to the other, and how I feel about having it. Such feelings and values are often so powerful that they can actually distort or overbalance what might commonly be considered the accepted truth. For instance, consider a female, who is five feet four inches tall, and weighs 115 lbs., a weight which appears to other people to be very attractively distributed. However, she may consider herself short, fat, and generally unattractive. She may therefore avoid the beach, where her figure will be in view, wear badly-fitting clothes, and torture herself with an unreasonable reducing diet, denying herself gastronomic pleasures as well as many forms of social interaction.

The Effect of the "Unknown" Sections of the Self

It is important at this point to consider a fifth idea about the self. While the self-concept is most *directly* responsible for our behavior, the other two sections of the self—*KO* and *UK*—can have a powerful indirect influence on behavior through their ability to change the self-concept itself. If people think of me as repulsive and shun me, even if it is because of characteristics I have of which I am not conscious, it will certainly cause my self-concept to be affected. I may not know that I have bad breath, but I do know I am shunned. A sexual experience in early childhood, which is now repressed and therefore not known to me, may prevent me from having enjoyable sexual experiences now, an occurrence which will affect my self-concept. These unknown parts of the self *do* affect behavior, largely indirectly, by means of their influences on the conscious areas of the self.

The sixth important point about the self comes to us in the form of two very crucial questions: How can the self, through the self-concept, be developed and changed in desirable directions? How can we become what we want to be?

In order to do justice to this discussion, we must recognize that we are not born with a self-concept. At birth the human infant doesn't really have a self at all. We denote this by referring to an infant as "it." Very quickly material in *KO* develops as the baby begins to make its presence felt. From *KO*, with the efforts of the family, *KIO* begins to emerge. We must remember that this development is difficult. At first the infant does not even know how to distinguish its body from its mother's body, much less any of its more abstract attributes. As *KIO* develops factually, values quickly follow. One needs acceptance in order to be warm, so one learns which acts are acceptable and which acts are equally desirable to us but are not acceptable to others. Therefore, one learns to suppress consciously and then to repress unconsciously, and in so doing the material in *KI* and *UK* is developed. The crucial points here are that the self-concept is learned, not genetically inherited; and that this learning takes place in a social context—it is learned from others by interacting with them in various ways.

Furthermore, many of these patterns of interaction are largely beyond the conscious control of the infant or even of the small child. Our feeling that we—our *selves*—are unchangeable is due largely to the social straight-jacketing into which we are born, rather than to inherent rigidity within ourselves. Therefore the crucial factor for producing behavioral change and learning in order to become what we want to be is to seek for more growth-producing—less rigid—social contexts in which to be involved and thus change and enhance our self-concept, and correspondingly make our behavior more satisfying and enriching. For those people whose self-concepts are painted in negative colors, this means we must call on the other pigments of the psychic palette, which will generally be found in *KO* and *UK*, and are probably tightly locked in there. To release them requires an atmosphere where camouflage can be gradually removed and privacy gently and gradually reduced. In such an atmosphere, self-disclosure will develop, and as the individual discloses himself to others, he will learn from them positive things about himself which were formerly stored in *KO*. As this process continues, he and others will also gradually open *UK*. In these two sections positive facts and values will begin to emerge, and the permeability of the compartments of the self can be restored so that the energy used to keep them impermeable, or permeable in only one direction, can be used more fully for the creative enjoyment of a self-fulfilling life.

The Self-Ideal

We are now ready to consider the seventh important idea about the self. This idea has to do with what is called the self-ideal, that which the individual would like to become, or achieve, in the future. This concept is closely related to the sixth point—how to facilitate desirable changes in the self. It might be considered a facilitating agent—something which, correctly developed, makes the change easier. But it may also be an inhibiting agent—something which incorrectly developed, makes the change more difficult.

If the self-ideal is clear, realistic, and not too far from possible achievement, then it may be a facilitating agent. If it is vague, unreal, or far beyond what can be expected, then it may inhibit change in the self in any desirable way. The self-ideal starts to form in childhood, and is strongly influenced by "significant others" who are present at that time. The competence of these "others"—or their lack of it—can have a strong influence on what the child wants to become or fears he will become.

For example, a child whose parents are effective in living their own lives, as well as supportive of him in his efforts to achieve, will probably develop a clear, realistic self-ideal—one which he can reasonably expect to achieve. A child whose parents are not effective in life, and for this reason have negative attitudes, and are also repressive with respect to his efforts to succeed, will probably have only the vaguest kind of self-ideal or one which cannot be achieved. For example, he may be a 140-pound youth who wants to be an all-American tackle, or a mathematically inept student who wants to be a research scientist. In general, only if such a child finds his competence model and support elsewhere, can he be expected to form a positive self-ideal and become what he wants to be.

In summary, everybody has a self. It can never be completely known, but it is always possible to know it better than we know it currently. As we get to know our self better, we will find that the self and its parts are not fixed or rigidly set. The self is actively directed by a self-concept—the way the individual sees himself—and this self-concept is influenced by feelings and values even more than by facts. The self-concept is also indirectly influenced by the unknown and subconscious aspects of the self. Hence in order to change the self the divisions between conscious and unconscious sections must be kept permeable; in other words, subject to the transmission of items from one section to another. It is also important for the individual to seek social contexts where he can share disclosures about himself with others as well as to form a realistic self-ideal with the help of the significant others in his life.

HOW DOES THE SELF DEVELOP?

In spite of all the pleasures and enjoyment we experience in life, one of the most illuminating ways to analyze our behavior and understand how our self develops is in terms of the frustration we experience. We mean by frustration any interruption of a particular act which stops us from achieving the goal we had in mind.

There are three ways in which frustration usually comes about: (1) *by delay,* (2) *by blocking,* and (3) *by conflict.* Waiting for a letter or phone call from someone special is frustration by delay. All forms of undesirable waiting can usually be classified as this kind of frustration. Frustration by blocking is sometimes deliberate, as shown by the football player who uses and experiences blocking as an essential part of the game. However, we are often blocked in life by obstacles not under our control—by lack of money, by the color of our skin, or by our lack of ability in school when we seek a job. The third type of frustration—that caused by conflict—is much more complicated than the other two forms of frustration. The four ways in which conflict may develop are described below.

Approach-Approach Conflict++

This form of conflict is one in which we are blocked in choosing which of two desirable objects we want. The conflict arises because we cannot have both of them, so one must be rejected. Examples of this are choosing a husband from two very attractive men; choosing one of two equally delicious desserts; or choosing to attend one of two equally exciting athletic events which occur at the same time. This type of conflict is usually resolved by moving closer to the choice of one of the alternatives. When one of two desirable alternatives is brought closer to us, it usually becomes considerably more or less desirable, and therefore the conflict is broken.

Avoidance-Avoidance Conflict— —

In this form of conflict we are faced with the choice of one of two alternatives, *neither* of which is attractive to us. However, the situation is such that one alternative *must* be chosen. The situation of the college student who does not like to study but must maintain a certain grade-point average in order to avoid the draft is typical of this type of conflict. Another example is the voter who must choose between two equally drab candidates, or the woman who feels that her last chance to avoid being an old maid is to marry a man she considers rather repugnant and unloved. The usual attempted response to this type of conflict is escape, if that outlet is at all possible. The student may dodge both college and the draft by going to Canada. The voter may not vote, or may write in a candidate.

The single woman may seek means other than marriage to find rewarding social relationships.

Approach-Avoidance Conflict±

This type of conflict develops due to the fact that an object of choice has at the same time both desirable and undesirable characteristics. The desire of a child to pet a dog of which he is afraid is an example of this type of conflict, as is a man who wants a life companion in marriage but doesn't want to be tied down, or a girl who wants to marry a particular man but does not want to be associated with his family. This type of conflict can only be overcome if one of the two sets of characteristics— positive or negative—can be seen to clearly outweigh the other, so that a choice or a rejection is clearly indicated as being the desirable alternative.

Double Approach-Avoidance Conflict± ±

This type of conflict is usually the most frustrating type. A girl with two lovers, both of whom are asking to marry her, finds herself in this situation: Each man has desirable characteristics; one is handsome, but the other is wealthy. Handsome Harry has a very over-protective mother. Roger Moneybags insists on living in what she perceives as a very undesirable location. What can she do? Of course, a third alternative is to marry someone else, but these two men are far more attractive than anyone else she could imagine. Only if personal attractiveness can outweigh an undesirable family, or if money can outweigh location, can she solve this dilemma—unless she discovers some new qualities about one of the men which throw the balance clearly for or against him.

We all know that frustration is far too upsetting a phenomenon to be experienced without any reaction. Therefore, whenever we experience any of these frustrations, we tend to react with one of the three types of *behavioral mechanisms* described below.

Defensive Behavior

In this type of adjustment to frustration, we employ some means to defend or protect ourselves against the discomfort of the frustration.

One of these mechanisms is *rationalization*. In this mechanism the frustrated person attempts to explain his inability by means of some other reason which sounds better to his ego. For instance, a boy who does not make the football team may say that he didn't want to play football anyway. He would rather save himself for basketball or be free to have more fun with his friends at times when the team will be practicing. A girl who wasn't invited to the prom by a particular boy may say that she really didn't want to go with him anyway, and would rather stay home and watch her favorite television program. Furthermore, she might say that the band that was going to play for the prom was lousy, and besides she could have much better entertainment on TV or listening to her stereo.

A second defensive type of adjustment is *projection*. A person who uses this mechanism attributes to someone else feelings, attitudes, or motives which are really his own and are probably not the feelings, attitudes, or motives of the other person. For example, a student who cheats on an exam may use as his excuse that "everyone else cheats anyway," or a person who falls in love may say "You made me love you. I didn't want to do it," in the attempt to excuse his intense feelings for the other person.

A third mechanism of the defensive type is *identification*. In this case the frustrated person loses his frustration with his own inability by identifying with a group or another person who is successful. For example, a parent who is an immigrant from another country and has had little education may compensate for his lack of literacy by identifying with his child and feeling pride in every step of the child's progress in school, or a boy who is crippled and thus cannot compete in athletics may become strongly identified with the whole group of athletes at his school and lose his frustration by following every minute of each athletic contest.

A fourth form of defensive adjustment is *emotional isolation*. In this type of mechanism the person who feels inadequate in dealing with conflict, tension, or even love, adjusts by removing all emotion from his reactions and simply approaching each situation of potential conflict in a strictly intellectual way. He says "I understand your hostility towards me. Therefore I feel no pain from it!" He always understands everything. He has no intense feelings and does not think they are necessary. He always talks softly and never "lets himself go." In this way he defends himself against the frustration and damage which an emotional explosion or "flood" would do to his social relationships.

Avoidance or Withdrawal

In this second general type of adjustment to frustration, we usually avoid the frustration or find some means to withdraw from the whole conflict scene.

The most obvious kind of avoidance is simple or *direct avoidance*. Thus, the person who feels inadequate with the opposite sex simply avoids all members of that sex. The person who is frustrated in school drops out and avoids all contact with educational institutions.

A second means of withdrawal is *regression*. An individual who is frustrated withdraws from the present frustrating scene to a past social context where he felt more secure. A child at the age of six or seven may therefore resort to thumb-sucking or bed-wetting when frustrated, or a grown man may throw a temper tantrum and yell at his associates when frustrated—as he used to do as a child with his parents.

A third form of withdrawal is *fantasy*. When faced with the frustration of loneliness we often resort to daydreams (or even night dreams) of association with pleasant companions, or if we are poor and need money, food, clothes, and the like, we may dream—with the help of our television—of a more affluent life. The unloved person may dream of his overs, the unsuccessful person may dream of his conquests, and the ugly person may dream of being beautiful.

The fourth form of withdrawal is a very complicated one, of which there are many perplexing examples. It is puzzling often because it seems that the individual has no control over it. This is the *flight into illness.* This is the case in which a child gets sick at school time, but never on Saturday. A tooth stops aching as the dentist's office is approached. One becomes fatigued and sleepy whenever a difficult job must be done. A person forgets to do a disagreeable task or keep an appointment which will result in conflict or embarrassment. A man develops ailments such as asthma, eczema, or hay fever (which makes him dependent, incapacitated or "explains" his unattractiveness to others); blindness—partial or total; paralysis of certain kinds; deafness; dizziness. All of these reactions may be used—unconsciously—as a means of escaping from coping with conflict, anxiety and frustration. Dual personalities, amnesia, compulsions to act in a particular way, and obsessive ideas from which we "cannot escape," are also mechanisms used to withdraw from rational coping with the problems of life. One must continually keep in mind that these flights into seeming organic disabilities are not consciously chosen by the person. Therefore, asking him to stop only makes the flight more intense and adds insult to injury.

Aggressive Behavior

People who use this type of reaction to frustration do so by venting emotion or action towards some object. This object may or may not be the object which is really causing the frustration.

The simplest form of aggressive behavior is direct *extra-punitive behavior.* The person who is blocked physically or verbally assaults the person or thing which is blocking him. We kick at a biting dog. We punish an unruly child. We attack someone who invades the privacy of our home. We argue with the policeman or teacher who has treated us unreasonably.

A second form of aggression is *intro-punitive behavior,* in which we do not attack the external offender, but rather blame ourselves. The student says, "I am stupid. I deserve to fail," or the driver says "I was careless. I deserve to get the traffic ticket."

A third form of aggressive behavior is *displacement.* In this form of behavior we are overly aggressive, but not to the cause of our frustration. The student who needs very much to succeed in school may take his reprimand from the teacher quietly, and then punch one of his friends in the nose to "let off steam." A girl who has split up with her boyfriend may rant and rail at her parents.

One interesting form of displacement is so-called *juvenile delinquency.* Here an oppressed group of adolescents may beat out their frustrations by destructive behavior against property of persons who had nothing to do with their oppression and who may, in fact, be actively working in their behalf.

Sometimes feelings of aggression are *compensated* for by letting these feelings out in a non-destructive way. One who feels physically pent up may let out his feelings by chopping wood or by indulging in contact sports or other forms of athletics. These feelings may even be *sublimated* by directing them to a more inactive level physically, but one which still releases much of the pent-up emotion. Such activities might be painting, plastic art, writing poetry or fiction, or dramatics.

Finally, some of us use *reaction-formation* as a way of dealing with our feelings of aggression. Here we may be overly considerate to someone whom we feel we *should* love but whom we actually hate: for example, a child or parent. We may be overly quiet or polite to the teacher or the policeman who is reprimanding us. This display of reversed emotion is acceptable, and yet it does provide us with an emotional outlet.

In conclusion, it is important to understand that most of us use a variety of mechanisms to deal with the problems of life. The mechanisms are generally *not* maladjustments and only become so when they tend to incapacitate us. Some mechanisms—fantasy, for example—can be very creative and can often be cultivated to great advantage.

The list of mechanisms above by which we may adjust to frustration is by no means complete. However, it is at least a start in understanding how we come to be the kind of self we are, and how this self develops. If we are to become what we *want* to be, this knowledge is very important. But it must be "understood" with the feelings and emotions as well as with the mind.

FOR DISCUSSION

1. Examine your own Johari window with special reference to those items known only to you. Why are these items restricted to you alone? Why are you unwilling to let others become aware of them?

2. How can you go about discovering what is now known only to others? Which people are most likely to tell you? Why do you suppose that for most people this area of unknowns would contain a vast number of items?

3. Construct a diagrammatic model of your ideal self, i.e., the self that you want to become. Include in this model the objects, events, people, feelings, etc. that would be part of your ideal self, their specific kind of relationship to you, their relative importance, and so on.

4. In an effort to relate the four basic kinds of conflict to your own behavior and to ensure understanding of the concepts, try to provide a recent personal example that illustrates each type of conflict. How were the conflicts eventually resolved?

5. How do you respond most often to' frustration? with defensive behavior? with avoidance or withdrawal? with aggressive behavior? What kinds of frustrations lead to what type of behavioral mechanisms?

6. Explain what Levy means when he says that these mechanisms for dealing with frustrations must be understood "with the feelings and emotions as well as the mind."

Active Listening

Carl R. Rogers and Richard E. Farson

THE MEANING OF ACTIVE LISTENING

One basic responsibility of the supervisor or executive is the development, adjustment, and integration of individual employees. He tries to develop employee potential, delegate responsibility, and achieve cooperation. To do so, he must have, among other abilities, the ability to listen intelligently and carefully to those with whom he works.

There are, however, many kinds of listening skills. The lawyer, for example, when questioning a witness, listens for contradictions, irrelevancies, errors, and weaknesses. But this is not the kind of listening skill we are concerned with in this booklet. The lawyer usually is not listening in order to help the witness adjust or cooperate or produce. On the other hand, we will be concerned with listening skills which *will help* employees gain a clearer understanding of their situations, take responsibility, and cooperate with each other.

Two Examples

The kind of listening we have in mind is called "active listening." It is called "active" because the listener has a very definite responsibility. He does not passively absorb the words which are spoken to him. He actively tries to grasp the facts and the feelings in what he hears, and he tries, by his listening, to help the speaker work out his own problems.

To get a fuller picture of what is meant by active listening, let us consider two different approaches to the same work problem.

From Carl R. Rogers and Richard E. Farson. By permission of the authors and the University of Chicago Industrial Relations Center.

Example No. 1

> **Foreman:** *Hey, Al, I don't get this production order. We can't handle this run today. What do they think we are?*
>
> **Supervisor:** *But that's the order. So get it out as soon as you can. We're under terrific pressure this week.*
>
> **Foreman:** *Don't they know we're behind schedule already because of that press breakdown?*
>
> **Supervisor:** *Look, Kelly, I don't decide what goes on upstairs. I just have to see that the work gets out and that's what I'm gonna do.*
>
> **Foreman:** *The guys aren't gonna like this.*
>
> **Supervisor:** *That's something you'll have to work out with them, not me.*

Example No. 2

> **Foreman:** *Hey, Ross, I don't get this production order. We can't handle this run today. What do they think we are?*
>
> **Supervisor:** *Sounds like you're pretty sore about it, Kelly.*
>
> **Foreman:** *I sure am. We were just about getting back to schedule after that press breakdown. Now this comes along.*
>
> **Supervisor:** *As if you didn't have enough work to do, huh?*
>
> **Foreman:** *Yeah. I don't know how I'm gonna tell the guys about this.*
>
> **Supervisor:** *Hate to face 'em with it now, is that it?*
>
> **Foreman:** *I really do. They're under a real strain today. Seems like everything we do around here is rush, rush.*
>
> **Supervisor:** *I guess you feel like it's unfair to load anything more on them.*
>
> **Foreman:** *Well, yeah. I know there must be plenty of pressure on everybody up the line, but—well, if that's the way it is . . . guess I'd better get the word to 'em.*

There are obviously many differences between these two examples. The main one, however, is that Ross, the supervisor in the second example, is using the active-listening approach. He is listening and responding in a way that makes it clear that he appreciates both the meaning and the feeling behind what Kelly is saying.

Active listening does not necessarily mean long sessions spent listening to grievances, personal or otherwise. It is simply a way of approaching those problems which arise out of the usual day-to-day events of any job.

To be effective, active listening must be firmly grounded in the basic attitudes of the user. We cannot employ it as a technique if our fundamental attitudes are in conflict with its basic concepts. If we try, our behavior will be empty and sterile and our associates will be quick to recognize this. Until we can demonstrate a spirit which genuinely respects the potential worth of the individual which considers his rights and trusts his capacity for self-direction, we cannot begin to be effective listeners.

What We Achieve by Listening

Active listening is an important way to bring about changes in people. Despite the popular notion that listening is a passive approach, clinical and research evidence clearly shows that sensitive listening is a most effective agent for individual personality change and group development. Listening brings about changes in people's attitudes toward themselves and others, and also brings about changes in their basic values and personal philosophy. People who have been listened to in this new and special way become more emotionally mature, more open to their experiences, less defensive, more democratic, and less authoritarian.

When people are listened to sensitively, they tend to listen to themselves with more care and make clear exactly what they are feeling and thinking. Group members tend to listen more to each other, become less argumentative, more ready to incorporate other points of view. Because listening reduces the threat of having one's ideas criticized, the person is better able to see them for what they are, and is more likely to feel that his contributions are worthwhile.

Not the least important result of listening is the change that takes place within the listener himself. Besides the fact that listening provides more information than any other activity, it builds deep, positive relationships and tends to alter constructively the attitudes of the listener. Listening is a growth experience.

These, then, are some of the worthwhile results we can expect from active listening. But how do we go about this kind of listening? How do we become active listeners?

HOW TO LISTEN

Active listening aims to bring about changes in people. To achieve this end, it relies upon definite techniques—things to do and things to avoid doing. Before discussing these techniques, however, we should first understand why they are effective. To do so, we must understand how the individual personality develops.

The Growth of the Individual

Through all of our lives, from early childhood on, we have learned to think of ourselves in certain, very definite ways. We have built up pictures of ourselves. Sometimes these self-pictures are pretty realistic but at other times they are not. For example, an overage, overweight lady may fancy herself a youthful, ravishing siren, or an awkward teenager regard himself as a star athlete.

All of us have experiences which fit the way we need to think about ourselves. These we accept. But it is much harder to accept experiences which don't fit. And sometimes, if it is very important for us to hang on to this self-picture, we don't accept or admit these experiences at all.

These self-pictures are not necessarily attractive. A man, for example, may regard himself as incompetent and worthless. He may feel that he is doing his job poorly in spite of favorable appraisals by the company. As long as he has these feelings about himself he must deny any experiences which would seem not to fit this self-picture, in this case any that might indicate to him that he is competent. It is so necessary for him to maintain this self-picture that he is threatened by anything which would tend to change it. Thus, when the company raises his salary, it may seem to him only additional proof that he is a fraud. He must hold onto this self-picture, because, bad or good, it's the only thing he has by which he can identify himself.

This is why direct attempts to change this individual or change his self-picture are particularly threatening. He is forced to defend himself or to completely deny the experience. This denial of experience and defense of the self-picture tend to bring on rigidity of behavior and create difficulties in personal adjustment.

The active-listening approach, on the other hand, does not present a threat to the individual's self-picture. He does not have to defend it. He is able to explore it, see it for what it is, and make his own decision as to how realistic it is. And he is then in a position to change.

If I want to help a man reduce his defensiveness and become more adaptive, I must try to remove the threat of myself as his potential changer. As long as the atmosphere is threatening, there can be no effective communication. So I must create a climate which is neither critical, evaluative, nor moralizing. It must be an atmosphere of equality and freedom, permissiveness and understanding, acceptance and warmth. It is in this climate and this climate only that the individual feels safe enough to incorporate new experiences and new values into his concept of himself. Let's see how active listening helps to create this climate.

What to Avoid

When we encounter a person with a problem, our usual response is to try to change his way of looking at things—to get him to see his situation the way we see it, or would like him to see it. We plead, reason, scold, encourage, insult, prod—anything to bring about a change in the desired direction, that is, in the direction we want him to travel. What we seldom realize, however, is that, under these circumstances, we are usually responding to *our own* needs to see the world in certain ways. It is always difficult for us to tolerate and understand actions which are different from the ways in which *we* believe *we* should act. If, however, we can free ourselves from the need to influence and direct others in our own paths, we enable ourselves to listen with understanding, and thereby employ the most potent available agent of change.

One problem the listener faces is that of responding to demands for decisions, judgments, and evaluations. He is constantly called upon to agree or disagree with someone or something. Yet, as he well knows, the question or challenge frequently is a masked expression of feeling or needs which the speaker is far more anxious to communicate than he is to have the surface questions answered. Because he cannot speak these feelings openly, the speaker must disguise them to himself and to others in an acceptable form. To illustrate, let us examine some typical questions and the type of answers that might best elicit the feeling beneath it.

Employee's Question	*Listener's Answer*
Just whose responsibility is the tool room?	Do you feel that someone is challenging your authority in there?
Don't you think younger able people should be promoted before senior but less able ones?	It seems to you they should, I take it.
What does the super expect us to do about those broken-down machines?	You're pretty disgusted with those machines, aren't you?
Don't you think I've improved over the last review period?	Sounds as if you feel like you've really picked up over these last few months.

These responses recognize the questions but leave the way open for the employee to say what is really bothering him. They allow the listener to participate in the problem or situation without shouldering all responsibility for decision-making or actions. This is a process of thinking *with* people instead of *for* or *about* them.

Passing judgment, whether critical or favorable, makes free expression difficult. Similarly, advice and information are almost always seen as efforts to change a person and thus serve as barriers to his self-expression and the development of a creative relationship. Moreover, advice is seldom taken and information hardly ever utilized. The eager young trainee probably will not become patient just because he is advised that "The road to success in business is a long, difficult one, and you must be patient." And it is no more helpful for him to learn that "only one out of a hundred trainees reach top management positions."

Interestingly, it is a difficult lesson to learn that positive *evaluations* are sometimes as blocking as negative ones. It is almost as destructive to the freedom of a relationship to tell a person that he is good or capable or right, as to tell him otherwise. To evaluate him positively may make it more difficult for him to tell of the faults that distress him or the ways in which he believes he is not competent.

Encouragement also may be seen as an attempt to motivate the speaker in certain directions or hold him off rather than as support. "I'm sure everything will work out O.K." is not a helpful response to the person who is deeply discouraged about a problem.

In other words, most of the techniques and devices common to human relationships are found to be of little use in establishing the type of relationship we are seeking here.

What To Do

Just what does active listening entail, then? Basically, it requires that we get inside the speaker, that we grasp, *from his point of view,* just what it is he is communicating to us. More than that, we must convey to the speaker that we are seeing things from his point of view. To listen actively, then, means that there are several things we must do.

Listen for Total Meaning.   Any message a person tries to get across usually has two components: the *content* of the message and the *feeling* or attitude underlying this content. Both are important, both give the message *meaning*. It is this total meaning of the message that we try to understand. For example, a machinist comes to his foreman and says, "I've finished that lathe set-up." This message has obvious content and perhaps calls upon the foreman for another work assignment. Suppose, on the other hand, that he says, "Well, I'm finally finished with that damned lathe set-up." The content is the same but the total meaning of the message has changed—and changed in an important way for both the foreman and the worker. Here sensitive listening can facilitate the relationship. Suppose the foreman were to respond by simply giving another work assignment. Would the employee feel that he had gotten his total message across? Would he feel free to talk to his foreman? Will he feel better about his job, more anxious to do good work on the next assignment?

Now, on the other hand, suppose the foreman were to respond with, "Glad to have it over with, huh?" or "Had a pretty rough time of it?" or "Guess you don't feel like doing anything like that again," or anything else that tells the worker that he heard and understands. It doesn't necessarily mean that the next work assignment need be changed or that he must spend an hour listening to the worker complain about the set-up problems he encountered. He may do a number of things differently in the light of the new information he has from the worker—but not necessarily. It's just that extra sensitivity on the part of the foreman which can transform an average working climate into a good one.

Respond to Feelings.   In some instances the content is far less important than the feeling which underlies it. To catch the full flavor or meaning of the message one must respond particularly to the feeling component. If, for instance, our machinist had said, "I'd like to melt this lathe down and make paper clips out of it," responding to content would be obviously absurd. But to respond to his disgust or anger in trying to work with his lathe recognizes the meaning of this message. There are various shadings of these components in the meaning of any message. Each time the listener must try to remain sensitive to the total meaning the message has to the speaker. What is he trying to tell me? What does this mean to him? How does he see this situation?

Note All Cues.   Not all communication is verbal. The speaker's words alone don't tell us everything he is communicating. And hence, truly sensitive listening requires that we become aware of several kinds of communication besides verbal. The way in which a speaker hesitates in his speech can tell us much about his feelings. So too can the inflection of his voice. He may stress certain points loudly and clearly, and may mumble others. We should also note such things as the person's facial expressions, body posture, hand movements, eye movements, and breathing. All of these help to convey his total message.

What We Communicate By Listening

The first reaction of most people when they consider listening as a possible method for dealing with human beings is that listening cannot be sufficient in itself. Because it is passive, they feel, listening does not communicate anything to the speaker. Actually, nothing could be farther from the truth.

By consistently listening to a speaker you are conveying the idea that: "I'm interested in you as a person, and I think that what you feel is important. I respect your thoughts, and even if I don't agree with them, I know that they are valid for you. I feel sure that you have a contribution to make. I'm not trying to change you or evaluate you. I just want to understand you. I think you're worth listening to, and I want you to know that I'm the kind of a person you can talk to."

The subtle but most important aspect of this is that it is the *demonstration* of the message that works. While it is most difficult to convince someone that you respect him by *telling* him so, you are much more likely to get this message across by really *behaving* that way—by actually *having* and *demonstrating* respect for this person. Listening does this most effectively.

Like other behavior, listening behavior is contagious. This has implications for all communications problems, whether between two people, or within a large organization. To insure good communication between associates up and down the line, one must first take the responsibility for setting a pattern of listening. Just as one learns that anger is usually met with anger, argument with argument, and deception with deception, one can learn that listening can be met with listening. Every person who feels responsibility in a situation can set the tone of the interaction, and the important lesson in this is that any behavior exhibited by one person will eventually be responded to with similar behavior in the other person.

It is far more difficult to stimulate constructive behavior in another person but far more profitable. Listening is one of these constructive behaviors, but if one's attitude is to "wait out" the speaker rather than really listen to him, it will fail. The one who consistently listens with understanding, however, is the one who eventually is most likely to be listened to. If you really want to be heard and understood by another, you can develop him as a potential listener, ready for new ideas, provided you can first develop yourself in these ways and sincerely listen with understanding and respect.

Testing for Understanding

Because understanding another person is actually far more difficult than it at first seems, it is important to test constantly your ability to see the world in the way the speaker sees it. You can do this by reflecting in your own words what the speaker seems to mean by his words and actions.

His response to this will tell you whether or not he feels understood. A good rule of thumb is to assume that one never really understands until he can communicate this understanding to the other's satisfaction.

Here is an experiment to test your skill in listening. The next time you become involved in a lively or controversial discussion with another person, stop for a moment and suggest that you adopt this ground rule for continued discussion: Before either participant in the discussion can make a point or express an opinion of his own, he must first restate aloud the previous point or position of the other person. This restatement must be accurate enough to satisfy the speaker before the listener can be allowed to speak for himself.

This is something you could try in your own discussion group. Have someone express himself on some topic of emotional concern to the group. Then, before another member expresses his own feelings and thought, he must rephrase the *meaning* expressed by the previous speaker to that individual's satisfaction. Note the changes in the emotional climate and the quality of the discussion when you try this.

PROBLEMS IN ACTIVE LISTENING

Active listening is not an easy skill to acquire. It demands practice. Perhaps more important, it may require changes in our own basic attitudes. These changes come slowly and sometimes with considerable difficulty. Let us look at some of the major problems in active listening and what can be done to overcome them.

The Personal Risk

To be effective at all in active listening, one must have a sincere interest in the speaker. We all live in glass houses as far as our attitudes are concerned. They always show through. And if we are only making a pretense of interest in the speaker, he will quickly pick this up, either consciously or unconsciously. And once he does, he will no longer express himself freely.

Active listening carries a strong element of personal risk. If we manage to accomplish what we are describing here—to sense deeply the feelings of another person, to understand the meaning his experiences have for him, to see the world as he sees it—we risk being changed ourselves. For example, if we permit ourselves to listen our way into the psychological life of a labor leader or agitator—to get the meaning which life has for him—we risk coming to see the world as he sees it. It is threatening to give up, even momentarily, what we believe and start thinking in someone else's terms. It takes a great deal of inner security and courage to be able to risk one's self in understanding another.

For the supervisor, the courage to take another's point of view generally means that he must see *himself* through another's eyes—he must be able to see himself as others see him. To do this may sometimes be unpleasant, but it is far more *difficult* than unpleasant. We are so accustomed to viewing ourselves in certain ways—to seeing and hearing only what we want to see and hear—that it is extremely difficult for a person to free himself from his needs to see things these ways.

Developing an attitude of sincere interest in the speaker is thus no easy task. It can be developed only by being willing to risk seeing the world from the speaker's point of view. If we have a number of such experiences, however, they will shape an attitude which will allow us to be truly genuine in our interest in the speaker.

Hostile Expressions

The listener will often hear negative, hostile expressions directed at himself. Such expressions are always hard to listen to. No one likes to hear hostile action or words. And it is not easy to get to the point where one is strong enough to permit these attacks without finding it necessary to defend himself or retaliate.

Because we all fear that people will crumble under the attack of genuine negative feelings, we tend to perpetuate an attitude of pseudo-peace. It is as if we cannot tolerate conflict at all for fear of the damage it could do to us, to the situation, to the others involved. But of course the real damage is done to all these by the denial and suppression of negative feelings.

Out-of-Place Expressions

There is also the problem of out-of-place expressions, expressions dealing with behavior which is not usually acceptable in our society. In the extreme forms that present themselves before psychotherapists, expressions of sexual perversity or homicidal fantasies are often found blocking to the listener because of their obvious threatening quality. At less extreme levels, we all find unnatural or inappropriate behavior difficult to handle. That is, anything from an "off-color" story told in mixed company to seeing a man weep is likely to produce a problem situation.

In any face-to-face situation, we will find instances of this type which will momentarily, if not permanently, block any communication. In business and industry any expressions of weakness or incompetency will generally be regarded as unacceptable and therefore will block good two-way communication. For example, it is difficult to listen to a supervisor tell of his feelings of failure in being able to "take charge" of a situation in his department because *all* administrators are supposed to be able to "take charge."

Accepting Positive Feelings

It is both interesting and perplexing to note that negative or hostile feelings or expressions are much easier to deal with in any face-to-face relationship than are truly and deeply positive feelings. This is especially true for the business man because the culture expects him to be independent, bold, clever, and aggressive and manifest no feelings of warmth, gentleness, and intimacy. He therefore comes to regard these feelings as soft and inappropriate. But no matter how they are regarded, they remain a human need. The denial of these feelings in himself and his associates does not get the executive out of the problem of dealing with them. They simply become veiled and confused. If recognized they would work for the total effort; unrecognized, they work against it.

Emotional Danger Signals

The listener's own emotions are sometimes a barrier to active listening. When emotions are at their height, when listening is most necessary, it is most difficult to set aside one's own concerns and be understanding. Our emotions are often our own worst enemies when we try to become listeners. The more involved and invested we are in a particular situation or problem, the less we are likely to be willing or able to listen to the feelings and attitudes of others. That is, the more we find it necessary to respond to our own needs, the less we are able to respond to the needs of another. Let us look at some of the main danger signals that warn us that our emotions may be interfering with our listening.

Defensiveness.   The points about which one is most vocal and dogmatic, the points which one is most anxious to impose on others—these are always the points one is trying to talk oneself into believing. So one danger signal becomes apparent when you find yourself stressing a point or trying to convince another. It is at these times that you are likely to be less secure and consequently less able to listen.

Resentment of Opposition.   It is always easier to listen to an idea which is similar to one of your own than to an opposing view. Sometimes, in order to clear the air, it is helpful to pause for a moment when you feel your ideas and position being challenged, reflect on the situation, and express your concern to the speaker.

Clash of Personalities.   Here again, our experience has consistently shown us that the genuine expression of feelings on the part of the listener will be more helpful in developing a sound relationship than the suppression of them. This is so whether the feelings be resentment, hostility, threat, or admiration. A basically honest relationship, whatever the nature of it, is the most productive of all. The other party becomes secure when he learns that the listener can express his feelings honestly and openly to him. We should keep this in mind when we begin to fear a clash of personalities in the listening relationship. Otherwise, fear of our own emotions will choke off full expression of feelings.

Listening to Ourselves

To listen to oneself is a prerequisite to listening to others. And it is often an effective means of dealing with the problems we have outlined above. When we are most aroused, excited, and demanding, we are least able to understand our own feelings and attitudes. Yet, in dealing with the problems of others, it becomes most important to be sure of one's own position, values, and needs.

The ability to recognize and understand the meaning which a particular episode has for you, with all the feelings which it stimulates in you, and the ability to express this meaning when you find it getting in the way of active listening, will clear the air and enable you one again to be free to listen. That is, if some person or situation touches off feelings within you which tend to block your attempts to listen with understanding, begin listening to yourself. It is much more helpful in developing effective relationships to avoid suppressing these feelings. Speak them out as clearly as you can, and try to enlist the other person as a listener to your feelings. A person's listening ability is limited by his ability to listen to himself.

FOR DISCUSSION

1. Define "active listening." What are the advantages of active listening over "just plain listening?"

2. Construct a dialogue to illustrate the failure to listen actively and a dialogue to illustrate the operation of active listening—as Rogers and Farson do. Build your dialogues around issues that are important to you—for example, your school, your home, your work. Discuss the specific ways in which these dialogues and their implications differ.

3. Select a person you have difficulty communicating with at least fairly frequently, for example, a brother or sister, a parent, a friend, or an employer. With reference to this specific person explain how the "problems in active listening" discussed by Rogers and Farson may be operating in these situations. Be especially careful that you consider—with an open mind—how you might be causing some or all of these difficulties by failing to listen actively.

Feedback

Larry L. Barker

Communication is a circular process. As a message is transmitted from sender to receiver, a return message, known as *feedback,* is transmitted in the opposite direction. Feedback is a message that indicates the level of understanding or agreement between two or more communicators in response to an original message. Feedback represents a listener's verbal or nonverbal commentary on the message being communicated.

Feedback is an ongoing process, which usually begins as a reaction to various aspects of the initial message. For example, a definite response is being fed back to the speaker when we shake our heads affirmatively or look quizzically at him. Feedback plays an essential role in helping us to determine whether or not our message has been understood, whether it is being received positively or negatively, and whether our audience is open or defensive, self-controlled or bored. Feedback can warn us that we must alter our communication to achieve the desired effect. If we are not aware of feedback, or don't pay any attention to it, there is a strong possibility that our efforts at communicating will be completely ineffective.

To emphasize the importance of the feedback mechanism in communication, you need only imagine yourself growing up for the last eighteen years or so, never having received any feedback. No one has praised you as you learned to walk or ride a bike. No one has warned you not to chase a ball into the street or put your hand on a hot stove. No one has shared your tears or laughter. You probably would not function well at all. How would you appraise your self-concept? What values or morals would you possess? While such an existence is impossible, since a certain

Larry L. Barker, *Communication* (Englewood Cliffs, N.J.: Prentice-Hall, 1978), pp. 59–65. Reprinted by permission of Prentice-Hall, Inc.

148

amount of feedback comes from you yourself as well as from others in the environment, this example does suggest the various functions and effects of feedback in the communication process.

TYPES OF FEEDBACK

There are two types of feedback: self-feedback and listener feedback.

Self-feedback applies to the words and actions that are fed back into your central nervous system as you perceive your own muscular movements and hear yourself speak. Feeling your tongue twist as you mispronounce a word or, in a library, suddenly realizing that you are speaking too loudly are examples of self-feedback. Another example would be hearing yourself use a word incorrectly, or reversing sounds, such as asking, "Were you sappy or had?" instead of "happy or sad."

Research indicates that self-feedback is both enjoyable and necessary for normal development. Linguists maintain, for example, that a baby in the "babbling stage" finds pleasure in the actual production of sounds, as well as in hearing those sounds. The importance of self-feedback is indicated by findings showing that deaf babies start to babble at the same time that hearing babies do, but because they can't hear their babblings they begin to lose interest, which limits their vocal play.[1] Interestingly enough, visual feedback through the use of mirrors suspended over deaf babies' cribs has increased babbling and vocal activity.

The other major type of feedback, *listener feedback,* involves verbal and nonverbal responses. Verbal feedback may take the form of questions or comments. A listener may, for instance, ask a speaker to explain the last point or may give praise for making the story so interesting. Nonverbal feedback may be transmitted by applause or laughter to indicate approval, or a blank stare, which might indicate disinterest or confusion. Even silence can act as feedback. If a teacher asks a question and no one answers, the silence may indicate lack of knowledge, misunderstanding, or perhaps dislike of the teacher. If a father asks his son if he has finished his homework and the son doesn't reply, that silence is meaningful.

FUNCTIONS OF FEEDBACK

Feedback serves various functions in the communication process. The first of these functions is to evaluate what is right or wrong about a particular communication. If you give a speech to the class, your teacher will offer criticism and suggestions for improving your delivery. If someone is watching you hang a painting, he or she will give you feedback as you try various positions, to help you find the right place for it. . . nonverbal feedback in the form of nods and hand movements helps to regulate turn taking in conversation.

[1]Charles Van Riper, *Speech Correction,* 4th ed. (Englewood Cliffs, N.J.: Prentice-Hall, 1963), p. 79.

Feedback can also serve to stimulate change. For example, a popular entertainment magazine, after changing its format by drastically shortening the descriptions of programs in the TV section of the magazine, received so much feedback in the form of angry letters from readers that the publisher not only resumed th program descriptions, but elaborated on them.

A third function of feedback is to reinforce, to give reward or punishment. A father says, "I'm proud of you, son," or "Jim, can't you ever keep quiet!" When used in this way, rewarding feedback encourages certain behaviors, while punishing feedback is intended to discourage certain behaviors. A comedian relies on positive reinforcement from his audience in the form of laughter—and his performance may improve if he senses that the audience feedback is positive.

EFFECTS OF FEEDBACK

If you have ever made a phone call and found yourself talking to an answering machine, you may have felt somewhat uncomfortable or even foolish. It is difficult to sound conversational when there is no one on the other end to respond. This example suggests that feedback is an essential part of the communication process. We can see this through the effects of feedback.

Probably the most important effect of feedback on the communication process is in improving the accuracy of understanding. For example, a teacher seeing only blank stares during a complicated lecture might make a conscious effort to repeat and clarify his or her points until the audience shows signs of nodding in agreement. As this example indicates, feedback may increase the amount of time necessary for a communication interaction to be completed. Nonetheless, it ensures a more thoroughly and clearly transmitted message.

In terms of intrapersonal and interpersonal communication, the most significant effect of feedback, and one that is often long range, is on self-concept. You surely know people who have very poor self-images and little feeling of self-worth. It is probable that such individuals have based this self-image on punishing feedback received from family and peers during crucial periods of identity development. On the other hand, an individual who has had considerable rewarding feedback from family and friends is likely to develop a favorable self-concept.

Feedback also affects performance. Sometimes improved performance results from improved self-image. An experiment conducted by music educator Elizabeth Elrod, for example, indicated that elementary education majors could improve their singing ability through the use of positive self-concept building and video feedback. Before the training session, 90 percent of the students claimed they could not sing, but after ten weeks those students who had heard taped replays of their singing were judged by independent observers as much improved.[2]

2"Everybody Sing," *Human Behavior* 4 (August 1975):63.

Feedback can work in two directions, however. For example, a beginning tennis player who has been praised for her skills at the sport (rewarding feedback) will probably perceive it to be an easier game than someone who performs equally well but who has received harsh criticism (punishing feedback). Similarly, a student who fails a test (punishing feedback) may set his mind on just passing the next one instead of working for an "A." Thus, we can see that feedback also affects performance expectations.

Another important effect of feedback on performance concerns task behavior, particularly in small groups. When people find themselves in small group situations in which they don't know the other members of the group, they often suffer from feelings of rejection and hostility. These negative feelings can keep the group from performing any type of cooperative work. Positive reinforcement from group members, as well as from outside observers, will help the group interact better and will ultimately improve performance. For example, a group of quarrelsome young children complimented on how well they are cleaning up their play area may continue the task with renewed enthusiasm.

Feedback can also affect your attitude toward your own messages, or toward the messages of others. There is an extensive body of research on this aspect of feedback. Basically, the findings indicate that feedback favorable to a particular message causes the communicator of the message to believe in it more strongly, and causes others to become more favorably disposed to the message than they had been at the start.[3] Punishing feedback, on the other hand, causes negative attitude change in both the speaker and the listener. We have all had experiences which, though less controlled than research studies, help to clarify the findings of these attitude-change experiments. Perhaps you remember a time when you were in a theater, watching a comedy that you and the rest of the audience did not find amusing. No one was laughing. Yet when several members of the audience later began to laugh loudly, your reaction somehow became more favorable. Soon you were laughing, too. This is the reason for using laugh tracks in television situation comedies.

GIVING EFFECTIVE FEEDBACK

Feedback is often so spontaneous that you are unaware of giving or receiving it. Nevertheless, there are ways to consciously make your feedback more effective. One method is to focus on observations rather than inferences. For example, consider the following situation: A young woman passes a friend whom she has dated several times. She says hello, but her friend walks right on by. The next time she sees him, she asks, "Hey, are you mad at me? You ignored me the other day when I saw you downtown." She has assumed a negative motive behind the man's action, although he may simply have been preoccupied. The woman's feedback to her friend

---

[3]John Gardiner, "A Synthesis of Experimental Studies of Speech Communication Feedback," *Journal of Communication* 21 (March 1971):23.

would have been more productive if she had relayed the facts, and only the facts, as she understood them: "Hey, I saw you the other day and called to you, but you didn't reply." This would permit the man to make an honest response rather than a defensive one.

Another method for increasing the effectiveness of your feedback is to use description rather than judgment. The captain of a basketball team would be more helpful in coaching his players if he said, "You're not running for the ball and you're moving too slowly," as opposed to, "You're really getting lazy."

It is also important to give immediate feedback. We often delay our responses to problems and conflicts and wait for emotions to die down. It is better to deal with anger or hurt when it occurs, when you are in touch with your reactions. Feedback at the time is more specific and accurate than it can be, say, two months later. Yet sometimes extreme emotions make you overreact or respond in ways you regret later on. Again, your feedback should be appropriate to the situation, as best as you can control it.

Limiting feedback is another means of increasing its effectiveness, particularly in a one-to-one situation in which you are the listener. Constantly nodding or interjecting comments in such situations is interfering, at best, and may show superficiality and insincerity, at worst. Thus it is necessary to guard against overresponding. A smile or nod of agreement to particularly significant statements does more to show that you understand than continuous "uh-huhs."

The act of using conscious feedback techniques may sometimes seem unnatural. However, it is important to remember that effective feedback does improve the communication process. While feedback that is entirely calculated tends to be stilted, awareness of the feedback mechanism and the messages you are transmitting is an asset to communication.

FOR DISCUSSION

1. What kind of feedback goes on in your communication class? Is there much feedback between teacher and student? Among students? What form does this feedback take? What are some of its effects?

2. How do you respond to feedback? Do you respond more positively to feedback that follows Barker's suggestions for "giving effective feedback?"

3. Are there additional guidelines that might prove useful in giving feedback that Barker has not included? Explain why you think this would be helpful to interpersonal communications.

4. How does feedback in interpersonal communication differ from feedback in public speaking? In mass communication?

Overcoming Barriers

Coping with Conflict

Richard L. Weaver II

So far I have talked a lot about openness, cooperation, and empathy in interpersonal communication. And those positive qualities are at the center of our success in communicating with others. . . . As we attempt to change the attitudes of others, we often run into problems. We all face a certain amount of unpleasantness, hostility, conflict, and defensiveness in our relationships. What do we do about this? We can ignore it. Our society values cooperation and has not taught us how to deal with conflict or even to admit it exists in most cases. But ignoring conflict is not the solution. We can start to deal with conflict by accepting the idea that it is part of life. Next we can learn ways to manage it or cope with it. Finally we can practice those methods or skills.

We'll begin this chapter by considering how our society views conflict and how each of us reacts to it personally. Then I'll discuss ways of coping with conflict with suggestions for some skills to practice. Understanding the nature of conflict will help us to facilitate cooperative behavior, resolve problems, and enhance our interpersonal relationships and contacts. We can't eliminate conflict, but we can start to look at it as something we can handle.

HOW SOCIETY VIEWS CONFLICT

Conflict is considered bad in our society. You may have come to believe that conflicts are the cause for marriages to be dissolved, for employees to be fired, and for demotions, demerits, demoralization, and divisiveness.

From *Understanding Interpersonal Communication* by Richard L. Weaver II. Copyright (©) 1978 by Scott, Foresman and Company. Reprinted by permission.

Certainly arguments, disagreements, and fights do force people apart and damage relationships. But more than likely it is not the conflict itself that causes the break in these relationships, but the poor handling of the conflict.

Anger, often one of the underlying causes of conflict, is also considered taboo in our society. This is supposed to be the age of reason and togetherness. Anger is not "gentlemanly," "ladylike," "nice" or "mature." The mere mention of fighting is enough to make some people uncomfortable. They may talk of their "differences" or of their "silly arguments" but not of "fights" because they feel "fight" implies a lack of maturity and self-control. Fighting here means verbal and nonverbal quarreling, not physical battle. Actually, not to admit to conflict or fighting implies a lack of maturity. People who are mature *do* fight. When we are on intimate terms with another person, our closeness may be characterized by quarreling and making up. We may try to live in harmony and agreement with another person but this desire alone creates a need for conflict—just to establish and maintain *our* notion of harmony and agreement.[1]

Our society has conditioned us to dislike and dread personal, aggressive openness. Well-liked people are described with such phrases as, "She is very kind; she'll do anything for anyone" or "He doesn't have a nasty bone in his body" or "She wouldn't raise her voice to anyone." Think of people you know who are admired and the phrases people use to describe them. Nonaggressiveness is praised and admired.[2] We are often taught that nobody will like us unless we are cheerful and that nice people do not fight.

Our society's attitude toward nonaggressiveness may be responsible for the vicarious pleasure many people get from watching the violent acts of other people. Sports such as hockey, football, and boxing include elements of violence; violence is also prominent in the news, in movies, and on television. Anger and aggressiveness are officially taboo, but as a society we are obsessed and fascinated with them and admire them. Our heroes and heroines are powerful, robust, forceful characters. There seems to be a difference between what we give lip service to and what we actually like. There is no doubt that conflict *can be* destructive. Whether it is harmful or helpful depends on how it is used.

HOW YOU VIEW CONFLICT

Healthy interpersonal communication is *not* conflict-free. Conflict is a part of all the relationships we have with other people. It can be constructive or destructive, depending on how we manage it.[3] Conflict is often the

---

[1] George R. Bach and Peter Wyden. *The Intimate Enemy: How to Fight Fair in Love and Marriage* (New York: Avon Books, 1968), pp. 25–26.

[2] George R. Bach and Herb Goldberg, *Creative Aggression: The Art of Assertive Living* (New York: Avon Books, 1974), p. 82.

[3] Robert J. Doolittle, "Conflicting Views of Conflict: An Analysis of Basic Communication Textbooks," *Communication Education* 26 (March 1977), 121.

constructive means we use to challenge established norms and practices and at times it is the means through which we are our most creative and innovative. Conflict often motivates us to summon up our untapped abilities. Some of our most eloquent moments result from impromptu situations that occur when we have been stopped from doing something or need to get our way. We should concentrate on managing interpersonal conflict to gain the maximum benefit, discovering our own best style of handling it in the process.

Any time we get together with another person for more than a short while, conflicts may arise that are serious enough to destroy our relationship if we do not know how to handle them. There are no magic formulas for overcoming barriers and resolving breakdowns. But we can look at those breakdowns in a fresh way. The fact that we are unique and that we experience the world in a unique way is enough to generate conflict because conflict occurs when human differences or uniquenesses meet. In addition to being unique, each of us is also able to make choices. We can decide how to handle the disagreements we encounter.

It may seem discouraging to think that even in the very best of relationships there is going to be conflict and that, on top of that, there is no guarantee that the conflict can be resolved. But we can change the way we deal with it. First we need to confront our own feelings. There are different styles of handling conflict. To know what happens when we disagree is a useful starting point.

WHAT HAPPENS WHEN YOU DISAGREE

Conflict is simply a situation in which we, our desires, or our intentions are in opposition to those of another person. Opposition means incompatibility: if our desires predominate, the other person's will not.[4] If we want to go to one movie and our friend wants to go to another one, a state of conflict results. If we feel we deserve an A and our instructor thinks a B is all we deserve, we are in conflict. If we believe that one interpretation of a poem is correct and our classmates think another one is more appropriate, we have another conflict situation. There are, of course, honest differences of opinion that lead to conflict. But there are also barriers and breakdowns in communication that create conflict and can be avoided.

Communication Barriers and Breakdowns

An atmosphere of acceptance is essential to preventing breakdowns in communication. Without acceptance, messages may not be received at all or may be distorted if they are received. Not receiving a message or distorting it causes conflicts. An atmosphere of acceptance can be affected

---

[4]Kenneth E. Boulding, *Conflict and Defense* (New York: Harper and Row, 1962), p. 5.

by contrary attitudes, newly acquired contrary opinions, jumping to conclusions, credibility, and hostility.[5]

Contrary attitudes. Our predjudices, biases, and predispositions affect the way we interact with and perceive others. When other people's views are contrary to ours, our reactions are aroused through a sense of irritation. This will become a barrier to communication unless we make a concerted attempt to be tolerant, understanding, and personally poised.

Newly acquired contrary opinions. Converts to a religious belief are generally thought to be stronger believers than those who have been brought up with the belief. The closer we are to the time we acquired a new opinion, attitude, or belief, the more rigid we will be in defending it. And the more rigid we are, the less vulnerable we are to change. Conflict is most frustrating when neither person is willing to be flexible. As time passes, we may begin to be more receptive to contrary ideas, even though we may still firmly hold our original belief. If we are conscious of the effects of the passage of time on creating an atmosphere of acceptance, we will be more careful about our timing when we need to present a new and potentially controversial idea to someone.

Jumping to conclusions. The problem with jumping to conclusions is that the climate of acceptance is destroyed when we rush to make a decision before we have enough facts on which to base the judgment. When we do not really listen, review the facts, or try to examine all the messages we are receiving, we create an atmosphere of misinformation and distrust which works against effective communication.

Credibility. Acceptance is affected if one of us perceives the other to be a person of low credibility. If we suspect someone of being unfair, biased, unreliable, hostile, or contradictory, we are not likely to hear what he or she says. This basic lack of acceptance creates a serious handicap to communication. To focus on the content of the message and not on the person will help, but a climate of low credibility is difficult to overcome.

Hostility. In the presence of outright hostility, it is very hard to achieve an atmosphere of acceptance. Hostility begets hostility. When we become aware of hostility directed toward us, we are likely to respond with a potentially hostile posture—prepared, alert, and equipped for a self-defensive action. Hostility then intensifies and communication is blocked.

Styles of Handling Conflict

Conflict can evolve from situations that are critically important as well as from seemingly irrelevant ones. By "important" I mean situations

[5]Based on pgs. 172–176 from *Elements of Interpersonal Communication* by John W. Keltner. © 1973 by Wadsworth Publishing Company, Inc., Belmont, California 94002. Reprinted by permission of the publisher.

where basic moral or ethical values are challenged. Such a situation might occur in a family where some members hold politically conservative views and other members have strong liberal tendencies—conflicts may spring up about military service, tax laws, and countless other subjects. Seemingly irrelevant situations occur daily as we must decide what to wear, whether or not to go to class, or where to eat lunch.

It is not for us to judge the importance of conflict to anyone else. What is a conflict situation to one person may not be for another person. Just as people view conflict differently, they deal with it differently. Some people tend to be more conflict-prone than others; they are sometimes less adaptable and their points of view tend to oppose other people's. Some people, too, get certain satisfactions from setting up competitive, win-lose situations. I won't explore all the psychological reasons, but this is a type of person most of us have known. When someone else takes a stand, you can almost predict that this conflict-prone person will stand squarely against that position and an argument will ensue.

Whether we are conflict-prone or not, we can ignore conflict by actively denying that it exists or by running away from it. We can attack the other person directly by challenging his or her credibility. Direct attacks can take many forms; all are destructive to effective communication. There are, fortunately, some other alternatives:

1. We can give in or agree to meet the other person halfway.

2. We can postpone the confrontation, hoping that the passage of time will eliminate the conflict, shed new light on the situation, make one side in the conflict predominate, or cause the other person to forget about it.

3. We can work through the problem until differences are resolved or both of us agree to disagree.

Using the wrong approach can do irreparable damage to a relationship. On the other hand, interpersonal communication can be enhanced if the conflict is handled effectively. People essentially take one of two positions: they may "erupt" or they may "withhold."[6]

"Erupters" tend to enter a conflict situation with vigor. They might lash out at the opposition, bystanders, and whoever else is available, venting their emotions. When these people believe they are right, they may be unwilling to compromise. They may find it hard to apologize or to forgive. They use this means of reacting because they know of no other alternatives, or they know them but do not practice them.

"Withholders" tend to be afraid of conflict. Because of exposure to highly emotional people, because of upbringing, or because of certain personality characteristics, these people may avoid expressing any conflict-oriented feelings. They withhold their frustrations, anger, hate, resentment, irritations, and annoyances. Sometimes these feelings build up and are let out all in one emotional avalanche, but more often they build up

---

[6]Ron Adler and Neil Towne, *Looking Out/Looking In: Interpersonal Communication* (San Francisco: Rinehart Press, 1975), p. 303.

inside, causing mental and physical harm. Self-hate is just one of the possible side effects resulting from the containment of strong feelings.
Neither of these ways leads to satisfactory solutions. Only the third way—working through the problem until differences are resolved—makes any sense for strengthening interpersonal relationships, yet this alternative is not often used. I will label people who take this approach "confronters" or "copers."

COPING WITH CONFLICT: A SUCCESSFUL APPROACH

An approach has been designed for managing all stressful conflict situations that puts a high priority on creative coping and on maintaining self-esteem. How successfully we use these coping behaviors depends on our recognition of a conflict situation and on our ability to keep our wits about us as we put this approach into action. The four main elements of this approach to coping are gaining information, organizing our selves, striving for independence, and anticipating conflict situations.[7]

Information: Get Enough of the Right Kind

In any communication setting, whether conflict-laden or not, we act best when we are well informed. In a conflict situation, we need to find out all we can about the problem to assure our selves that we have more than one way to deal with it. The information we pick up may involve the nature of the communication itself or it may involve the other person. Problems with information may develop in three major ways: through overload, manipulation, and ambiguity.

Communication overload. If one person provides another person with more information than he or she can handle, a problem will arise.[8] We call this "overload." The information I am referring to here has to do with the content of a communicator's message to a listener, not with information of a general nature about a conflict situation, as discussed above.

A human being can handle only so much information at one time. This has to do with the capability of the human brain to decipher material but also with the various ways the emotions get bound to certain experiences. Often the root causes for conflict are closely tied to our emotional response pattern. In such cases, as sure as conflicts are bound to come up, so are the emotions that go along with them. If we are having an emotionally involving experience, it is difficult to take on and fully comprehend a new "load" of information at the same time. Our senses

[7]Julius Fast, *Creative Coping: A Guide to Positive Living* (New York: William Morrow and Co., Inc., 1976), pp. 187–188.

[8]W. Charles Redding, *Communication Within the Organization* (New York: Industrial Communication Council, 1972), p. 87.

are preoccupied. If someone else tries to share some vital news with us while our feelings are thus tied up, interpersonal conflicts may result. We may experience this when we try to listen to a classroom lecture just after we've heard some upsetting news. The intensity of the emotional experience overshadows any material the teacher could offer. We simply don't have room for any more information; trying to fit it in would be overloading.

Manipulative communication. Communication breakdowns are likely to occur when a listener feels information is being offered with manipulative intent. You may have experienced manipulation at one time or another when you felt someone was using you or trying to control you. People manipulate other people for various reasons. In some cases, a person looks to others *for support*. Not trusting them to give it, he or she manipulates them to steer them in the right direction. Manipulation may also result *from* love. The problem is described by Everett Shostrom:

> We seem to assume that the more perfect we appear—the more flawless— the more we will be loved. Actually, the reverse is more apt to be true. The more willing we are to admit our weaknesses as human beings, the more lovable we are. Nevertheless, love is an achievement not easy to attain, and thus the alternative that the manipulator has is a desperate one—that of complete power over the other person, the power that makes him do what we want, feel what we want, think what we want, and which transforms him into a thing, *our* thing.[9]

Erich Fromm has said that the ultimate relationship between human beings is that of love—knowing a human being as he or she is and loving that person's ultimate essence.[10] Loving someone's "ultimate essence" is just the opposite of manipulation.

A third reason that manipulation occurs is *out of frustration with life*. People who feel overwhelmed may decide that since they cannot control everything, they will control nothing. They become passive manipulators. They may use various devices and tricks to accentuate their helplessness. They will try to get other people to make decisions for them and carry part of their burden, manipulating through their own feeling of powerlessness.

There are two other reasons that people manipulate that appear to be near opposites. People may deal with others ritualistically in an effort *to avoid intimacy or involvement*. An example of ritualistic communication is the teacher who cannot deal with students in other than stictly teacher-student terms. The same type of ritualistic behavior might be seen in employer-employee and doctor-patient relationships.

[9]Adapted from *Man, the Manipulator* by Everett Shostrom, Copyright © 1967 by Abingdon Press. Used by permission of Abingdon Press.

[10]Erich Fromm, "Man is Not a Thing," *Saturday Review* (March 16, 1957), pp. 9–11.

Another reason people manipulate is *to gain the approval of others*. There are people who think they need to be approved of by everyone. They may be untruthful, trying to please everyone in their quest for acceptance. An example of this behavior is the friend who tells us everything we do is "great" just to keep us as a friend.

Ambiguous communication.   Ambiguous information may contribute to a conflict situation because ambiguity almost always leads to misunderstanding.[11] Ambiguity can result when not enough information is provided or when it is too general. If one of your friends told you that everyone was going to the show tonight and that you should meet them downtown, you might easily misunderstand. Who is "everyone"? Where exactly should you meet them? What time? Also, the more abstract our language is, the more likely it is to be ambiguous and conflict-promoting.

Whenever we find our selves in a conflict situation, we should pay special attention to the kind of information we are exchanging: Is there enough? Is there too much? Is it manipulative? Is it ambiguous? It will be helpful to remember that every receiver of messages creates his or her own meaning for that communication based upon what he or she perceives. We can never know exactly which stimulus aroused meaning in someone else's head. The kinds of phenomena that can provoke meaning are limitless—there is no way anyone can control with certainty all the variables that will eliminate potential conflict situations.

Finally, remember that the message a receiver gets is the only one that counts in a conflict situation. The message that he or she acts upon may be quite different from the information that was sent. To discover precisely what message was received is useful in coping with conflict. We may need to ask the other person, "Now, what did you hear?" or "What is it that you understand?" or "What are you going to do?" As far as possible, we need to know where the other person is coming from if we are to deal successfully with conflict.[12]

Organization: Sort Things Out

Think of a situation to which you had a powerful emotional response: fear, anger, grief, or passion. If you needed to cope with conflict at that time, you may have found your judgment was affected. To reestablish stability and a sense of right and wrong we need to organize our selves within our selves—we need to get our selves together.[13]

This is not to say we should avoid emotional experiences. Feelings of fear, anger, grief, and passion are healthy and normal and should not be

---

[11]Richard C. Huseman, James M. Lahiff, and John D. Hatfield, *Interpersonal Communication in Organizations: A Perceptual Approach* (Boston: Holbrook Press, Inc., 1976), p. 99.

[12]Redding, *Communication Within the Organization*, pp. 28, 30, and 37.

[13]Fast, *Creative Coping*, p. 187.

repressed. But when in the throes of extreme emotional experiences, we must remember that our senses are affected, that we cannot depend on our perceptions. This is why, for example, people are wise to make funeral arrangements *before* a person dies. In the emotional aftermath of the death of a loved one, decision making is difficult and judgments are not as rational as they are at other times.

When our perceptions are distorted, conflict is likely to escalate because of the misunderstandings exchanged. One such misunderstanding has been labeled by David W. Johnson as "mirror image." In conflict, "mirror image" occurs when both people think they are right, both think they were the one maligned, both think the other person is wrong, and both think they are the only one who wants a just solution.

Another kind of misunderstanding occurs when one person sees identical acts committed by both sides but considers those of the other person illegitimate, unfair, unjust, and unreasonable while viewing his or her own as legitimate, fair, just, and reasonable considering the circumstances. This is known as the "double standard."

In conflict situations, too, thinking becomes polarized. Both individuals might come to have an oversimplified view of the conflict. In this uncomplicated view, anything the other person does is bad and everything we do is good. Obviously, when such misunderstandings are at work, it is difficult to organize our thinking.

When we are aware that we are not coping rationally, we would do well to seek help from others. It's a good idea to go to trusted friends for help in making decisions and carrying out plans. To recognize that we cannot make competent decisions until we have reorganized our thinking is not a weakness; it is realistic and mature.

To be organized within our selves is an awareness function. People who "have it together" are responsive, alive, and interested. They listen to themselves.[14] The attitudes they express are based on firmly rooted values. An organized person takes time to think, to monitor, and to reevaluate before responding.

Independence: Be Your Own Person

Most conflict situations we deal with on a daily basis are not the extremely taxing kind. The better we know our selves, the better we will be able to cope with daily conflict. The better organized we are, too, the more likely we are to be our own person—autonomous. We need to be free to act and to deal with conflict and we must avoid being pushed into action before we are ready.[15]

The people best prepared to cope with conflict are spontaneous. They have the freedom to be, to express their full range of potentials, to be the masters of their own lives and not to be easily manipulated.

[14]Ibid., pp. 187–188.

[15]Shostrom, *Man, the Manipulator,* p. 50.

Successful copers are open and responsive. They can assert their own independence without trying to stifle another person's. They show their independence by expressing their wants and needs instead of demanding them, by expressing their preferences instead of ordering, by expressing acceptance of each other rather than mere tolerance, and by being willing to surrender genuinely to the other person's wishes rather than simply pretending to submit.[16]

Anticipation: Be Prepared for Conflict

Conflicts are more likely to become cries when they catch us totally unaware. Try to anticipate conflict situations. Try to cut your emotional reactions off at the pass. If we are ready for conflict and confident in our ability to deal with it, we'll be much less anxious if and when conflict develops.

By anticipating a conflict situation, we will be more likely to have some control over the context in which it occurs. Instead of focusing, for example, on whose fault the conflict is, we can try to get in touch with where we and the other person are and attempt to work from there.

In addition, with some anticipation, we can take responsibility for our feelings and actions. We can plan, in advance, to say such things as "I am angry" instead of "You make me angry," or "I feel rejected" instead of "You are excluding me again," or "I am confused" instead of "You don't make sense." In this way, we own our feelings—we take full responsibility for them. And we convey our feelings to others, creating trust in the process.

Finally, anticipation can cause us to be more aware. Resolving interpersonal conflict is easiest when we listen to the other person and respond to him or her with feedback. Conflict is likely to be reduced when we try to support and understand the other person.

IMPROVING SKILLS IN CONFLICT MANAGEMENT

The following ideas will aid in developing a constructive approach to dealing with conflict situations.[17] Remember that there are no guaranteed solutions or sure-fire approaches. Remember, too, that not all conflicts can be resolved but that we can always choose how to handle them.

Define the conflict.[18] How we view the cause, size, and type of conflict affects how we manage it. If we know what events led up to the conflict and especially the specific event that triggered it, we may be able to

[16]Ibid., p. 53.

[17]David W. Johnson, *Reaching Out* (Englewood Cliffs, N.J.: Prentice-Hall, Inc., 1972), pp. 217–219.

[18]This approach is a variation of Dewey's problem-solving method. See John Dewey, *How We Think* (Chicago: D. C. Heath, 1910).

anticipate and avoid future conflicts. We should learn to see the true size of a conflict: the smaller and more specific it is, the easier it will be to resolve. When a large, vague issue or principle is involved, the conflict itself is often escalated and enlarged. We can get very upset over how the system of higher education stifles individual initiative and growth, but that is a large, vague issue. To narrow the cause of the conflict, we might focus directly on a particular professor we are having problems with.

View the conflict as a joint problem.   There are two general ways of looking at a conflict: as a win-or-lose situation or as a joint problem. If we look at a conflict as a joint problem, there is a greater possibility for a creative solution which results in both of us being satisfied. If we are having trouble with our English professor, we could easily turn the situation into a win-lose confrontation. We might say, "She thinks she's so great, I'm going to show her. I'll go the the department head. . . ." If we perceive the conflict as a joint problem, we might say, "Perhaps she has a point; maybe if I go in to see her, we could talk about this." The way we label a conflict partly determines the way we resolve it.

Defining conflict as a joint problem means trying to discover the differences and samenesses between our selves and the other person. There is always the question of not just how *we* define the problem but also of how the *other person* defines the problem and how our definitions differ.

State the problem.   We'll have a better chance of resolving a potential conflict quickly if we have a clear idea of what behavior is acceptable or unacceptable to us and if we express our position to the other person. When we say to another person, "When you interrupt me when we are talking to other people, I feel put down and unimportant" or "Every time you publicly criticize how I dress, I get angry with you," we explain specific behaviors that are unacceptable to us. And we can then discuss or change those behaviors.

When we focus on a specific bothersome behavior, we reveal what is going on inside us. We take responsibility for our feelings by using "I" language instead of "you" language. This lessens the likelihood of defensiveness by not placing the blame on the other person as we would if we said, "You insult me" or "You make me angry."

Check your perceptions.   Under any circumstances, it is easy to be misunderstood, misquoted, or misinterpreted. Especially in a conflict situation, we should always check to make certain our message has been received accurately. We should also make sure we understand the other person's responses by paraphrasing them before we answer. Because our emotions quicken in times of conflict, further hurt or resentment can occur quickly through distortions caused by expectations or predispositions. Empathic listening is essential. We can determine where we are in our conversation with another person through paraphrases and summaries.

Generate possible solutions. It is important, once we have shared what is bothering us, to consider how change can occur. We need not come up with all the solutions ourselves. A joint, cooperative solution is more likely to work. Flexibility is important in this process. Julius Fast views flexibility as extremely valuable, calling it "an awareness of alternative solutions as well as the ability to discard one solution if it doesn't work and select another."[19] What is needed? What can the other person do? What can we do? What can be done together? These are realistic questions that should be raised. As we get possible answers to these questions, we should paraphrase and summarize them so that we are certain that both of us know what has been suggested and what alternatives exist.

Reach a mutually acceptable solution. When we have considered all the possible alternative we and the other person could generate, we should decide which of them would be mutually acceptable. It is important that we find an answer somewhat agreeable to everyone involved. But we cannot stop there. We all should understand the possible outcomes of implementing the solution. What is likely to happen? We should also understand what needs exist for cooperative interaction. In what ways, for example, will a particular solution require us to work together? When we have come to a final agreement on how to settle our conflict, we should make certain everyone fully understands what we agreed on by paraphrasing and summarizing the results.

If we cannot reach an agreement we should stop. Plan another meeting. Try again later. To get away from the problem for a while may result in new insights being generated.

Implement and evaluate the solution. Before we put the proposed solution into effect, we should try to agree on how we will check it later to see if it solved the problem. Plan a check-up meeting to evaluate progress. After we implement the solution, we'll want fo find out if the results are mutually satisfying. If they aren't, we might have to go back to the beginning, possibly to our original definition of the conflict. We should have some way of knowing how to tell if the implemented solution worked well or did not work at all. If we have moved through the conflict successfully or are at least making progress, some gesture of appreciation might be appropriate.

Conflict in interpersonal communication is an inevitable human experience. We are unique, the next person is unique; when these uniquenesses meet, conflict can occur. Conflict does not need to fracture friendships, split marriages, or break up other interpersonal relationships. There is nothing inherently destructive, threatening, or mysterious about conflict. How well we handle it while maintaining our values and our self-esteem and, at the same time, protecting the values and self-esteem of

---

[19]Fast, *Creative Coping*, p. 53.

other people will help determine our effectiveness in interpersonal relationships.

FOR DISCUSSION

1. Do you agree with Weaver that conflict is not necessarily bad or negative? Can you identify specific instances from your own experiences in which conflict served a positive function?

2. How do you generally deal with interpersonal conflict? Try to describe your specific behavior patterns in as much detail as you can. To what degree do you naturally follow the suggestions of Weaver? How might you alter your conflict behavior to make it more productive?

3. Can you distinguish your friends from your enemies on the basis of the way in which they handle interpersonal conflict with you and the way in which you handle interpersonal conflict with them?

4. Can you provide any additional suggestions for effectively dealing with interpersonal conflict? In what ways might these additional suggestions prove useful?

5. If you had to formulate one principle of "communication and conflict" what would it be? That is, formulate in the form of a principle one specific guideline to follow in dealing with conflict in communication.

SERIAL AND SMALL GROUP COMMUNICATION

In this section we focus on serial and small group communication. Serial or sequential communication refers to communication that takes place through some linear kind of sequence, going from A to B to C to D and so on. It is a kind of small group situation but the participants do not meet at the same time; rather, the messages, passed from one person to another, create a kind of group network. William V. Haney's "Serial Communication of Information in Organizations" is a particularly good introduction to this area. His analysis of the trends in serial transmission and the correctives that might be employed to prevent some or all of these potential distortions in the messages is especially valuable.

In "Gossiping as a Way of Speaking" Sally Yerkovich analyzes one of the most important types of serial communication. This article should provide an excellent opportunity to analyze your own gossiping behavior as a source and as a receiver. Once we recognize that we all engage in gossip—willingly or unwillingly, as source or receiver of both—we will be better prepared to deal with some of the implications and consequences of gossiping.

Robert Freed Bales, in his "Communication in Small Groups," provides a readable and informative overview of small group communication, identifying some of the significant dimensions of small group interaction and suggesting some of the ways in which small group communication is influenced. Each paragraph in this article could be expanded into an entire article; Bales is here providing a kind of skeletal outline of the tremendously complex area of small group communication. Dennis Gouran, in his Participating in Decision-Making Discussions offers some suggestions on how you might improve your own effectiveness as a participant in a small group communication situation. The guidelines should enable you to function more effectively and should be considered carefully. Intellectually it will be easy to see yourself following all of these guidelines; but try to see if these are evident in your actual behaviors at the time you are functioning in small group situations.

These articles should fit neatly with the previous articles dealing with intrapersonal and interpersonal communication. Serial communication is surely a type of interpersonal interaction and small group communication may be viewed as a slightly enlarged form of interpersonal communication. Both the similarities and the differences among these several forms need to be appreciated if you are to function effectively in all forms.

Serial Communication of Information in Organizations

William V. Haney

An appreciable amount of the communication which occurs in business, industry, hospitals, military units, government agencies—in short, in chain-of-command organizations—consists of serial transmissions. A communicates a message to *B; B* then communicates *A*'s message (or rather his *interpretation* of *A*'s message) to *C; C* then communicates his interpretation of *B*'s interpretation of *A*'s message to *D;* and so on. The originator and the ultimate recipient of the message[1] are separated by "middle men."

"The message" may often be passed down (but not necessarily all the way down) the organization chain, as when in business the chairman acting on behalf of the board of directors may express a desire to the president. "The message" begins to fan out as the president, in turn, relays "it" to his vice presidents; they convey "it" to their respective subordinates; and so forth. Frequently "a message" goes up (but seldom all the way up) the chain. Sometimes "it" travels laterally. Sometimes, as with rumors, "it" disregards the formal organization and flows more closely along informal organizational lines.

Regardless of its direction, the number of "conveyors" involved, and the degree of its conformance with the formal structure, serial transmission is clearly an essential, inevitable form of communication in organizations. It is equally apparent that serial transmission is especially susceptible to

---

[1]"The message," as already suggested, is a misnomer in that what is being conveyed is not static, unchanging, and fixed. I shall retain the term for convenience, however, and use quotation marks to signify that its dynamic nature is subject to cumulative change.

From Sidney Mailick and Edward H. Van Ness, eds., *Concepts and Issues in Administrative Behavior*, pp. 150–65. © 1962. Reprinted by permission of Prentice-Hall, Inc., Englewood Cliffs, N. J.

distortion and disruption. Not only is it subject to the shortcomings and maladies of "simple" person-to-person communication but, since it consists of a series of such communications, the anomalies are often *compounded*.

This is not to say, however, that serial transmissions in organizations should be abolished or even decreased. We wish to show that such communications *can be improved* if communicators are able (1) to recognize some of the patterns of miscommunication which occur in serial transmissions; (2) to understand some of the factors contributing to these patterns; (3) to take measures and practice techniques for preventing the recurrence of these patterns and for ameliorating their consequences.

I shall begin by cataloguing some of the factors which seemingly influence a serial transmission.[2]

MOTIVES OF THE COMMUNICATORS

When *B* conveys *A*'s message to *C* he may be influenced by at least three motives of which he may be largely unaware.

The Desire to Simplify the Message

We evidently dislike conveying detailed messages. The responsibility of passing along complex information is burdensome and taxing. Often, therefore, we unconsciously simplify the message before passing it along to the next person.[3] It is very probable that among the details most susceptible to omission are those we already knew or in some way presume our recipients will know without our telling them.

The Desire to Convey a "Sensible" Message

Apparently we are reluctant to relay a message that is somehow incoherent, illogical, or incomplete. It may be embarrassing to admit that one does not fully understand the message he is conveying. When he

---

[2]During the past three years I have conducted scores of informal experiments with groups of university undergraduate and graduate students, business and government executives, military officers, professionals, and so on. I would read the "message" (below) to the first "conveyor." He would then relay his interpretation to the second conveyor who, in turn, would pass along his interpretation to the third, etc. The sixth (and final member of the "team") would listen to "the message" and then write down his version of it. These final versions were collected and compared with the original.

Every year at State University, the eagles in front of the Psi Gamma fraternity house were mysteriously sprayed during the night. Whenever this happened, it cost the Psi Gams from $75 to $100 to have the eagles cleaned. The Psi Gams complained to officials and were promised by the president that if ever any students were caught painting the eagles, they would be expelled from school.*

[3]On an arbitrary count basis the stimulus message used in the serial transmission demonstrations described in footnote 2 contained 24 "significant details." The final versions contained a mean count of approximately 8 "significant details"—a "detail loss" of 65%.

*Adapted from "Chuck Jackson" by Diana Conzett, which appears in Irving J. Lee's *Customs and Crises in Communication* (New York: Harper & Bros., 1954), p. 245. Reprinted by permission.

receives a message that does not quite make sense to him he is prone to "make sense out of it" before passing it along to the next person.[4]

The Desire to Make the Conveyance of the Message as Pleasant and/or Painless as Possible for the Conveyor

We evidently do not like to have to tell the boss unpleasant things. Even when not directly responsible, one does not relish the reaction of his superior to a disagreeable message. This motive probably accounts for a considerable share of the tendency for a "message" to lose its harshness as it moves up the organizational ladder. The first line supervisor may tell his foreman, "I'm telling you, Mike, the men say that if this pay cut goes through they'll strike—and they mean it!" By the time "this message" has been relayed through six or eight or more echelons (if indeed it goes that far) the executive vice president might express it to the president as, "Well, sir, the men seem a little concerned over the projected wage reduction but I am confident that they will take it in stride."

One of the dangers plaguing some upper managements is that they are effectively shielded from incipient problems until they become serious and costly ones.

ASSUMPTIONS OF THE COMMUNICATORS

In addition to the serial transmitter's motives we must consider his assumptions—particularly those he makes about his communications. If some of these assumptions are fallacious and if one is unaware that he holds them, his communication can be adversely affected. The following are, in this writer's judgment, two of the most pervasive and dangerous of the current myths about communication:

The Assumption that Words Are Used in Only One Way

A study[5] indicates that for the 500 most commonly used words in our language there are 14,070 different dictionary definitions—over 28 usages per word, on the average. Take the word *run*, for example:

---

[4]The great majority (approximately 93%) of the final versions (from the serial transmission demonstrations) made "sense." Even those which were the most bizarre and bore the least resemblance to the original stimulus were in and of themselves internally consistent and coherent.

For example,

"At a State University there was an argument between two teams—the Eagles and the Fire Gems—in which their clothing was torn."

"The Eagles in front of the university had parasites and were sprayed with insecticide."

"At State U. they have many birds which desecrate the buildings. To remedy the situation they expelled the students who fed the birds."

[5]Lydia Strong, "Do You Know How to Listen?" *Effective Communication on the Job*, Dooher and Marquis, eds. (New York: American Management Association, 1956), p. 28.

Babe Ruth scored a *run*.
Did you ever see Jesse Owens *run?*
I have a *run* in my stocking.
There is a fine *run* of salmon this year.
Are you going to *run* this company or am I?
You have the *run* of the place.
Don't give me the *run* around.
What headline do you want to *run?*
There was a *run* on the bank today.
Did he *run* the ship aground?
I have to *run* (drive the car) downtown.
Who will *run* for President this year?
Joe flies the New York–Chicago *run* twice a week.
You know the kind of people they *run* around with.
The apples *run* large this year.
Please *run* my bath water.

We could go on at some length—my small abridged dictionary gives eighty-seven distinct usages for *run*. I have chosen an extreme example, of course, but there must be relatively few words (excepting some technical terms) used in one and in only one sense.

Yet communicators often have a curious notion about words *when they are using them*, i.e., when they are speaking, writing, listening, or reading. It is immensely easy for a "sender" of a communication to assume that words are used in only one way—the way he intends them. It is just as enticing for the "receiver" to assume that the sender intended his words as he, the receiver, happens to interpret them at the moment. When communicators are unconsciously burdened by the assumption of the mono-usage of words they are prone to become involved in the pattern of miscommunication known as *bypassing*.

A foreman told a machine operator he was passing: "Better clean up around here." It was ten minutes later when the foreman's assistant phoned: "Say, boss, isn't that bearing Sipert is working on due up in engineering pronto?"

"You bet your sweet life it is. Why?"

"He says you told him to drop it and sweep the place up. I thought I'd better make sure."

"Listen," the foreman flared into the phone, "get him right back on that job. It's got to be ready in twenty minutes."

. . . What the foreman had in mind was for Sipert to gather up the oily waste, which was a fire and accident hazard. This would not have taken more than a couple of minutes, and there would have been plenty of time to finish the bearing.[6]

Bypassing: Denotative and Connotative.   Since we use words to express at least two kinds of meanings there can be two kinds of bypassings.

---

[6]Reprinted from *The Foreman's Letter* with permission of National Foremen's Institute, New London, Conn.

Suppose you say to me, "Your neighbor's grass is certainly green and healthy looking, isn't it?" You could be intending your words merely to *denote*, i.e., to point to or to call my attention, to the appearance of my neighbor's lawn. On the other hand, you could have intended your words to *connote*, i.e., to imply something beyond or something other than what you were ostensibly denoting. You might have meant any number of things: that my own lawn needed more care; that my neighbor was inordinately meticulous about his lawn; that my neighbor's lawn is tended by a professional, a service you do not have and for which you envy or despise my neighbor; or even that his grass was not green at all but, on the contrary, parched and diseased; and so forth.

Taking these two kinds of meanings into account it is clear that bypassing occurs or can occur under any of four conditions:

1. *When the sender intends one denotation while the receiver interprets another.* (As in the case of Sipert and his foreman.)

2. When the sender intends one connotation while the receiver interprets another.

A friend once told me of an experience she had had years ago when as a teenager she was spending the week with a maiden aunt. Joan had gone to the movies with a young man who brought her home at a respectable hour. However, the couple lingered on the front porch somewhat longer than Aunt Mildred thought necessary. The little old lady was rather proud of her ability to deal with younger people so she slipped out of bed, raised her bedroom window, and called down sweetly, "If you two knew how pleasant it is in bed, you wouldn't be standing out there in the cold."

3. *When the sender intends only a denotation while the receiver interprets a connotation.*

For a brief period the following memorandum appeared on the bulletin boards of a government agency in Washington:

Those department and sections heads who do not have secretaries assigned to them may take advantage of the stenographers in the secretarial pool.

4. *When the sender intends a connotation while the receiver interprets a denotation only.*

Before making his final decision on a proposal to move to new offices, the head of a large company called his top executives for a last discussion of the idea. All were enthusiastic except the company treasurer who insisted that he had not had time to calculate all the costs with accuracy sufficient to satisfy himself that the move was advantageous. Annoyed by his persistence, the chief finally burst out: "All right, Jim, all right! Figure it out to the last cent. A penny saved is a penny earned, right?"

The intention was ironic. He meant not what the words denoted but the opposite—forget this and stop being petty. For him this was what his words connoted.

For the treasurer "penny saved, penny earned" meant exactly what it said. He put several members on his staff to work on the problem and, to test the firmness of the price, had one of them interview the agent renting the proposed new quarters without explaining whom he represented. This indication of additional interest in the premises led the agent to raise the rent. Not until the lease was signed, did the agency discover that one of its own employes had, in effect, bid up its price.[7]

The Assumption That Inferences Are Always Distinguishable from Observations

It is incredibly difficult, at times, for a communicator (or anyone) to discriminate between what he "knows" (i.e., what he has actually observed—seen, heard, read, etc.) and what he is only inferring or guessing. One of the key reasons for this lies in the character of the language used to express observations and inferences.

Suppose you look at a man and observe that he is wearing a white shirt and then say, "That man is wearing a white shirt." Assuming your vision and the illumination were "normal" you would have made a statement of *observation*—a statement which directly corresponded to and was corroborated by your observation. But suppose you now say, "That man bought the white shirt he is wearing." Assuming you were not present when and if the man bought the shirt that statement would be *for you a statement of inference*. Your statement went *beyond* what you observed. You inferred that the man bought the shirt; you did not observe it. Of course, your inference may be correct (but it could be false: perhaps he was given the shirt as a gift; perhaps he stole it or borrowed it; etc.).

Nothing in the nature of our language (the grammar, spelling, pronunciation, accentuation, syntax, inflection, etc.) prevents you from speaking or writing (or thinking) a statement of inference *as if* you were making a statement of observation. Our language permits you to say "Of course, he bought the shirt" with certainty and finality, i.e., with as much confidence as you would make a statement of observation. The effect is that it becomes exceedingly easy to confuse the two kinds of statements and also to confuse inference and observation on nonverbal levels. The destructive consequences of acting upon inference as if acting upon observation can range from mild embarrassment to tragedy. One factual illustration may be sufficient to point up the dangers of such behavior.

THE CASE OF JIM BLAKE[8]

Jim Blake, 41, had been with the Hasting Co. for ten years. For the last seven years he had served as an "inside salesman," receiving phone calls from customers and writing out orders. "Salesman," in this case, was somewhat of a euphemism as the customer ordinarily knew what he wanted and was prepared to place an order. The "outside salesmen," on the other hand, visited industrial accounts and enjoyed considerably more status and income. Blake had aspired to an outside position for several years but no

---

[7]Robert Froman, "Make Words Fit the Job," *Nation's Business* (July 1959), p. 78. Reprinted by permission.

[8]The names have been changed.

openings had occurred. He had, however, been assured by Russ Jenkins, sales manager, that as senior inside man he would be given first chance at the next available outside job.

Finally, it seemed as if Jim's chance had come. Harry Strom, 63, one of the outside men, had decided in January to retire on the first of June. It did not occur to Jenkins to reassure Blake that the new opening was to be his. Moreover, Blake did not question Jenkins because he felt his superior should take the initiative.

As the months went by Blake became increasingly uneasy. Finally, on May 15 he was astonished to see Strom escorting a young man into Jenkins' office. Although the door was closed Blake could hear considerable laughing inside. After an hour the three emerged from the office and Jenkins shook hands with the new man saying, "Joe, I'm certainly glad you're going to be with us. With Harry showing you around his territory you're going to get a good start at the business." Strom and the new man left and Jenkins returned to his office.

Blake was infuriated. He was convinced that the new man was being groomed for Strom's position. Now he understood why Jenkins had said nothing to him. He angrily cleaned out his desk, wrote a bitter letter of resignation and left it on his desk, and stomped out of the office.

Suspecting the worst for several months, Blake was quite unable to distinguish what he had inferred from what he had actually observed. The new man, it turned out, was being hired to work as an inside salesman—an opening which was to be occasioned by Blake's moving into the outside position. Jenkins had wanted the new man to get the "feel" of the clientele and thus had requested Strom to take him along for a few days as Strom made his calls.

TRENDS IN SERIAL TRANSMISSION

These assumptions,[9] the mono-usage of words, and the inference-observation confusion, as well as the aforementioned motives of the communicators, undoubtedly contribute a significant share of the difficulties and dangers which beset a serial transmission. Their effect tends to be manifested by three trends: omission, alteration, and addition.

Details Become Omitted

It requires less effort to convey a simpler, less complex message. With fewer details to transmit the fear of forgetting or of garbling the message is decreased. In the serial transmissions even those final versions which most closely approximated the original had omitted an appreciable number of details.

[9]For a more detailed analysis of these assumptions and for additional methods for preventing and correcting their consequences, see William V. Haney, *Communication: Patterns and Incidents* (Homewood, Ill.: Irwin, 1960), chs. III, IV, V.

> There are eagles in front of the frat house at the State University. It cost $75 to $100 to remove paint each year from the eagles.

The essential question, perhaps, which details *will be retained?* Judging from interviewing the serial transmitters after the demonstrations these aspects will *not* be dropped out:

1. those details the transmitter wanted or expected to hear.

2. those details which "made sense" to the transmitter.

3. those details which seemed important *to the transmitter.*

4. those details which for various and inexplicable reasons seemed to stick with the transmitter—those aspects which seemed particularly unusual or bizarre; those which had special significance to him; etc.

Details Become Altered

When changes in detail occurred in the serial transmissions it was often possible to pinpoint the "changers." When asked to explain why they had changed the message most were unaware that they had done so. However, upon retrospection some admitted that they had changed the details in order to simplify the message, "clarify it," "straighten it out," "make it more sensible," and the like. It became evident, too, that among the details most susceptible to change were the qualifications, the indefinite. Inferential statements are prone to become definite and certain. What may start out as "The boss seemed angry this morning" may quickly progress to "The boss was angry."

A well-known psychologist once "planted" a rumor in an enlisted men's mess hall on a certain Air Force base. His statement was: "Is it true that they are building a tunnel big enough to trundle B-52's to—(the town two miles away)?" Twelve hours later the rumor came back to him as: "They are building a tunnel to trundle B-52's to—." The "Is-it-true" uncertainty had been dropped. So had the indefinite purpose ("big enough to").

It became obvious upon interviewing the serial transmitters that bypassing (denotative and connotative) had also played a role. For example, the "president" in the message about the "eagles" was occasionally bypassed as the "President of the U.S." and sometimes the rest of the message was constructed around this detail.

> The White House was in such a mess that they wanted to renovate it but found that the cost would be $100 to $75 to paint the eagle so they decided not to do it.

Details Become Added

Not infrequently details are added to the message to "fill in the gaps," "to make better sense," and "because I thought the fellow who told it to me left something out."

The psychologist was eventually told that not only were they building a tunnel for B-52's but a mile-long underground runway was being constructed at the end of it! The runway was to have a ceiling slanting upward so that a plane could take off, fly up along the ceiling and emerge from an inconspicuous slit at the end of the cavern! This, he admitted, was a much more "sensible" rumor than the one he had started, for the town had no facilities for take-offs and thus there was nothing which could have been done with the B-52's once they reached the end of the tunnel!

PICTORIAL TRANSMISSION

An interesting facet about serial transmission is that the three trends— omission, alteration, and addition—are also present when the "message" is pictorial as opposed to verbal. Our procedure was to permit the "transmitter" to view the stimulus picture (upper left corner of drawing below) for thirty seconds. He then proceeded to reproduce the picture as accurately as possible from memory. When he finished his drawing he showed it to transmitter$_2$ for thirty seconds, who then attempted to reproduce the first transmitter's drawing from memory, etc. Drawings 1 through 5 represented the work of a fairly typical "team" of five transmitters.

Details Become Omitted. Note the progressive simplification of the configuration in the lower right and the eventual omission of it altogether. Note the omission of the border.

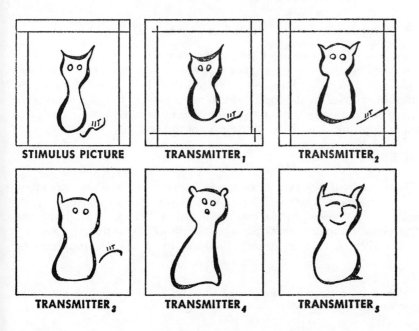

STIMULUS PICTURE   TRANSMITTER$_1$ TRANSMITTER$_2$

TRANSMITTER$_3$ TRANSMITTER$_4$ TRANSMITTER$_5$

Details Become Altered. The border is an interesting example of alteration. The original border is quite irregular, difficult to remember. Transmitter$_1$ when interviewed afterward said, "I remembered that the frame was incomplete somehow but couldn't remember just how it was incomplete." Note how indefinitely irregular his border is. So subtle, in fact, that Transmitter$_2$ said he never recognized it as purposefully asymmetrical. "I thought he was just a little careless." Transmitter$_2$ drew a completely regular border—easy to remember but also easy to fail to notice. Transmitter$_3$ was surprised afterwards to discover that the drawing he had tried to memorize had had a border. It had apparently seemed so "natural," so much a part of the background, that he had failed to attend to it.

Details Become Added. Transmitter$_1$ perceived the stimulus picture as a cat and a cat it remained through the series. When shown that he had added a nose Transmitter$_4$ admitted, "You know, I knew there was something missing from that cat—I knew it had a body, a head, ears, and eyes. I thought it was the mouth that was missing but not the nose." Providing everything *except* a mouth was far too enticing for Transmitter$_5$. "I thought the other fellow made a mistake so I corrected it!"

CORRECTIVES[10]

Even serial transmissions, as intricate and as relatively uncontrolled communications as they are, can be improved. The suggestions below are not sensational panaceas. In fact, they are quite commonplace, common sense, but uncommonly used techniques.

1. *Take notes.*

   Less than five percent of the serial transmitters took notes. Some said that they assumed they were not supposed to (no such restriction had been placed upon them) but most admitted that they rarely take notes as a matter of course. In the cases where all transmitters on a team were instructed to take notes the final versions were manifestly more complete and more accurate than those of the non-notetakers.

2. *Give details in order.*

   Organized information is easier to understand and to remember. Choose a sequence (chronological, spatial, deductive, inductive, etc.) appropriate to the content and be consistent with it. For example, it may suit your purpose best to begin with a proposal followed by supporting reasons or to start with the reasons and work toward the proposal. In either case

---

[10]Most of these suggestions are offered by Irving J. and Laura L. Lee, *Handling Barriers in Communication* (New York: Harper & Bros., 1956), pp. 71–74.

take care to keep proposals and reasons clearly distinguished rather than mixing them together indiscriminately.

3. *Be wary of bypassing.*

If you are the receiver, query (ask the sender what he meant) and paraphrase (put what you think he said or wrote into your own words and get the sender to check you). These simple techniques are effective yet infrequently practiced, perhaps because we are so positive we *know* what the other fellow means; perhaps because we hesitate to ask or rephrase for fear the other fellow (especially if he is the boss) will think less of us for not understanding the first time. The latter apprehension is usually unfounded, at least if we can accept the remarks of a hundred or more executives questioned on the matter during the last four years. "By all means," they have said almost to a man, "I *want* my people to check with me. The person who wants to be sure he's got it straight has a sense of responsibility and that's the kind of man (or woman) I want on my payroll."

Although executives, generally, may take this point of view quite sincerely, obviously not all of them practice it. Querying and paraphrasing are *two-way* responsibilities and the sender must be truly approachable by his receivers if the techniques are to be successful.

This check-list may be helpful in avoiding bypassing:

Could he be denoting something other than what I am?
Could he be connoting something other than what I am?
Could he be connoting whereas I am merely denoting?
Could he be merely denoting whereas I am connoting?

4. *Distinguish between inference and observation.*

Ask yourself sharply: Did I *really* see, hear, or read this—or am I guessing part of it? The essential characteristics of a statement of observation are these:

1. It can be made only by the observer. (What someone tells you as observational is still inferential for you if you did not observe it.)
2. It can be made only *after* observation.
3. It stays with what has been observed; does not go beyond it.

This is not to say that inferential statements are not to be made—we could hardly avoid doing so. But it is important or even vital at times to know *when* we are making them.

5. *Slow down your oral transmissions.*

By doing so, you give your listener a better opportunity to assimilate complex and detailed information. However, it is possible to speak *too* slowly so as to lose his attention. Since either extreme defeats your purpose, it is generally wise to watch the listener for clues as to the most suitable rate of speech.

6. *Simplify the message.*

This suggestion is for the *originator* of the message. The "middlemen" often simplify without half trying! Most salesmen realize the inadvisability of attempting to sell too many features at a time. The customer is only confused and is unable to distinguish the key features from those less important. With particular respect to oral transmission, there is impressive evidence to indicate that beyond a point the addition of details leads to disproportionate omission. Evidently, you can add a straw to the camel's back without breaking it, but you run the decided risk of his dropping two straws.

7. *Use dual media when feasible.*

A message often stands a better chance of getting through if it is reinforced by restatement in another communication medium. Detailed, complex, and unfamiliar information is often transmitted by such combinations as a memo follow-up on a telephone call; a sensory aid (slide, diagram, mockup, picture, etc.) accompanying a written or oral message, etc.

8. *Highlight the important.*

Presumably the originator of a message knows (or should know) which are its important aspects. But this does not automatically insure that his serial transmitters will similarly recognize them. There are numerous devices for making salient points stand out as such; e.g., using underscoring, capitals, etc., in writing; using vocal emphasis, attention-drawing phrases ("this is the main point . . . ," "here's the crux . . . ," "be sure to note this . . ."), etc., in speaking.

9. *Reduce the number of links in the chain.*

This suggestion has to be followed with discretion. Jumping the chain of command either upward or downward can sometimes have undesirable consequences. However, whenever it is possible to reduce or eliminate the "middle-men," "the message" generally becomes progressively less susceptible to aberrations. Of course, there are methods of skipping links which are commonly accepted and widely practiced. Communication downward can be reduced to person-to-person communication, in a sense, with general memos, letters, bulletins, group meetings, etc. Communication upward can accomplish the same purpose via suggestion boxes, opinion questionnaires, "talk-backs," etc.

10. *Preview and review.*

A wise speech professor of mine used to say: "Giving a speech is basically very simple if you do it in three steps: First, you tell them what you're going to tell them; then you tell; then, finally, you tell them what you've told them." This three-step sequence is often applicable whether the message is transmitted by letter, memo, written or oral report, public address, telephone call, etc.

SUMMARY

After the last suggestion I feel obliged to review this article briefly. We have been concerned with serial transmission—a widespread, essential, and yet susceptible form of communication. Among the factors which vitiate a serial transmission are certain of the communicator's motives and fallacious assumptions. When these and other factors are in play the three processes—omission, alteration, and addition—tend to occur. The suggestions offered for strengthening serial transmission will be more or less applicable, of course, depending upon the communication situation.

An important question remains: What can be done to encourage communicators to practice the techniques? They will probably use them largely to the extent that they think the techniques are needed. But *do* they think them necessary? Apparently many do not. When asked to explain how the final version came to differ so markedly from the original, many of the serial transmitters in my studies were genuinely puzzled. A frequent comment was "I really can't understand it. All I know is that I passed the message along the same as it came to me." If messages *were* passed along "the same as they came," of course, serial transmission would no longer be a problem. And so long as the illusion of fidelity is with the communicator it is unlikely that he will be prompted to apply some of these simple, prosaic, yet effective techniques to his communicating. Perhaps a first step would be to induce him to question his unwarranted assurance about his communication. The controlled serial transmission experience appears to accomplish this.

REFERENCES

ALLPORT, G. W., and L. POSTMAN, "The Basic Psychology of Rumor," *Transactions of the New York Academy of Sciences*, Series II, 8 (1945), 61–81.
ALLPORT, G. W., and L. POSTMAN, *The Psychology of Rumor.* New York: Holt, Rinehart & Winston, 1947.
ASCH, S., "Group Forces on the Modification and Distortion of Judgments," *Social Psychology.* Englewood Cliffs, N.J.: Prentice-Hall, 1952.
BACK, K. W., "Influence through Social Communication," in *Readings in Social Psychology,* eds. Swanson, Newcomb, and Hartley. New York: Holt, Rinehart & Winston, 1952.
BACK, K. W. and others, "A Method of Studying Rumor Transmission," in *Theory*

and *Experiment in Social Communication,* Festinger and others. Ann Arbor, Mich.: Research Center for Group Dynamics, University of Michigan, 1950.

BORST, M., "Recherches experimentales sur l'éducabilité et la fidèlité du témoignage," *Archives de Psychologie,* 3 (1904), 204–314.

BRUNER, J. S., "The Dimensions of Propaganda," *Journal of Abnormal and Social Psychology,* 36 (1941), 311–37.

BRUNER, J. S., and L. POSTMAN, "Emotional Selectivity in Perception and Reaction," *Personality,* 16 (1947), 69–77.

CANTRIL, H., H. GOUDET, and H. HERZOG, *The Invasion from Mars.* Princeton: Princeton University Press, 1940.

CARMICHAEL, L., H. P. HOGAN, and A. A. WALTER, "An Experimental Study of the Effect of Language on the Reproduction of Visually Perceived Form," *Journal of Experimental Psychology,* 15 (1932), 73–86.

CARTER, L. F., and K. SCHOOLER, "Value, Need, and Other Factors in Perception," *Psychological Review,* 56 (1949), 200–207.

CLAPARÈDE, E., "Expériences sur le témoignage: témoignage simple; appréciation; confrontation," *Archives de Psychologie,* 5 (1906), 344–87.

Communicating with Employees, Studies in Personnel Policy No. 129. New York: National Industrial Conference Board, 1952.

DE FLEUR, M. L., and O. N. LARSEN, *The Flow of Information.* N.Y.: Harper & Bros., 1958.

GARDINER, RILEY W., and LEANDER J. LOHRENZ, "Leveling-Sharpening and Serial Reproduction of a Story," *Bulletin of the Menninger Clinic,* 24 (November 1960).

HANEY, W. V., *Measurement of the Ability to Discriminate Between Descriptive and Inferential Statements.* Unpublished doctoral dissertation, Northwestern University, 1953.

HIGHAM, T. M., "The Experimental Study of the Transmission of Rumor," *British Journal of Psychology, General Section,* 42 (1951), 42–55.

IRVING, J. A., "The Psychological Analysis of Wartime Rumor Patterns in Canada," *Bulletin of the Canadian Psychological Association,* 3 (1943), 40–44.

JACOBSON, D. J., *The Affairs of Dame Rumor.* New York: Holt, Rinehart & Winston, 1948.

KATZ, D., "Psychological Barriers to Communication," in *Mass Communications,* ed., Schramm. Urbana, Ill.: University of Illinois Press, 1949.

KATZ, E., and P. LAZARSFELD, *Personal Influence: The Part Played by People in the Flow of Mass Communications.* Glencoe, Ill.: The Free Press, 1955.

KNAPP, R. H., "A Psychology of Rumor," *Public Opinion Quarterly,* 8 (1944), 23–37.

OTTO, M. C., "Testimony and Human Nature," *Journal of Criminal Law and Criminology,* 9 (1918), 98–104.

POSTMAN, L., and J. S. BRUNER, "Perception under Stress," *Psychological Review,* 55 (1948), 313–23.

POSTMAN, L., J. S. BRUNER, and E. MCGINNIES, "Personal Values as Selective Factors in Perception," *Journal of Abnormal and Social Psychology,* 43 (1948), 142–54.

SMITH, G. H., "The Effects of Fact and Rumor Labels," *Journal of Abnormal and Social Psychology,* 42 (1947), 80–90.

STEFANSSON, V., *The Standardization of Error.* London: Routledge & Kegan Paul, 1928.

WHIPPLE, G. M., "The Observer as Reporter: A Survey of the 'Psychology of Testimony,'" *Psychological Bulletin,* 6 (1909), 153–70.

FOR DISCUSSION

1. Haney places quotation marks around the word "message" to call attention to its dynamic and changing nature. What types of messages appear most subject to change as they pass through the communication system? What types of messages seem least subject to change? Why?

2. In discussing "the desire to simplify the message" Haney says: "It is very probable that among the details most susceptible to omission are those we already knew or in some way presume our recipients will know without our telling them." What other kinds of details seem easily susceptible to omission? Why? What implications does this kind of omission have for the communicator? For the receiver?

3. A message that moves up the organizational ladder tends to lose its harshness, according to Haney. How would you tell a fellow student that you hated a particular course and the instructor? How would you tell your instructor? What factors might account for the differences in these two messages?

4. Illustrate the pattern of miscommunication Haney calls "bypassing" by reference to a communication breakdown that you have witnessed or been involved in.

5. The humor of comic strips and cartoons frequently revolves around bypassing. Locate some examples and discuss them with particular reference to the four types of bypassing Haney considers.

6. The confusion between factual and inferential statements can lead to considerable problems in all forms of communication. Identify at least one instance from your own experience in which fact-inference confusion occasioned a breakdown in communication.

Gossiping as a Way of Speaking

Sally Yerkovich

What is one difference between gossiping and the simple exchange of information about people?

During a year living in and sharing the life of an upper middle-class white Anglo-Saxon urban community, I observed gossiping in informal settings and ongoing relationships in order to discover the expressive and social features which distinguish gossiping from other ways of speaking. My observations were recorded as field notes written at the end of each day or, if possible, immediately after individual encounters. Conversations were reconstructed and other details of the interactions I either participated in or observed (e.g., participants involved, setting, movement within the interactional surround) were recorded. These notes constitute the data used to formulate conclusions about gossiping as a communicative process.

I found that gossiping is a form of sociable interaction, which depends upon the strategic management of information through the creation of others as "moral characters" in talk. Because it is a sociable process, the content of the talk is not as important as the interaction which the talking supports.

Three factors affecting the gossiping interaction derived from the data: the familiarity of the participants, a congenial definition of the situation, and a moral characterization of the subject. To be able to gossip together, individuals must know one another. They need not be friends

Reprinted from "Gossiping as a Way of Speaking" by Sally Yerkovich in the *Journal of Communication*, vol. 27, no. 1, Winter 1977.

or intimates, but they must be familiar enough with one another to minimize intervening social distance. Where social distance is not minimized initially (for example, in the case of two individuals from different age groups with dissimilar social statuses or roles), the amassing of shared biographical information allows for its gradual minimization.

Biographical information is usually exchanged before gossiping occurs in a relationship which by desire will (or by circumstance must) endure over a period of time. It is put together not only by interacting with someone and observing him or her but also by conversing about the individual with others. Part of getting to know someone well enough to gossip *with* may be gossiping *about* that person with others. Gossiping without knowing someone well is risky, for if the gossiping is disagreeable to one of the participants, it may cause dissatisfaction or misunderstandings which can make the further development of a social relationship difficult.

The mutual recognition of a group of names is also part of the information which gossipers must share, and arriving at this recognition is part of the process of becoming familiar with someone. "Do you know so-and-so?" exchanges—so much a part of meeting new people that they are often dubbed a "game"—may provide initial recognition of commonly known individuals. These exchanges are short and allow only for an analysis of the participants' social status and social network.

In subsequent encounters the people recognized as mutually known or known about in the "do you know" exchanges or by other means can be talked about. Participants express an interest in talking about someone frequently by asking "What do you think of so and so?" or similar questions. At this point, preliminary opinions about this person are exchanged. If it turns out that the opinions coincide, evaluative categorizations are developed concerning the individual and his/her way of doing things. These evaluative categorizations, developed from the initial, shared recognition of a name, lead to the possibility for gossip. At least for the group studied here, the recognition of a name and the identification of a person as a close friend or relative precludes the possibility of gossiping about him or her.[1]

As the relationship develops, the evaluative categorizations (evaluations of specific instances of behavior) gell into evaluative categories—abstractions concerning attitudes towards types of behavior. These categories are similar to types or typifications as discussed by Schutz (1, p. 120) because they transform unique individual actions into typical ones.

---

[1]It should be noted that complaining about a friend or relative is different from gossiping about the same individual except in cases where all the participants are close friends or relatives. Where the latter is not the case, the complaining cannot be reciprocal. For example, I can complain to you about my mother at length, but unless you are my brother or sister, your reinforcing and supporting my complaints with your own about my mother will usually cause me to take a defensive position toward her.

The categories, once established, take a part in the store of shared knowledge that familiar individuals use when they interact with one another.

Thus, familiarity for gossiping implies a social relationship in which social distance is minimized, in which biographical information about selves and others is shared, and in which mutual concerns lead to the development of shared knowledge about not only everyday and esoteric interests but also evaluative categories concerning ways of acting and interacting.

Participants are either active or passive gossipers depending upon their interest in and attitude toward the gossiping and upon their gossip reputation—how they are known to deal with what they hear.

Familiarity among individuals is necessary for gossiping but it is not sufficient—the situation of a particular interaction must be constituted and defined by the participating individuals to provide a backdrop for sociable communinion. The identities projected by the individuals (as either active or passive gossipers) and their analysis of each other's identities in these terms define the situation as congenial or uncongenial for gossiping. All participants must also express an interest in gossiping (either verbally or nonverbally). This interest is necessary so that serious contradictions which might interrupt the flow of conversation and the sociability of the interaction can be avoided. Such contradictions call attention to the gossiping and cause embarrassment and unpleasantness.

People who listen with interest to gossip, take part in gossiping, and occasionally pass on what they hear are active gossipers. They create a congenial situation for gossiping if they are interested in the immediate activity and if their gossip reputation is acceptable to their fellow gossiper.

"Gossips," on the other hand, enjoy gossiping to such an extent that others may think that they will talk to anyone about anything. The Gossip's fondness for the form of expression causes others to be cautious when they are in his or her presence, especially when they want to retain a sense of control over reports of their interaction. This caution increases when there is the danger that the Gossip will gossip *about* the person who gossips *with* him or her. The presence of a Gossip, also certainly an active participant, creates a situation uncongenial to gossiping particularly when the co-participants don't want to be talked about or don't want what they say to be spread.

Between the extremes there are individuals who are neither Gossips nor congenial active participants ("benign" gossipers). These gossip troublemakers fall into two groups. The "Unwitting Troublemaker," a person who repeats what he or she hears without due consideration of his or her participants in conversation, is sometimes said not to know how to manage information and becomes known as a person to be gossiped with cautiously.

Unlike the Unwitting Troublemaker, the "Knowing Troublemaker" repeats information in order to stir things up. He or she may have playful intentions, may do it just to see what happens, or may intentionally wish to cause trouble. Both these active participants are known as Troublemakers whose presence creates a situation uncongenial to gossiping.

Passive participants are part of the conversational surround but do not gossip. They may not know the people gossiped about or may have no vested interest in the gossip but may be considered participants by virtue of their presence. They create a situation congenial to gossiping if they do not call attention to the ongoing interaction in a disruptive manner.

An observer may become an uncongenial passive participant if she/he makes his/her presence as an observer known. An observer may do this directly by making a meta-comment on the conversation as gossip or by trying to participate in it and upsetting the interaction by asking inappropriate questions or by making too many comments in an overzealous attempt to keep the conversation going. Especially for groups which consider gossiping a stigmatized form of speech—"not the thing to do" —an observer can call attention to the fact that gossip is going on, thus making the gossipers self-conscious and inhibiting conversation.

The presence of a passive participant who is known to disapprove of gossiping as a form of expression also creates an uncongenial situation. As in the case of the observer, his/her presence calls attention to the ongoing interaction making the participants reluctant to indulge in their sport as freely as they would were the disapproving person not present.

Once the situation is defined as having appropriate personnel, the gossiping may begin.

This conversational practice uses information in a manner such that it becomes more than an exchange of information about absent people. Structurally, the process involves an agreement on the part of all participants to gossip, gossiping statements made by the gossiper (a role which any one of the active participants may take), and supporting and elaborating statements or comments from the people not in the role of the gossiper. Closure in gossiping or transitions from gossiping to other ways of speaking may be in the form of a generalizing statement made by one or more of the participants (e.g., "Well, you never know," "People do act crazy," or "Isn't that something?").

Because gossiping is a dynamic process, the structure is highly variable. The distinctive features that make talk about others "gossip" is an important focal point. How is this done?

The gossiper strategically relays relevant information about an absent individual in a certain manner and then implicitly or explicitly justifies the manner of presentation. The gossiper's comments are "moral": they describe an individual's behavior and present it as sanctionable. The moral comments need not be evaluative—they may simply present the behavior as interesting or salient. The immediacy of the sociable communicative event and the style in which the information is presented (e.g., with overtones of urgency, newness, scandal) make the information salient. Out of this context, the information relayed in gossiping takes on a "so-what?" quality, evoking a justifying comment on the part of the speaker to the effect of "Oh, you just have to know him or her to understand." Information, no matter how salient or scandalous, isn't gossip unless the participants know enough about the people involved to experience the thrill of revelation.

The gossipers draw their comments from the store of knowledge they have about the person to be talked about, and as one individual is talked about repeatedly by the same people, the moral comments about that person increase in number. "Immoral characterization" emerges. The characterization is selective rather than complete for it must include only the elements of knowledge about an individual which support and justify the stance taken by the gossiper. The strategic use of information in gossiping descriptions requires that "moral" not be interpreted in the sense of an absolute. Just as we talk with different people about different things according to our common concerns and interests, our moral comments and thus our moral characterizations of individuals are tempered by the people we are gossiping with and the position we wish to take toward the people we gossip about.

Individuals gossiping about someone for the first time often exchange a great deal of information about the person and create an initial moral character. This initial characterization is both used and referred to implicitly or explicitly in subsequent conversations. The later conversations continue to build upon the initial characterization and to develop it. When the characterization is well-established, gossiping can be done in very short remarks about the already characterized individual (e.g., "He's been in a state of constant sexual excitement since he proposed"). Although the remarks may be appreciated on the surface for their wittiness, viciousness, etc., by anyone who hears them, they can only be completely understood with a knowledge of the shared characterization.

Thus the moral characterizations which draw upon the participants' shared knowledge of one another and their shared evaluative categories (i.e., their familiarity) form another part of their shared universe. While describing an absent party, the substance of the moral characterization serves also to reinforce the existing social bond of the gossipers. Gossiping as sociable interaction allows the gossipers to update their relationship in terms of their own and others recent activities and in terms of their shared view of social interaction.

Viewing gossiping as a process allows for a focus upon more than just the information relayed and its functions. Features which distinguish gossiping from ways of speaking are located not only within the content of the speech itself but also within the social relationships and situations in which they are used.

REFERENCES

1. SCHUTZ, A. *On Phenomenology and Social Relations.* Edited by H.R. Wagner. Chicago: University of Chicago Press, 1970.

FOR DISCUSSION

1. Describe your own gossip behavior—as source and as receiver. Do you engage in much gossip? Why? That is, what rewards do you derive from it? Are you a good subject for the gossip of others? Why do you think this?

2. Yerkovich notes that "all participants must also express an interest in gossiping (either verbally or nonverbally). This interest is necessary so that serious contradictions which might interrupt the flow of conversation and the sociability of the interaction can be avoided. Such contradictions call attention to the gossiping and cause embarrassment and unpleasantness." Do you agree with this observation? Do you do this in your own gossiping behavior? How do you determine the interest of another in gossiping? That is, what kind of responses would you look for in ascertaining interest?

3. Have you ever functioned as a "benign gossiper"? As either an unwitting troublemaker or a knowing troublemaker? Explain the circumstances, the interactions, and the consequences. Did you learn anything from these experiences?

Communication in Small Groups

Robert Freed Bales

For one reason or another, everyone spends a sizable fraction of his life interacting with other people in small groups. Whether for work or pleasure, such groups comprise a large part of our social lives, so it is not surprising that social scientists have been interested in understanding what goes on in such groups.

Our communication with each other in face-to-face situations is very subtle and complex. In addition to the meanings of the words used, there is a rich flow of contextual information by mutual eye contact. Bodily attitudes, gestures, and facial expressions play an important part. The obvious meaning of what is said in words is only a part, sometimes only a small part, of what is communicated, as we all know.

It has been found that a surprising amount of information is carried by the form of the interaction itself. For example, one can usually infer something about the relative dominance of members in a small group simply by counting the number of remarks each makes to the others. The number of remarks is roughly equivalent to the time consumed. In a small group, time is like money or property. It is not distributed equally among members, but in a gradient that has some relation to the social status of the members. Talking time in a group is not something that a member has with security—it is usually something for which he must compete. Some members take it almost by force, in that they take more than others are willing to give them. They exercise power in the taking of time, though

From Robert Freed Bales, "Communication in Small Groups," in *Communication, Language, and Meaning*, ed., George A. Miller (New York: Basic Books, 1973), pp. 208–218.

they may not gain legitimate status. An increase in the amount of participation initiated by a given member may signal a bid for power.

Information about the positive or negative attitude of one group member toward another is also revealed by the formal characteristics of their communication. It is a relatively simple matter to count the number of acts of agreement versus disagreement group members give to each other. It is usually felt that one should not agree with another simply because one likes him, but in fact the rates of agreement and disagreement received by a man over a time period can reveal how well he is liked.

Formal characteristics of communication also give information as to where the individual member stands with regard to the work of the group. For this purpose it is useful to count the acts commonly called "giving opinion" and "giving suggestion." Persons give opinions and suggestions in the attempt to persuade each other. Attempts to persuade are central to the work of the group. A person who gives many opinions and suggestions is likely to be regarded as work-oriented by other members of the group. Joking and laughing, on the other hand, often show resistance to the work.

All of the kinds of activity I have mentioned can be recognized by characteristics that do not depend on what the group is talking about. In fact, the three dimensions I have mentioned (dominance versus submissiveness, friendliness versus unfriendliness, and work-acceptance versus work-resistance) could be distinguished reasonably well even if the observer did not understand the language spoken by the persons in the group. These dimensions formulate important and probably universal distinctions.

Methods of study that concentrate upon the type of interaction rather than upon the content of communication are called methods of *interaction process analysis*. *Process* analysis is similar to *content* analysis in that it provides information about the underlying attitudes and values of the communicator. But process analysis is unlike content analysis in that it concentrates on the action and reaction of individuals rather than on the content of their messages. Both owe something to *psychoanalysis*. The technique of psychoanalytic interpretation of dreams and free-associations has been a fertile source of insight into unrecognized or poorly controlled aspects of personality and group life. What the psychoanalyst does is not usually called content analysis, nor process analysis, but it is basically similar to both, in that it uses the surface characteristics of interpersonal communication to infer the underlying determinants. The interpretive techniques of psychoanalysis have made a tremendous contribution to our understanding of communication in small groups. It is by now quite commonly understood that highly animated chatter, entertaining conversations, gossip, unusually heated arguments, jokes, and other familiar phenomena of interpersonal interaction are basically quite similar to free association as known to the psychoanalyst. They are subject to interpretation in much the same way, and can be used as sources of insight by group members as to their underlying, unrecognized concerns.

People can be taught to utilize more effectively these partially hidden types of information about the attitudes and emotions of others. Groups called sensitivity training groups are increasingly being used for this kind of psychological education. Gains of knowledge and skill in this area are important across a broad front of practical applications—in sensitivity and leadership training for persons in business, government, community affairs, in education, and in clinical settings concerned with the assessment of personality and the treatment of individual and social problems. Face-to-face interaction of an intensive kind in small groups is being increasingly utilized, not only for group therapy, but for psychologically oriented education or attitude change of many specialized kinds. Alcoholics Anonymous is a classical example. Similar group methods are employed in the treatment of drug addiction, smoking, obesity, gambling, and in the changing of attitudes underlying social problems such as prejudice, poor race relations, poor working relationships, delinquency, and criminality.

Skilled work in the conduct of such groups requires an ability to utilize to the utmost the clues about personality, attitudes, and beliefs that are presented naturally in spontaneous interaction. In such groups members learn psychological skills in a practical form from their leaders or mentors, and then pass them on to new members or recruits. The clinical skills of the psychological professional are thus being rapidly democratized and passed on in the most relevant concrete form to individuals with problems. They learn to help themselves as they pass the skills on to still others, new recruits. The use of groups for psychological purposes, and the accompanying democratization of clinical skills has by now gathered tremendous momentum in the United States. Theoretical psychologists have much to learn from studying the successful instances of psychological group work. On the other hand, there is also an encouraging growth of technically based knowledge of natural communication in small groups; there is, indeed, more knowledge than has been put together and utilized.

Modes of participation in small groups are closely related to familiar types of neurotic problems and personality disorders. Fellow participants, though untrained in technical psychology, often agree surprising well in their characterization of an individual. If he is also a patient, or a prospective patient, these lay descriptions can be translated into a diagnosis that is about as reliable as one by trained clinical psychologists. The average group wisdom as to what such a person needs by way of interpersonal treatment is often surprisingly good.

The main dimensions of the distinctions group members make without technical training are essentially the same as those I described earlier: dominance versus submissiveness, friendliness versus unfriendliness, and work-acceptance versus work-resistance. The traits measured by many written personality tests are distributed in this same interpersonal space and may be inferred from observation of interpersonal communication. Even attitudes about political and economic affairs in the larger society, and values related to religious and philosophical beliefs appear to be related to these same interpersonal characteristics. A person who is very conservative in his political beliefs, for example, often also wants to be treated as a legitimate authority in the small group in which he participates. He is likely to be high on giving opinion or suggestion, and to be low on joking and laughing.

A theoretical model of a three-dimensional space can be used to summarize much of what is known about the relations of personality, attitudes, and values to interpersonal style of communication. As I describe each dimension in turn, it may help to visualize it as located in actual physical space.

The vertical dimension in the space, upward and downward, is related to dominance versus submissiveness as a personality trait. It is shown in interpersonal communication in the amount a person talks, and also in the amount of communication that is directed to him. A person lower in the dominance hierarchy tends to address his communications to a higher person in the hope that his ideas will be accepted and that he will thereby gain greater status in the group. The person in the higher position, however, is not so motivated to direct his communications to the lower, but rather to some other person still higher, or to the group as a whole. It turns out, then, that the lower person addresses a little more, generally, to the higher person than the higher person addresses to him. The higher person, especially if he is the highest in the group, is likely to address a large portion of his communication to the group as a whole.

Persons high in this hierarchy are likely to measure high on person-ality traits of dominance, extroversion, activity, adventuresomeness, and are likely to have values of material success and power. It is possible to be dominant, and also friendly, with a tendency to agree and ask others for their opinion. Such a person is likely to measure high on personality tests of sociability, and perhaps leadership. He tends to value social success and popularity. Dominance, on the other hand, may also be combined with unfriendliness and a tendency to disagree. These persons are likely to measure high on personality tests of domination, and may show some tendencies toward the more hostile and overactive personality disorders. They are likely to value a kind of tough-minded assertiveness in their dealings with others.

On the downward or submissive end of the vertical dimension are those who talk little, receive little, and seldom address the group as a whole. They are seen as introverted and perhaps depressed by their fellow group members, and measure so on written personality tests. They tend to confine themselves to giving information when they do talk, rather than giving opinion or suggestion, and they avoid joking or doing anything exhibitionistic or dramatic. In their attitudes and beliefs they tend to devalue themselves, and to wish there were a world in which desires and appetites did not exist, rather than one in which their desires are actively satisfied.

At right angles to the upward and downward dimension is another dimension one may think of as horizontal, extending from side to side, concerned with positive versus negative feelings. The positive end is marked by friendly behavior, asking others for their opinions, and agree-ing with them. Persons on the far positive end of this dimension are likely to measure high on tests of calm, stable, and trustful feelings, and to have what some clinicians call "ego strength," that is, integrated control of their feelings and intellectual functions. Such persons tend to be liked by others, and to like and appreciate them in return. They tend to have an equalitarian and humanitarian set of values and attitudes. Persons on the negative end of this dimension tend to seem unfriendly in their behavior, alienated or isolated, and to disagree. Personality tests show them to have feelings of anxiety, suspicion, jealousy, fearfulness, doubt, indecision, and guilt. Neurotic personality problems of various kinds tend to put a person in this position. These persons are likely to value individual isolation and self-sufficiency.

Dislike is not the simple opposite to liking. Dislike in most groups does not center on the person simply at the negative end of the dimension, but on the one who is negative and at the same time dominating, and work-acceptant, that is, moralistic and dictatorial. This type of person is often called the authoritarian type, but probably should be called the dominating or autocratic authoritarian. There are also more submissive and positive authoritarians who tend to be more agreeable and are somewhat positively regarded by their fellow group members.

The work-acceptant versus work-resistant dimension is at right angles to both the preceding, and may be thought of as extending in the direction forward and backward from the intersection of the other two dimensions. Both types of authoritarians just mentioned are on the forward or work-acceptant end of the dimension. In groups that are concerned with the performance of tasks assigned to them by an external authority, the persons who are found far forward on the work-acceptant end of the dimension are themselves likely to accept authority, or to view themselves as legitimate representatives of authority. They are likely to be conventional or conservative in socioeconomic attitudes, and often in religious orientation as well. In interpersonal communication they are likely to be high in giving opinion, and in asking for and giving suggestions. The more submissive ones may seem somewhat overpersistent and dutiful. Those on the submissive *positive* side will seem altruistic and docile, those on the submissive *negative* side will seem somewhat self-punishing and complaining.

The acknowledged leader of the group, if there is one, is likely to be found somewhere on the work-acceptant end of this dimension. Usually he is also somewhat on the dominant side, and somewhat on the positive side in his behavior. A task leader who is simply dominant and work-acceptant, with no positive component in his behavior, is likely to encounter trouble. He is likely to be identified sooner or later as an authoritarian autocrat, and to suffer a revolt in which he is provoked into negative and dominating behavior.

Persons who make many jokes are found at the work-resistant end of the dimension, along with those who seem to have a preference for fantasy as the organizing process in their action. These persons often prefer to "act out" or dramatize their wishes rather than to analyze problems by logic and try to persuade others. There are both positive and negative varieties, and sometimes they seem quite different. Although the work-resistant type who is both dominant and negative is a rugged individualist, indeed a kind of outlaw, the dominant and positive work-resistant type is often an advocate of unconditional love, who tends to be emotionally supportive to those who cannot or will not conform, and seems warm and spontaneous to his fellows.

The submissive persons on the work-resistant end of the dimension tend to show various restless and inhibited signs of restraint and conflict that we may call showing tension. They tend to hold back from the task or from the suggestions or demands of authority. In their socioeconomic attitudes and beliefs, they are likely to be radical and heretical, rejecting authority, orthodoxy, conventionality, and established modes of social organization.

Personality differences among group members strongly affect their ability to work together. To see how this comes about in more detail, let us consider a group trying to come to a decision about a problem. The most frequently observed sequence in many groups is an act of giving opinion by one participant, followed by an act of agreement on the part of another. Both giving opinions and agreeing with them are frequent types of acts, and it is important for the success of the work that opinions should be produced that can command voluntary acceptance. But agreement on the basic facts underlying the problem is often also essential. Many decision-making groups start a problem-solving cycle with a review of facts. That sends the rate of giving information up for a while at the beginning. Only after they have essential agreement about the facts do they allow themselves to go on to an analysis and evaluation of the facts, and thus allow the rate of giving opinion to rise above that of giving information.

However, the needs of the dominant work-acceptant members may conflict, especially at the beginning, with the demands of such a task sequence. A work-acceptant person who likes to analyze and give his opinion is generally more active than one who is cautious and likes to confine his contributions, so far as possible, to giving information only. And the one who likes to give suggestions is more dominant still. Dominant members not only have a high total rate of participation, but they are likely to want to participate as early as possible in the meeting, and to get ahead with the action immediately. A quarrel among the most dominant and negative members is all too likely to begin early and to prevent an optimal approach to the task. Negative and unfriendly acts tend to lead to further negative and unfriendly acts. Once negativity starts in this circular fashion it has a tendency to build up and to spiral out of control.

One of the principal functions of the leader of such a group is to prevent such a negative buildup, or to bring it within control if it begins. A successful leader, if the group is fortunate enough to have one, is usually himself somewhat dominant, but not too much so. He must be able to cope with the most dominant and negative members, but he must not be too dominant or negative himself, or he will also alienate other group members. He usually needs the help of one or more other members on the positive side who often form a kind of coalition with him. Acting as their agent, and with their help, the successful leader is able to control the negative elements.

The successful and acknowledged task leader is usually positive in his behavior rather than negative, and so is able to inspire enough liking and admiration to keep the coalition around him strong. He needs also to be work-acceptant in a task-oriented group, but should not be too impatiently so. It is usually due to him, if it happens at all, that the relevant persons, including the most submissive, are asked for information, and later for their opinion, and that the group is kept in an information reviewing phase for a sufficiently long time. The task leader is also often the principal receiver of their information, and provides as high a rate of agreement with them as he can, consistent with his feeling for the real demands of the task.

In many groups the problem of keeping the negative buildup from occurring is a constant one, and it is all the more difficult if the group contains many members with negative and dominant personalities. The composition of the group in terms of personalities may make it impossible to prevent negative buildups, but a skillful leader, especially one who is able to expose and analyze with insight the causes and operation of the negative feelings, can make a tremendous difference. The approach through group self-analysis however, assumes, or even requires, that the negative feelings be allowed to show themselves in sufficiently full play to be recognized and analyzed. The process of psychological self-analysis in training or therapy groups is often full of conflict. It may involve a hostile revolutionary attack on the leadership, and the uncovering of negative and psychologically primitive tendencies altogether too frightening for the inexperienced leader, and for some of the participants. It is in this area that the growth and diffusion of psychological knowledge and skill about group communication will probably contribute most to practical affairs. In any group there are personal and interpersonal problems to be solved in addition to those that are clearly related to the assigned task. Every group decision tends to put the whole group structure under strain—the delicate balance of power and status among the members, their liking and disliking of each other, and their modes of suppressing or expressing work-resistant tendencies.

The strains that accompany group problem solving and decision making may be held in check for a period, in order to get the job done, but they tend increasingly to break through the normal work facade as the effort continues. Eventually, often after the group has reached a decision, or even if there has been none, the group may break into a phase of joking and laughing, a circular interchange that tends to build up through some period of time while the tensions that have been held in check are dealt with. The atmosphere in this phase is quite different from that in the work-acceptant phase. Suppressed feelings or fantasies are expressed symbolically in the form of jokes, allusions, anecdotes, or spontaneous dramatization.

Activity of this kind is a natural form of therapy in most groups. It is generally recognized to have a legitimate time and place, even though it is work-resistant in direction. It is the result, in part, of work, and it is preliminary to more work. In groups where education or re-education is a part of the work goal, it is essential to have the level of tension lowered or the perception of new information will be impaired. The active part in the expression of fantasies and the lowering of tension is often taken by a joker or persons other than the usual task leader. If others are not available to take the lead in this direction, however, the task leader should optimally be able to switch from his work-acceptant orientation and take the lead in the direction of fantasy expression and spontaneous therapy.

In the most effectively operating groups, of whatever concrete kind, *leadership, therapy,* and *education* in some form *all* play a vital part. They are all three necessary and are normally present in the natural processes of interpersonal communication. We may hope that as knowledge and skills concerning these elementary necessities of group life are gained and diffused more widely, the quality of our attempts to solve special problems in many applied areas can be improved correspondingly. Research on communication in small groups promises many practical benefits.

FOR DISCUSSION

1. Here is a representation of the three dimensions discussed by Bales. Where would you place the interactions that take place in this class? Compare your responses and the reasons for it with the responses of others. Where would you place yourself interacting with your peers? Where do you think they would place you? If there is a difference in placement, try to explain why this happened.

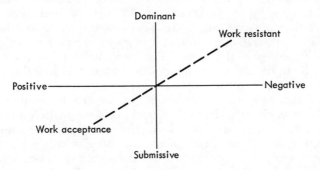

2. How do personality differences influence the small group interactions that take place in your family? How might these family interactions be improved?

3. Describe your own leadership behavior. Do you want to change such behaviors? How might you go about affecting such changes?

Groupthink

Joseph A. DeVito

After examining the decisions and the decision-making processes of large government organizations: the catastrophic decisions of the Bay of Pigs and Pearl Harbor; the decision processes that went into the development of the Marshall Plan; and President Kennedy's handling of the Cuban missile crisis, Irving Janis developed a theory he calls "groupthink." Groupthink, according to Janis (1971, p. 43), may be defined as "the mode of thinking that persons engage in when *concurrence seeking* becomes so dominant in a cohesive ingroup that it tends to override realistic appraisal of alternative courses of action." The term itself is meant to signal a "deterioration in mental efficiency, reality testing, and moral judgments as a result of group pressures."

There are many specific behaviors of the group members that may be singled out as characteristic of groupthink. One of the most significant behaviors is that the group limits its discussion of possible alternatives to only a small range. It generally does not consider other possibilities as alternatives. Once the group has made a decision it does not reexamine its decisions even when there are indications of possible dangers. Little time is spent in discussing the reasons why certain of the initial alternatives were in fact rejected. For example, if high cost led the group to reject a certain alternative, the group members will devote little time, if any, to the ways in which the cost may be reduced. Similarly, the group members make little effort to obtain expert information even from people within their own organization.

The group members are extremely selective in the information they

From *Communicology: An Introduction to the Study of Communication* by Joseph A. DeVito. Copyright © 1978 by Joseph A. DeVito. By permission of Harper & Row, Publishers, Inc.

consider seriously. Facts and opinions contrary to the position of the group are generally ignored while those facts and opinions that support the position of the group are welcomed. The group members generally limit themselves to the one decision or one plan. They fail to discuss alternative decisions or plans in the event that their initial decision fails or if it should encounter problems on the way to implementation.

The following symptoms should help in recognizing the existence of groupthink in the groups we observe or in which we participate.

1. Group members think the group and its members are invulnerable to dangers.

2. Members create rationalizations to avoid dealing directly with warnings or threats.

3. Group members believe their group is moral.

4. Those opposed to the group are perceived in simplistic stereotyped ways.

5. Group pressure is put on any member who expresses doubts or questions the group's arguments or proposals.

6. Group members censor their own doubts.

7. Group members believe all members are in unanimous agreement whether such agreement is stated or not.

8. Group members emerge whose function is to guard the information that gets to other members of the group, especially when such information may create diversity of opinion.

Participating in Decision-Making Discussions:
Behavioral and Procedural Considerations

Dennis S. Gouran

INTRODUCTION

Much of the material presented in the preceding chapters is scientifically and theoretically oriented. This chapter represents an attempt to distill from that body of information concrete suggestions for participating in decision-making discussions. The suggestions offered are merely guidelines and not formulas. Nevertheless, a substantial foundation for each has been laid, and the reader should discover that, by adhering as much as possible to the principles enumerated, he can begin to contribute more significantly to the decision-making discussions in which he takes part.

BEHAVIORAL GUIDELINES

Always Have the Group's Goal Firmly in Mind

As difficult as it is to believe, individual members of decision-making groups sometimes lose sight of their objective. In so doing, they may engage in much irrelevant and unproductive behavior. The reasons for failure to keep a group goal in mind are varied and not altogether understood; the principal reason for this difficulty, however, appears to be motivational. People participate in decision-making discussions for many different reasons. In some instances, they are obligated; in others, they see their participation as a vehicle for satisfying personal needs. Reluctant participants simply do not care about the issues being considered or if a decision is reached. The personally motivated individual, on the

Dennis S. Gouran, *Discussion: The Process of Group Decision-Making* (NY: Harper & Row, 1974).

other hand, might care about the group's work but abandon his responsibility to the group as he tries to satisfy his own needs first.

In classroom exercises, I have frequently witnessed individuals in groups working at cross purposes. Rather than trying to find the most appropriate answer to a discussion question, some participants seem bent on gaining acceptance of their positions, "winning" the discussion, or becoming acknowledged leaders. Such behavior almost invariably precludes intelligent inquiry, and even if a good decision is reached, under the circumstances, it is most likely to be a product of chance.

Problems such as these are by no means limited to the classroom. One can easily find evidence in a variety of social settings, for example, in city councils having members who aspire to higher office, in university faculty committees whose members are more concerned with their own visibility than the interests of the university community, or in organizational groups in which service is perceived as a means of enhancing one's position and opportunities for advancement. Although these kinds of motivations cannot be eliminated, it is important for discussion participants to realize that pursuit of personal objectives need not necessarily come at the expense of the group as a whole. However, if one allows his personal ambitions to supplant his commitment to the group's objectives, he is rendering a serious disservice to the group.

Introduce Information
That is Relevant to the Issue
or Point Being Discussed

Many discussions fail to terminate with a useful decision simply because some participants do not process information with any depth of analysis. Recently, a discussion on obscenity laws illustrated the point. The chairman of the group called for definitions of obscenity, and, in response, several members complied. One participant, however, began to sketch the outlines of a policy for controlling the distribution of unsolicited obscene material. The rest of the group followed suit and completely abandoned the attempt to find a working definition on which they could all agree. As a result, the group was unable to reach a decision because the members were not sure what they wanted to regulate.

If the chairman of a group fails to keep the members' attention properly focused, then it is reasonable for any other participant to point out that the discussion is going astray or that the point under consideration has not been fully explored. Such initiative may mildly antagonize other members, but, in most instances, they are not offended when someone suggests that they have moved to another, possibly irrelevant, point without having reached a conclusion about the previously discussed point.

When Changing from One Point to Another,
Be Sure that Other Group Members
Understand What You Are Doing

A great deal of confusion could be eliminated from many discussions if the participants would only make clear to others that they wish to change the subject. Valuable time usurped by unproductive discussion can easily pass before the other members of a group realize that a colleague is talking about something different from what they are talking about. If more than one person consistently exhibits this kind of behavior pattern without indicating his intentions, a group has very little chance of succeeding.

In a study of problem-solving discussions, an associate and I (see Gouran and Baird, 1972) found that discussion participants do, in fact, change themes with great regularity. On the average, every third statement represented a shift in focus. Berg (1963) also discovered that the average amount of time devoted to each theme in a series of decision-making discussions was approximately 50 seconds. Because of this kind of fluidity, it is extremely important that group members signal their intentions to one another. Otherwise, chaos is likely to be the only measurable group product.

Ask for Clarification of Points that You Do Not Understand

Most of us find it embarrassing to publicize our lack of understanding of what someone else is saying. If one cannot understand a point being developed, however, he will be unable to evaluate its utility or to determine its logical connections to other ideas. In a discussion on noise pollution, one of the participants reported a great deal of technical information on the relationship between decibel level and hearing loss. It was apparent that no other members of the group had clear conceptions of what kinds of sounds the various decibel levels might encompass; yet no one in the group asked for concrete examples, such as the decibel level of car horns, turned-up stereo equipment, and mealtime clatter in dormitory cafeterias. Such examples might have helped to clarify the kinds of noise on which an effective regulatory policy would have to focus.

Lack of understanding can only serve to frustrate the efforts of a group in making intelligent decisions. Therefore, those who participate in decision-making discussions must learn to overcome their fear of appearing ignorant. Maintaining a facade of understanding may give one comfort in the short run, but when it comes to the serious business of establishing a final position, he may not fully comprehend the decision and its implications.

Even if one is reasonably certain that he understands what others are saying, there is no harm in asking for clarification of a statement. The results are occasionally surprising. A few years ago, I attended a conference on black rhetoric. One of the speakers made continual references to the "rhetoric" of Martin Luther King, Stokely Carmichael, Julian Bond, and other prominent black speakers. At one point, a member of the audience objected rather vigorously to labeling the speeches of these men as rhetoric. *Rhetoric* is a term used in the field of speech simply as a classification for certain kinds of communication; in common parlance, however, it has very negative connotations. Many students, in fact, these days use it synonymously with the expression "bullshit." Unfortunately for the conference, the speaker used the term in a professional sense, and the listener used it quite differently. Had there been an attempt to clarify the concept, the incident might never have occurred.

Anticipate Possible Misunderstanding of Your Ideas, and Be Prepared to Explain Them in Alternative Ways

The preceding illustrations should dramatize the need for not assuming that one will be automatically understood in the sense he intends. If communication scholars have discovered anything about human interaction, it is that there are probably more failures than successes in the enterprise. As a result, it is usually a good idea to anticipate misunderstanding.

A former student prefers to think of himself as a socialist, yet whenever I hear this young man talk about political and economic reform, he always suggests that government power be decentralized, and his thoughts on economics almost invariably smack of the laissez-faire doctrine. When he was in my class, the other students had a difficult time understanding the relationship between what he said and what he called himself. He apparently has something quite different in mind from what others mean when they are referring to socialism, or, at least, he does not seem to be able to explain adequately how his notions mesh with commonly accepted conceptions of socialism. His discussions with other people would probably be more profitable if he worked more on clarifying for them his meaning of the concept.

Be Willing To Challenge the Ideas of Others, Especially When Those Ideas Have No Apparent Support

A recurrent theme of this book has been that the quality of a group's decision is no better than the quality of the interaction giving rise to the decision. Consequently, it is important that individual members be willing to scrutinize one another's ideas. The aftermath of the 1972 presidential election provides a good illustration of the need for such scrutiny. Having suffered one of the most substantial defeats in history, leading members of the Democratic party looked for explanations. Some alleged that the "Eagleton Affair" was the major reason for the loss; others pinned responsibility on the chairman of the national committee; and still others alleged that reform of the methods for selecting delegates to the national convention was the critical factor. Some journalists and new commentators were quick to seize on these explanations and offer them as their own. Yet, with all of the discussion in the weeks following the election, one could find very little evidence to support any of these explanations. If decisions about the strategy for the 1976 campaign are based on a consideration of these possibilities (and if no evidence is forthcoming to establish which, if any, was the most crucial factor), the Democratic party could easily adopt an inappropriate approach for winning the next election. To make an intelligent decision, party leaders probably would have invested their time more profitably by challenging one another's ideas to find one that provided the most satisfactory explanation rather than promoting their own personal opinions on the matter.

In many decision-making discussions, unsubstantiated or poorly supported generalizations are made with almost frightening regularity. "Our high schools are failing miserably," "You can't trust politicians," "Cops are enemies of the people," "The young are disenchanted with society," "Prisons are an abomination," "Industrialists are destroying the quality of life," "Welfare recipients are too lazy to work," "Men are sexists," and "College professors are interested only in research, not students" are a few of the kinds of assertions I have heard made in classroom discussions over the past several years. Most distressing about these kinds of statements is the lack of willingness by many group participants to try to discover the bases on which such generalizations rest. If more people showed this kind of initiative, fewer categorical generalizations would be made in decision-making discussions. Knowing that he may be expected to account for the validity of his public pronouncements can have a quieting effect on one's tendency to overgeneralize.

Be Willing to Admit to the Possibility That You or Your Information Could Be Wrong

As soon as an individual makes a public statement, he tends to become committed to the position expressed (see, for example, Janis and King, 1954), even though he might not have been strongly convinced of the position before he made his statement. Unfortunately, this kind of behavior can have negative consequences for the performance of a decision-making group, such as a failure to reach consensus, inadequate analysis of issues, and disproportionate emphasis on maintaining the social-emotional climate. Retracting a discussion statement or admitting that he might be wrong can be embarrassing for a discussion participant; however, when such admissions are justified, one must weigh his potential embarrassment against the costs of maintaining his position to the group. This is not to say that a group member should always assume that he is wrong whenever his colleagues disagree with him. But if the weight of superior analysis and evidence indicates that his position is indefensible, he can help the group substantially by giving in and, thereby, allowing the discussion to move forward.

Recognize the Difference between Judgments of Fact and Judgments of Opinion

Opinions are very often cast in the same form as statements of fact. The critical difference between the two types of statements lies not in their formal properties but in the bases from which they are generated. Consider, for example, the following assertion: "President X was an effective leader." Is this a judgment of fact or opinion? With no other information than the statement itself, one could not make such a determination. Depending on how the conclusion was reached, the statement could be either. If one made such an observation from an analysis of the accomplishments (the indices of which are widely agreed on) of President X, then he would be expressing a judgment of fact. For instance, it might be that, as a result of the policies pursued by X's administration, unemployment was reduced to 2 percent, a favorable balance of trade was established, arms limitations agreements were reached, the crime rate was brought under control, and racial relations were improved. If relationships between presidential leadership and such indices of social progress could be clearly established, then to assert that President X was an effective leader could legitimately be taken as a judgment of fact. On the other hand, if one could find no such foundation for the assertion, the statement would have to be considered as merely a personal opinion.

Much of what any person thinks is partially determined by what other people think on the same subjects. We gauge the validity of our own ideas against the norms of influential reference groups, for example, parents, fellow parishioners, schoolmates, and various social organizations to which we belong. Effective decision-making, however, demands that we sometimes ignore these sources of influence and examine issues on more objective bases. This is not easy to do, but, in the long run, one increases the probability of contributing better input in discussions on controversial issues. Sensitivity to the distinction between factually based judgments and unsupported opinions is a starting point for achieving this objective.

Avoid Personality Conflicts with Other Group Members if at All Possible

As suggested earlier, personality conflicts can destroy the social-emotional climate of a group; consequently, one needs to exercise care in his relations with others to prevent these unwanted clashes from arising. We live at a time when openness is encouraged; being frank in dealing with others, however, does not necessarily entail being offensive. It is not unusual for some members of a group to dislike others, but allowing unfavorable impressions to dominate interaction with a continual undercurrent of antagonism can only serve to detract from the accomplishment of a group's central task.

Very often, seemingly trivial incidents can trigger a personality clash. Personal mannerisms, an unfortunately chosen word, a slip of the tongue, and an attitude of superiority are common examples. The genuinely sensitive participant will tend to overlook such things even if they bother him, for he recognizes that personalities are different and should not occupy a position of importance in the group's deliberative activities.

If you Observe a Personality Clash Starting to Develop, Try To Refocus Attention on the Substantive Aspects of the Discussion

The manner in which this can be best accomplished is controversial. Some would argue that hostility should be allowed to surface in a discussion, for only when people break down their facades by revealing their true feelings toward one another can they ultimately improve the group's performance. On the surface, this suggestion appears to have merit, but I feel that working out hostilities in public does little good in helping a group to make better decisions. I have found no evidence, either experimental or experiential, to warrant the assumption that direct confrontations by antagonistic personalities and public displays of hostility do anything to improve the quality of group decisions or to increase the facility with which they are reached. I have observed, however, that individuals who are able to refocus the group's attention on substantive agenda items do, in fact, facilitate greater productivity. The studies by Guetzkow and Gyr (1954), Gouran (1969), and Knutson (1972) lend empirical support to this notion.

Try To Become as Knowledgeable as Possible About Whatever Subject You Are Discussing

It probably seems unnecessary to give advice on becoming as knowledgeable as possible in decision-making discussions. This condition of participation is perhaps obvious; however, it is painfully evident to the seasoned observer that many decision-making discussions are carried on almost routinely without an adequate fund of knowledge. In fact, so-called experts are often more guilty of this affront to intelligent inquiry than beginners. Some school administrations, student governments, executive committees of governmental agencies, and the like have been known to make hasty decisions on controversial questions without a thorough consideration of the underlying issues. Such decisions can sometimes return to haunt the people who make them. The Bay of Pigs Invasion decision, for example, was apparently made without an adequate assessment of the possibilities for security leaks in executing the operation. Because of this problem, the invasion was crushed, and the mission became a disaster in American foreign policy (see Janis, 1972).

Whereas no group can be certain that it has made the right decision, being as knowledgeable as possible on the subject under consideration is a safeguard against making unwise or inappropriate decisions. Becoming well informed, however, requires the exercise of a great deal of initiative and time-consuming effort. In the long run, the value of one's contributions will have much more impact as a result of his thoroughness. The payoff, therefore, is well worth the investment.

Encourage the Expression of All Points of View

The need for being well informed is consistent with entertainment of all points of view in decision-making discussions. Because of the natural tendencies of groups to suppress the expression of positions contrary to those espoused by the majority, potentially valuable contributions may be precluded from consideration. History is filled with too many examples of unpopular or minority views' proving to be more fruitful than majority views to warrant close-minded behavior.

. . . I allude to a social action project in one of my classes. When the group first began to consider possibilities for research, much interest centered on the Student Health Service. The class was almost in total agreement at the outset of the semester that the university's service was poor and that something should be done about it. Second-hand information, rumors, and other types of anecdotal materials abounded in the early stages of discussion. One member of the class had the sense to suggest that it might be wise to have someone from the Student Health Service respond to the charges that the class was making so freely. The administrative director agreed to appear in class and answer the group's questions. As a result of his visit, his denial of many charges, his acknowledgement of the validity of some, and his promise to investigate others, the class members began to realize that their earlier feelings were not well founded. They ultimately decided that another project involving services and facilities for disabled students would be more worthwhile. An interesting footnote to this story is that the person who proved most helpful to the group in carrying out its project was the same one who had previously answered their charges about the health service.

Had the student who wanted to hear another point of view been afraid to make such a suggestion, the project that the other members of the class were so eager to undertake would have been biased at the outset. Fortunately, simple exposure to a new body of information helped the group to make a more realistic appraisal of areas in which a useful project could be developed. The lesson to be learned from the experience is that encouragement of the expression of diverse points of view is more likely to facilitate than to inhibit intelligent decision-making.

PROCEDURAL GUIDELINES

Decision-making discussions should not be staged; however, they can and should be well organized. . . . Without some semblance of structure, participants are more likely to miss important issues, to become confused, and to be more unsure of the wisdom of their decision.

In a class discussion of the 1972 presidential election, the group's chairman said, in effect, "Let's just discuss the election and see where we end up." His desire for openness was commendable, but his failure to suggest the need for systematic analysis was problematic, especially because the group's primary purpose was to determine why McGovern lost. In the ensuing discussion, ideas were injected almost at random until the group reached the not-too-startling conclusion that "the country was simply not ready for George McGovern."

Perhaps a more carefully planned pattern of analysis would have permitted this group to arrive at a more specific conclusion. The participants, for example, could have raised the following questions:

1. Did personal factors contribute to Senator McGovern's defeat? If they did what were they?

2. Did economic factors contribute? If they did, what were they?
3. Did strategic errors contribute? If they did, what were they?

By tackling such questions systematically, it would have been possible for the group to develop a list of explanations and to determine the relative importance of each. A more penetrating conclusion could then have been established.

A concern for structure need not imply inflexibility. One should avoid becoming so wedded to particular patterns of analysis that he cannot discern the circumstances under which those patterns might be inappropriate. Consider, for example, the question, "What can be done to reduce crime in the United States?" Also assume that one is accustomed to employing the following pattern of analysis in problem-solving discussions:

1. Is there a problem?
2. If so, what are its causes?
3. What are the possible solutions to the problem?
4. Which of the possible solutions is most workable?

Spending time on the first question would probably be ritualistic. Most of us would agree that there is a crime problem; consequently, a group's time would be better spent on questions 2, 3, and 4. On other subjects, however, the first question might be the only one worth pursuing. If, in reference to a particular topic, a group were to decide that there is no evidence to establish the existence of a problem, then, clearly, consideration of questions 2, 3, and 4 would be irrelevant.

Becoming preoccupied with the organizational structure of a discussion can be detrimental to the overall quality of a group's performance. A kind of restricted thinking, which some people call "tunnel vision," can develop. Aesthetic criteria replace the achievement of objectives as the basis for judging the value of a discussion; that is, the worth of the discussion is determined by the degree to which it conforms to accepted organizational patterns, regardless of their appropriateness to the issues involved. The point here is that, although a sound organizational structure can promote effective interaction, its role must be kept in perspective. Organization is a tool, not the objective, of decision-making discussions.

In addition to development of a useful structure for the analysis of issues, several other procedural matters concern the members of a decision-making group. The following suggestions are addressed to these concerns.

Be Cognizant of the Circumstances under which Discussion Should Be Suspended

Occasionally, a group will push on toward a conclusion, even though it lacks the necessary information for making an intelligent decision. This tendency occurs most frequently in response to external pressure. In such cases, it would be far better to suspend discussion until the required information becomes available, even if the external pressures for a decision are severe.

Be Prudent in the Use of Such Techniques as Majority Votes to Establish Group Positions

This suggestion may appear to be antidemocratic. The important consideration, however, is that one recognize that majority votes do not necessarily establish truth. If the chairman of a group were to ask how many members believed that the problem they are discussing is serious, and a majority were to respond affirmatively, it does not follow that a serious problem has been identified. This is not to imply that taking votes is always to be avoided. But when the members of a group rely on this technique as a substitute for inquiry, the consequences of their actions can be unfortunate. Establishing positions on the basis of what the majority believes or feels is a convenient technique but, nonetheless, it can also frequently be an undesirable escape from the responsibility of examining issues and evidence.

Be Responsive to the Contributions of Others

Decision-making discussions should not be viewed as a series of individualized presentations; yet they are often conducted as if they were. Some discussion participants act as if they were on a stage and other members of the group were merely part of the set. To meaningfully progress in a discussion, everyone must assume some responsibility for reacting to the contributions of others. Ideas are shaped, altered, developed, and/or rejected by means of joint participation. When too many participants function as individuals rather than as members of the group, the advantage of numbers is lost.

Recognize the Point at which Further Pursuit of an Issue Is No Longer Profitable

General semanticists have emphasized the impossibility of ever being able to say everything possible about anything. On the other hand, there are probably limits on what can be usefully said about particular discussion issues. Decision-making groups can easily fall into the trap of belaboring some points at the expense of others in need of consideration. When it becomes obvious that all the relevant information on a given issue has been exhausted, the discussion should move forward. The alert participant recognizes such instances of verbal overkill and indicates that, in the absence of new information or arguments on the matter under consideration, the group should probably move on.

Evaluate the Group's Overall Progress

For decision-making groups that have a continuing existence, it is a useful habit to devote a few minutes at the end of each session to evaluation. Recognizing trouble spots in any given discussion may prevent their recurrence in others. Raising such obvious questions as, "What did we accomplish?", "Could we have proceeded more expeditiously?", "How adequate was our information?", and "What problems should we try to avoid in our next meeting?" can sensitize group members to both the positive and negative aspects of each other's behavior. The payoff from such evaluative activity should be a more efficient utilization of group resources.

CONCLUSION

Although a large number of suggestions for participating in decision-making discussions have been presented here, one should not think that he is prepared to meet every contingency. The suggestions are intended only as general guidelines and not as a set of rules. As any experienced decision-maker knows, the kinds of factors that contribute to effective participation in one situation may not work well in another. Experience, of course, is a great teacher, and one needs to learn how to use it in assessing the potential value of the kinds of behavioral and procedural recommendations made in relation to the problems inherent in particular situations. Observing suggested guidelines can help one to make more meaningful contributions, but it will not assure universal success.

SUMMARY

Much remains to be learned about the factors that contribute to successful decision-making. On the basis of what is known, however, a number of principles of participation can be established:

1. Always have the group's goal firmly in mind.

2. Introduce information that is relevant to the issue or point being discussed.

3. When changing from one point to another, be sure that other group members understand what you are doing.

4. Ask freely for clarification of points that you honestly do not understand.

5. Anticipate possible misunderstanding of your ideas, and be prepared to explain them in alternative ways.

6. Be willing to challenge the ideas of others, especially when those ideas have no apparent support.

7. Be willing to admit to the possibility that you or your information could be wrong.

8. Recognize the difference between judgments of fact and judgments of opinion.

9. Avoid personality conflicts with other group members if possible.

10. If you observe a personality clash starting to develop, try to refocus attention on the substantive aspects of the discussion.

11. Try to become as knowledgeable as possible about whatever subject you are discussing.

12. Encourage the expression of all points of view.

Procedural considerations also play an important role in decision-making discussions. Chief among these is the need for development of a systematic analytical structure. Sound organization can promote effective interaction, but group members must be careful not to become so concerned about the organizational pattern of their discussions that they minimize the importance of the underlying issues.

In addition to considering structure, the members of a group should be concerned about several other procedural matters. As in the case of behavioral guidelines, a number of procedural recommendations can be offered:

1. Be cognizant of the circumstances under which discussion should be suspended.

2. Be prudent in the use of such techniques as majority votes to establish group positions.

3. Be responsive to the contributions of others.

4. Recognize the point at which further pursuit of an issue is no longer profitable.

5. Evaluate the group's overall progress.

REFERENCES

BERG, DAVID M. "A Descriptive Analysis of the Distribution and Duration of Themes Discussed by Task-Oriented Small Groups," *Speech Monographs* **34** (1967):172–175.

GOURAN, DENNIS S. "Variables Related to Consensus in Group Discussions of Questions of Policy," *Speech Monographs* **36** (1969):387–391.

GOURAN, DENNIS S., and JOHN E. BAIRD, JR. "An Analysis of Distributional and Sequential Structure in Problem-Solving and Informal Group Discussions," *Speech Monographs* **39** (1972):16–22.

GUETZKOW, HAROLD and JOHN GYR. "An Analysis of Conflict in Decision-Making Groups," *Human Relations* **7** (1954):367–382.

JANIS, IRVING L. *Victims of Groupthink: A Psychological Study of Foreign Policy Decisions and Fiascoes.* Boston: Houghton Mifflin, 1972, pp. 14–49.

JANIS, IRVING, and BERT T. KING. "The Influence of Role Playing on Opinion Change," *Journal of Abnormal and Social Psychology* **49** (1954):211–218.

KNUTSON, THOMAS J. "An Experimental Study of the Effects of Orientation Behavior on Small Group Consensus," *Speech Monographs* **39** (1972):159–165.

FOR DISCUSSION

1. What other behavioral guidelines might you suggest which might be appropriate for decision-making discussions? Are there guidelines which Gouran suggests with which you would take issue or which you would revise substantially? Explain.

2. To what extent are these behavioral guidelines applicable to discussions such as those that occur in your college courses with the instructor serving as leader? Are these guidelines followed?

3. To what extent are the behavioral guidelines offered by Gouran applicable to dyadic communication? Which ones are most appplicable? Why?

4. One of the procedural guidelines Gouran suggests is to "be cognizant of the circumstances under which discussion should be suspended." Can you identify two, three, or four such circumstances? Are these also applicable to dyadic communication?

Risky-Shift Phenomenon

Joseph A. DeVito

Many of our everyday decisions involve some degree of risk. Given two alternatives, one usually involves more risk than the other and the amount of risk we are willing to take will play some part in our decision-making process. A most interesting phenomenon concerning risk has emerged from research on small group communication and has come to be called the *risky-shift phenomenon*. Generally, it has been found that decisions reached after discussion are riskier than decisions reached before discussion. Thus, if we have to choose between two alternatives we would be more apt to choose the riskier alternative after discussion than before. It has also been found that decisions are more risky in group-centered rather than in leader-centered groups.

Although the procedures to investigate the risky shift have varied greatly from one researcher to another, the general procedure is to present participants with a number of cases involving a decision between a safe but relatively unattractive alternative and a risky but relatively attractive alternative. For example, M. A. Wallach, N. Kogan, and D. J. Bem (1962, p. 77) used the following case: "An electrical engineer may stick with his present job at a modest but adequate salary, or may take a new job offering considerably more money but no long-term security." The subjects would then indicate their decisions individually and then discuss the case in a small group. After the discussion each subject would indicate his or her decision a second time. In terms of our example, before

Pp. 360–361 from *Communicology: An Introduction to the Study of Communication* by Joseph A. DeVito. Copyright (c) 1978 by Joseph A. DeVito. Reprinted by permission of Harper & Row, Publishers, Inc.

discussion the engineer would be advised to stick with his present job but after discussion to take the job offering the higher salary but less security.

Research has indicated that the risky-shift phenomenon seems to hold for both sexes, for all subject areas, and for both hypothetical and real situations. The inevitable question that arises is, Why does this happen?

Some possibilities are: (1) risk is highly valued in certain roles; (2) taking risks is a cultural (American?) value and people raise their status by taking risks; (3) the risky individual is the most influential member of a group and therefore succeeds in influencing other group members in the direction of greater risk taking; and (4) individual responsibility is diffused in a group whereas when alone the responsibility is the individual's own.

PUBLIC
COMMUNICATION

The articles in this last section are designed to provide an overview of the area of public communication. The articles focus on you as a public speaker and also as a consumer of public speeches and public communications.

Ray Ross in "The General Purposes of Speaking" and "Organizing a Speech" takes you through the essential steps in the speech preparation process. These two articles should clarify the various types of speeches, the ways available for organizing your materials, and the factors to take into account in presenting and analyzing the material to the audience.

Wayne Thompson's "A Compendium of Persuasive Devices" covers some of the means used by persuaders to move an audience. These devices are valuable for the speaker looking for techniques of persuasion and also for the consumer who wants to recognize the attempts of others at persuasion. A knowledge of these devices should make us more effective persuaders as well as more effective, that is, more critical, consumers of public communications.

In "Retortmanship: How to Avoid Answering Questions" Chandler Washburne supplies us with a clearly developed picture of the frequently observed speaker who does everything but come to grips with the issues. Here is the teacher who, afraid to say "I don't know," attacks our questions as being poorly phrased or ill-timed. Here is the politician who, afraid to offend some voters, lets go with a mountain of words but never gets around to answering our questions. You should have no difficulty in locating specific instances of the retortmanship techniques Washburne discusses.

General Purposes of Speaking

Raymond Ross

The insurance agents who come to your door are interested primarily in selling you a policy. Though they may present an armload of practical information, their purpose is to persuade. A speech billed as an "Informative Talk on the Arts" may really turn out to be persuasion for abstract painting, even if most of the material is informative. There is probably no such thing as a purely informative, purely persuasive, or even purely entertaining speech. Even the most flowery oratory probably presents some information. Entertainment ranging from court jesters to comedy players has for ages been a means of gentle persuasion. Some very effective persuasive speeches have sounded like informative talks. Some, in fact, have been almost wholly information.

By itself the sheer volume of informative, entertaining, or persuasive elements in a speech does not determine the kind of speech or the speaker's purpose. The arrangement of the material, the audience, the speaker's style and voice, and many more factors must also be considered.

It is practical to discuss each of the purposes of speaking separately. If your instructor asks you to prepare an informative speech for the next class and you state your purpose as being "to inform the class why they should join the Republican party," you had better be prepared for criticism. The instructor will probably suggest that you save the subject for the persuasive speech assignment and state your purpose more accurately as being "to persuade the class to join the Republican party." You might choose as your purpose "to inform the class about the history of the

Raymond S. Ross, *Essentials of Speech Communication.* Englewood Cliffs, N.J.: Prentice-Hall, 1979.

Republican party." The speech could then be either informative or persuasive, depending on your treatment and emphasis.

Your real purpose can be determined by the primary reaction you want from your audience. The general purposes and goals of speaking are:

TO INFORM

One of the most frequent purposes of speaking is to inform people of something about which you have knowledge. This is the purpose of a typing teacher who is showing students how to use the keyboard. The speaker who would inform has an obligation to make the information or instruction clear, interesting, and easy for the audience to learn, remember, and apply. To achieve these goals, a speaker should know something of how humans learn (this will be discussed in detail in Chapter 7). But briefly, we learn through our previous knowledge and experience. We learn more easily when the material follows some sequence. We remember better because of reinforcement (repetition), verbal emphasis, organization, effective use of voice, and other techniques. The primary goal in informative speaking is *audience understanding*. The key means to this goal are *clarity, interest,* and *organization of material*.

TO PERSUADE

The goals of a persuasive speech are to convince people to believe or do something, or to stimulate them to a higher level of conviction.

These divisions (belief, action, and stimulation) often overlap. When no immediate action is being called for, the speaker may be attempting to convince or to bring about *belief*. Such persuasive speeches as "Foreign Policy," "The Threat of Fascism," or "Uphold the United Nations" might have this purpose. No specific and immediate action is asked. The listeners are only asked to agree with the speaker, to believe and be convinced. This, of course, assumes that the audience does not have the power to act. If the audience were the United States Congress, these belief purposes could become action purposes.

When the audience is asked to do something specific following the speech, the purpose is action—for example, a speech asking for donations

Purpose	Goals
To inform	Clarity
	Interest
	Understanding
To persuade	Belief
	Action
	Stimulation
To entertain	Interest
	Enjoyment
	Humor

to the Red Cross that is ended by passing a container for contributions. Election speeches asking people to vote or to sign petitions are further examples. Most sales talks are action speeches—even though the TV announcer does not really expect you to run out and buy a Chevrolet at 11:30 P.M. The desired action is specific and available.

When a speaker is seeking a higher degree of audience enthusiasm or devotion, the purpose is *inspiration* or *stimulation*. An example might be a speech for party unity at a political convention after the nominee has been selected. In short, speeches of stimulation are found in those situations where the speaker is (1) not trying to change any basic attitudes, but rather to strengthen them; (2) not trying to prove anything, but rather to remind the listeners; or (3) not calling for any unusual action, but rather to inspire the listeners.

TO ENTERTAIN

When you sincerely want people to enjoy themselves, your general purpose is to entertain. The "fun," after-dinner, or radio-television speeches that involve jokes, stories, and a variety of humor are examples. Their success depends upon the experience, skill, and personality of the speaker and mood of the audience. In a speech designed solely to entertain, the audience should understand that purpose and genuinely relax and enjoy themselves.

A word of warning to both beginning and experienced speakers: the speech to entertain is the most difficult of the three. Feedback is rapid and blunt. You know without doubt when a funny story or joke does not succeed. Practice is critical!

FOR DISCUSSION

1. Prepare an informative speech of approximately _____ minutes in length. Your goals—as stated by Ross—are clarity, interest, and understanding.
2. Prepare a persuasive speech of approximately _____ minutes in length. Your goal should be to convince your audience to believe in a certain way, to do something, or to strengthen their conviction about a particular issue.
3. For each of the following topics phrase a specific informative or persuasive speech purpose. Share these specific purposes with others in the class, asking yourselves the few questions presented below about each specific purpose.
  Topics: The high cost of education; problems of college students; making ends meet; drugs; morality in the 20th century.
  Questions: Is the purpose sufficiently narrow so that you would be able to cover it in the time allotted—say about 5 to 8 minutes? Can it be narrowed further? How does the audience feel about this purpose? Are they in favor of it? Against it? Neutral? What will this mean to the development of the speech? Is the specific purpose appropriate to you as a spokesperson? What might you do to make yourself a more appropriate and persuasive spokesperson for this particular topic and purpose?

Organizing a Speech

Raymond S. Ross

Let's look first at some useful methods for organizing the raw materials.

METHODS OF ORGANIZING IDEAS

Chronological Method

Materials are arranged according to the order in which events took place. In speaking on "Life on Earth," we would probably discuss the geologic periods chronologically. Most historical subjects lend themselves readily to this method; so do processes of a sequential 1–2–3 order, such as developing film. Remember, however, that these subjects do not have to be handled in this way. History, for example, is often more interesting and meaningful if discussed topically.

Topical Method

Material is ordered according to general topics or classifications of knowledge. To continue the example of history, we might concentrate on the history of religion, war, government, education, or science. The importance of the topic may be such that you'll ignore historical time. The topical method can help in breaking down very broad topics. One can, for example, look at integration of the races in several topical ways—educationally, socially, militarily, economically, and so forth. A city may be described topically in terms of its industry, employment opportunities, recreational facilities, schools, climate, and so on.

Raymond S. Ross, *Essentials of Speech Communication:* Englewood Cliffs, N.J.: Prentice-Hall, 1979.

Logical Method

This method is useful for subjects with generally accepted or obvious cause-and-effect relationships such as the fall of the Japanese empire or the building of a house or a boat. When the order is naturally present in the subject, it may be a convenient way to organize our speech materials. This method differs from the topical method in that subpoints almost always illustrate or explain whatever they are subordinate to. You must analyze your audience thoroughly before using this method. What seems logical to you may not seem logical to them.

Difficulty Method

For some subjects, particularly technical ones, it may help to organize your materials in their order of difficulty—that is, proceeding from the easiest aspect to the most difficult one.

Spatial Method

In a speech about the United Nations we might first describe each building, then discuss the offices in each building one floor at a time. The ideas are organized spatially. The ideas could also be organized topically if the audience were familiar with the political structure of the United Nations. In discussing "Nationalism in Africa," we might organize geographically and simply divide the ideas from north to south and east to west. This subject might also be organized historically.

Need-Plan Method

Materials are organized according to problems (needs) and solutions (plans). An affirmative debate team arguing government health programs will divide its material into needs and plans. The first speaker will concentrate on the needs. The second speaker will discuss the various plans and indicate why one is better than the others. The needs can be subdivided into economic needs, health needs, and social needs.

METHODS OF ARRANGING THE PARTS

The *major* parts of a speech are: *beginning, middle,* and *end,* or *introduction, body,* and *conclusion.* Other parts are the speech details and ideas. Before analyzing each part, let's look at three rhetorical principles that are important in the arranging of the parts. These are *unity, coherence,* and *emphasis.*

Unity

Aristotle once said that a play must be constructed so that the omission of any part damages the whole. He also noted that each part of the plot must contribute to the purpose or end of the play. He said a play must have a total unity in the same manner as a living thing. We still use the term *organic unity*. In speech, organic unity means that the material should be so unified that it can be summarized in a single statement of purpose. In some speeches this statement takes the form of a proposition that is openly announced. In others it is left unstated for strategic purposes. But the speaker must always understand his or her specific purpose if the speech is to have unity. This specific purpose helps the speaker evaluate materials and ideas during preparation. The arrangement of the parts of a speech should be so unified that the purpose is clear to both the audience and speaker.

Coherence

Coherence refers to the connections among the parts of the speech. It involves the methods of ordering ideas and speech details. To *cohere* is to be connected. The connecting of the parts and ideas of a speech is done with words or phrases. To achieve coherence, we must carefully consider our connecting words. Unlike the reader, the listener cannot go back and recheck the text to locate a lost thread of meaning. Thus, we must connect our thoughts carefully, often repeating the connectives. Coherence must involve the audience. In going from one point to another, we may lose our audience if we assume that it will see the relationship of ideas just because we do.

Emphasis

Emphasis involves the location, space, and form you give your ideas. Should you present your most important idea first, last, or as a climax? Does the amount of space you give the idea affect emphasis? Your main point should not be buried under some subpoint. Since a number of really important ideas may compete for attention, which idea should you emphasize most strongly? These questions can be answered best in terms of your subject, knowledge, audience, and the occasion. Location, space, form, and order do make a difference. They do affect emphasis. Successful emphasis involves the use of these devices.

Systems of Arrangement

Aristotle thought that good arrangement was related to normal thinking habits. So do modern rhetoricians. Aristotle suggested four steps: *introduction* (he called it proem), *statement* (of the purpose), *argument,* and *conclusion* (he called it epilogue). Hollingworth listed the parts of a speech as *attention, interest, impression, conviction,* and *direction.* Some parts may be eliminated as one adapts to the audience.

Monroe suggested that the basic parts are *attention, need, satisfaction, visualization,* and *action.* He believed that the emphasis given each element would depend on the audience's mood and knowledge as well as the purpose of the speech. A speech to inform might use only three elements. A speech to persuade might call for all five.

These systems of arrangement are useful. They show the complicated interaction of subject, audience, speaker, and arrangement.

Other divisions of your speech are possible. The *general* purpose of your speech (to persuade, to inform, or to entertain) will dictate how complex a system you will need. Let's view these parts in terms of the more common divisions of *introduction, body,* and *conclusion.*

SOME GENERAL SYSTEMS OF ARRANGEMENT

INTRODUCTION →	Attention	Attention	Attention	Attention
BODY →	Statement	Interest Impression	Need Satisfaction	Overview
	Argument	Conviction	Visualization	Information
CONCLUSION →	Conclusion	Direction	Action	Review

Let's look now at the requirements of a good introduction, body, and conclusion.

Introduction

The chart above shows that arousing attention is always an important first step. The number of attention-getting devices used depends on how attentive the audience already is. If listeners are on the edge of their seats and ready to hear what you have to say, a lengthy introduction to arouse their attention is unnecessary.

Arousing attention is only one requirement of an introduction. Your introduction should also attempt to establish or strengthen good will between you and the audience. In those rare cases where good will is hard to come by (as when you're facing a hostile audience), establishing a mood for a fair hearing is perhaps the most you can hope for. For example, Adlai Stevenson once used humor to establish rapport with a tough Labor Day audience: "When I was a boy I never had much sympathy for a holiday speaker. He was just a kind of interruption between hot dogs, a fly in the lemonade."

In some situations, a purpose of the introduction is *orientation.* That is, the speaker must supply certain background explanations to help the audience better understand the rest of the speech. Not defining new words, for example, will cause confusion in the audience. A brief historical sketch often helps orient the audience. A good example is John F. Kennedy's opening address to a conference on African culture in New York City on June 28, 1959.

Some 2,500 years ago the Greek historian Heredotus described Africa south of the Sahara as a land of "horned asses, of dog-faced creatures, the creatures without heads, whom the Libyans declared to have eyes in their breasts, and many other far less fabulous beasts." Apparently when Herodotus found himself short on facts, he didn't hesitate to use imagination—which may be why he is called the first historian.

But we must not be too critical of Herodotus. Until very recently, for most Americans, Africa was Trader Horn, Tarzan, and tom-tom drums. We are only now beginning to discover that Africa, unlike our comic strip stereotypes, is a land of rich variety—of noble and ancient cultures, some primitive, some highly sophisticated; of vital and gifted people, who are only now crossing the threshold into the modern world.

The introduction seeks to make your purpose clear. It is often a preview of what is to follow. Again, remember that an *audience*, unlike a *reader*, cannot go back to a previous page. Therefore, more repetition is called for.

To summarize, the purposes of an introduction are (1) to secure *attention*; (2) to establish *good will*; (3) to assure a *fair hearing*; (4) to *orient* your audience to the subject; and (5) to make your *purpose* clear.

You can achieve good introductions in many different ways. However, any introduction should relate to both the subject and the situation. An unusual story describing your troubles in getting to the meeting is acceptable. So are humorous anecdotes. Most experts agree that if you are going to use jokes or humorous stories, they should relate in some way to the subject or situation. Appreciation, personal reference, quotations, and related stories or experiences are also useful. When the purpose of the speech is obvious and both speaker and subject are well known, a related story or incident with built-in attention often gives the audience a fresh orientation. Booker T. Washington's introduction to his address at the Atlanta Exposition is a good example:

Attention

Mr. President and Gentlemen of the Board of Directors and Citizens: One-third of the population of the South is of the Negro race. No enterprise seeking the material, civil, or moral welfare of this section can disregard this element of our population and reach the highest success.

Good Will

I but convey to you, Mr. President and Directors, the sentiment of the masses of my race when I say that in no way have the value and manhood of the American Negro been more fittingly and generously recognized than by the managers of this magnificent Exposition at every stage of its progress. It is a recognition that will do more to cement the friendship of the two races than any occurrence since the dawn of our freedom.

Fair Hearing

Not only this, but the opportunity here afforded will awaken among us a new era of industrial progress. Ignorant and inexperienced, it is not strange that in the first years of our new life we began at the top instead of at the bottom; that a seat in Congress or the state legislature was more sought than real estate or industrial skill; that the political convention or stump speaking had more attractions than starting a dairy farm or truck garden.

Orientation

A ship lost at sea for many days suddenly sighted a friendly vessel. From the mast of the unfortunate vessel was seen a signal, "Water, water; we die of thirst!" The answer from the friendly vessel at once came back, "Cast down your bucket where you are." And a third and fourth signal for water was answered, "Cast down your bucket where you are." The captain of the distressed vessel, at last heeding the injunction, cast down his bucket, and it came up full of fresh, sparkling water from the mouth of the Amazon River.

Purpose

To those of my race who depend on bettering their condition in a foreign land or who underestimate the importance of cultivating friendly relations with the Southern white man, who is their next door neighbor, I would say: "Cast down your bucket where you are"—cast it down in making friends in every manly way of the people of all races by whom we are surrounded.

During World War II, President Roosevelt used a story in an introduction to one of the many appeals he made for the purchase of war bonds.

Once upon a time, a few years ago, there was a city in our Middle West which was threatened by a destructive flood in a great river. The waters had risen to the top of the banks. Every man, woman, and child in that city was called upon to fill sandbags in order to defend their homes against the rising waters. For many days and nights destruction and death stared them in the face. As a result of the grim, determined community effort, that city still stands. Those people kept the levees above the peak of the flood. All of them joined together in the desperate job that had to be done—businessmen, workers, farmers, and doctors, and preachers—people of all races.

To me that town is a living symbol of what community cooperation can accomplish.

Body

This is where the bulk of the information or argument is located. All the previous discussions of organization, rhetorical principles, and arrangement come into focus here.

Conclusion

Words from the arrangement chart on p. 223 are *direction, action* and *review.* We could add *visualization, restatement,* and *summary.* These devices are all intended to regain attention and to assist the memory. Aristotle suggested that the major purpose of the conclusion is to help the memory.

The conclusion is generally shorter than either the introduction or the body. It may and generally should include a short summary that reinforces the message and makes it easier to understand. It may call for clearly stated directions if certain actions are part of the speaker's purpose. When your purpose has been inspiration, you may need a more impressive conclusion. Some of the devices suggested in the discussion on introductions (an impressive quotation, incident, or experience) apply here. Martin

Luther King, Jr., gave an inspirational conclusion in his famous speech in support of civil rights legislation before an estimated 200,000 people.

> So let freedom ring—from the prodigious hilltops of New Hampshire, let freedom ring; from the mighty mountains of New York, let freedom ring—from the heightening Alleghenies of Pennsylvania!
> Let freedom ring from the snowcapped Rockies of Colorado!
> Let freedom ring from the curvaceous slopes of California!
> But not only that; let freedom ring from Stone Mountain of Georgia!
> Let freedom ring from Lookout Mountain of Tennessee!
> Let freedom ring from every hill and mole hill of Mississippi.
> From every mountainside, let freedom ring, . . .
> When we allow freedom to ring, when we let it ring from every village and every hamlet, from every state and every city, we will be able to speed up that day when all of God's children, black men and white men, Jews and Gentiles, Protestants and Catholics, will be able to join hands and sing in the words of the old Negro spiritual, "Free at last! thank God almighty, we are free at last!"[1]

Most important, make it evident when you are finished; consider your exit lines carefully. Speakers who do not know when they are going to finish appear awkward and confuse the audience. The never-ending conclusion, caused either by the ham in all of us or by poor preparation, is all too familiar. The remedy is obvious: prepare your conclusion as carefully as the rest of your speech. Doing so serves as a good check on unity. And quit while you're ahead. Don't let an audience hypnotize you so much that you ruin a good speech with an overly long conclusion.

AUDIENCE PSYCHOLOGY

Most of what was said about the model of person-to-person communication in Chapter 1 applies to communication with an audience. The audience model involves greater problems of physical setting and feedback. The analysis of audiences by types becomes in part an averaging process. But we must realize that such generalizing fits some members of the audience poorly and others not at all. That is why the model in Figure 1 places some of the members outside of the general audience (represented by the head).

The audience has frequently been considered as a statistical concept. As such, it is a means of assembling a large amount of information about individuals (average age, income, nationality, education, and so forth.)

Audiences have also been classified into many types—organized-unorganized, unified, apathetic, hostile, polarized, and bipolar to name a few. In general, the audience we are talking about is a fairly formal group of individuals who assemble for a specific purpose.

Several useful questions relating to *audience analysis* follow.

---

[1]Quoted in Robert T. Oliver and Eugene E. White. *Selected Speeches from American History* (Boston: Allyn & Bacon, 1966), pp. 289–94.

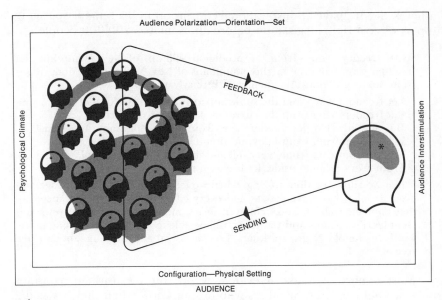

Audience Polarization—Orientation—Set

FEEDBACK

SENDING

Psychological Climate

Audience Interstimulation

Configuration—Physical Setting

AUDIENCE

Figure 1. Audience communication model.

1. **What is the significance of the subject for the audience?** Is its interest in the subject only casual, or is it motivated by real needs and wants? How far has its thinking about the problem progressed?

2. **What does the audience know about the subject?** Does it have essential factual information, or only opinions and sentiments? Are its sources of information sound ones, unbiased and complete?

3. **What beliefs or prejudices does the audience have about the subject?** In either case, what are the probable sources or influences in the formation of these existing notions?

4. **What is the attitude of the audience toward the subject?** Is it possible to estimate the percentage who are favorable, neutral, or unfavorable toward the problem?[2]

Some *general descriptive measures* worth considering in audience analysis are:

Age

It is obvious that an audience of ten-year-olds will call for different preparation by the speaker than will a group of forty-year-olds. Even if the subject is Little League baseball! A few children in an otherwise all-adult audience sometimes present a problem. Even if you choose (or are advised) to ignore them, you can be certain that the *audience* will not. They

[2]Jon Eisenson, J. Jeffrey Auer, and John V. Irwin. *The Psychology of Communication* (New York: Appleton-Century-Crofts, 1963), p. 279.

usually establish norms of appropriateness and understanding based on the youngsters. An off-color story is less well received when even a single child is present.

Sex

An audience of twenty men often differs considerably in outlook from an audience of twenty women or from an audience of ten men and ten women. An audience of nineteen men and one woman can cause a male speaker to alter many of his jokes and examples. This is not necessarily *because* of the one woman, but because the nineteen men expect the speaker to be conscious of the one woman. If you ignore the woman, the men will be unhappy.

Education

A person's education is the sum of that person's learning. Do not confuse schooling with education, for attending school does not guarantee an education. There are many uneducated college graduates! Nevertheless, formal schooling is in most cases a more efficient way of acquiring knowledge than other ways. Your audience's educational level and previous schooling should be taken into account when you select your language and vocabulary. An audience with a highly technical education requires a different approach than one with a liberal arts background. The problem again is a difference in educational background. Time invested in this kind of audience analysis is usually well spent.

Occupation

Stereotyping a person by his or her occupation is as dangerous as classifying a person according to schooling. Nevertheless, knowing a person's occupation is often useful. For instance, the average income level of your audience can often be predicted by knowing the occupations of most of its members. Furthermore, you can predict that teachers will have college degrees, that top management executives will have similar opinions about some kinds of legislation, and so on.

Primary Group Memberships

Most of us belong to many groups. Predicting what groups are represented in an audience is shaky at best. For example, an audience at a political convention may be all Republican or all Democratic. However, it may also represent many religious, ethnic, and occupational groups, not to mention attitudes. The more you can learn about the groups an audience does or does not belong to, the better you can prepare your speech.

Special Interests

Whatever their differences, audiences are often of one mind about some special interest they have in common. A small community with a

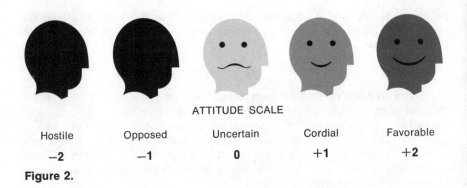

ATTITUDE SCALE

Hostile	Opposed	Uncertain	Cordial	Favorable
−2	−1	0	+1	+2

Figure 2.

winning high school basketball team may ignore a guest speaker who is unaware of this special interest. Sometimes these interests are temporary. Seek out and become familiar with any special interests that the audience *expects* you to know about.

Audience-Subject Relationships

This part of your analysis concerns an audience's *knowledge* about your speech topic. What *experience* and *interest* does the audience have in your subject? What is their *attitude* toward your specific purpose? It is often valuable to know to what extent the audience is uniform in its beliefs and knowledge.

Some audiences are very firm in their beliefs, whatever their level of knowledge or experience. In general, an audience is either interested or uninterested in your speech *subject,* but the audience's attitudes are directed toward your *purpose.* A useful scale for determining the general audience attitude toward the purpose of your speech is shown in Figure 2. Your preparation of a speech and your arrangement of its material will depend heavily on how accurately you analyze your audience.

FOR DISCUSSION

1. What method of organizing ideas would you use with each of the following topics? Before deciding on the organizational scheme, phrase a specific purpose for each of these topics and select the main points that you might cover in a 5 to 7 minute speech. Explain why you think the particular method of organization you selected would be appropriate.

The Causes of the Civil War
Great Movies of the 1940s
Violence on Television
Censorship
Capital Punishment

2. Create an introduction to a speech on one of the following topics. Be sure that your introduction serves all five functions noted by Ross: to secure attention, to establish good will, to assure a fair hearing, to orient your audience to the subject, and to make your purpose clear. Booker T. Washington's introduction to his Atlanta Exposition speech cited by Ross will provide an excellent guide to the preparation of this introduction.

Eliminate all required college courses.

Legalize marijuana.

Ban all cigarette advertising

Eliminate college athletics

3. Construct a conclusion to the speech for which you composed an introduction in the previous exercise. Be sure your conclusion summarizes the main points of the speech and that it clearly demonstrates that you are finished.

A Compendium of
Persuasive Devices

Wayne Thompson

Studies of successful persuaders show that a number of devices work much of the time. Knowing about them adds to the choices open to the communicator and to the critical resources of the wary respondent.

REPETITION

"The Do-Nothing Eightieth Congress" was a recurring phrase in Harry Truman's 1948 presidential campaign. "Trigger happy" was the tag applied repeatedly to Barry Goldwater in 1964, and "Come home, America" in 1972 was George McGovern's unsuccessful cry. A repeated phrase may be a stylistic feature of a single message, or it may be a strategy for a compaign. Each presentation, it is hoped, will heighten impact through a cumulative effect and eventually will bring persuasion.

Sometimes a dramatic event, such as a fire or a plane crash, leads to new safety laws, but effective social movements usually are campaigns in which repetition is a major strategy. In interpersonal relations repetitiveness at times becomes what one inventive student labeled "the fourth means of persuasion"—*logos, pathos, ethos,* and *nusos.* By persistence some individuals gain permission to buy a motorcycle, to live in their own apartments, to have their own telephones, or to buy new dresses or household appliances. More subtle is the interpersonal campaign in which invented situations demonstrate a need and in which the persuader slips sentences of argument into conversations. Whereas the *nusos* technique

"A Compendium of Persuasive Devices," pp. 438–445 in *The Process of Persuasion: Principles and Readings* by Wayne N. Thompson (1975). Reprinted by permission of Harper & Row, Publishers, Inc.

leaves the persuadee in a state of unhappy acquiescence, the subtle campaign culminates in his believing that the final decision is his own.

Nusos alone is unlikely to work with a public issue, even though some public relations men claim that irritating commercials are harmless to the seller so long as the consumer remembers the name of the product. Campaigns for more parking lots, student representation on faculty committees, lesser penalties for possessing marijuana, new community playgrounds, or passage of a bond issue, however, offer their own distinctive opportunities for using repetition, as well as other devices. The following questions suggest some specific procedures and opportunities:

> What slogan or catchy phrase, if any, will express the thesis or goal clearly and memorably? Statements containing rhyme, alliteration, or cadence are especially effective.
>
> Which medium or media should the communinator employ—radio or television spots, billboards, newspaper advertisements, editorials, letters to the editor, or speeches?
>
> Should the repetition be a restated phrase or idea, or should it be a series of messages that point in the same direction?
>
> If repetition is through diverse appeals, what are the available arguments, statistical data, examples, and authoritative opinions?
>
> How can these message elements be arranged for maximum effectiveness— from most believable to little known, in an order of increasing dramatic power, or in some other pattern?
>
> How much repetition will be tolerable before it produces a boomerang effect?
>
> How can one vary the presentations so that the respondents will remain attentive?
>
> How frequent should the repetitions be?

Why is repetition a sound persuasive strategy? First, so research studies indicate, it increases comprehension.[1] On the first presentation or even the second, some listeners do not grasp the communicator's ideas, but with repeated exposures the amount that they remember increases. Second, increasing the number of contacts between the respondent and the persuasive message results in added opportunities for shifts in belief. "What holds attention," William James wrote, "determines action."[2]

PRESTIGE AND TRANSFER

An example of a second common persuasive device arrived in the writer's mail box not long ago. An organization was seeking his membership—and dollars—in a lecture society with an impressive title. The letter carried the

---

[1]For a summary of studies, see Wayne N. Thompson, *Quantitative Research in Public Address and Communication* (New York: Random House, 1967), pp. 63–64.

[2]*Psychology* (New York: Holt, Rinehart & Winston, 1907), p. 448.

signature of a noted newscaster as general chairman and the names of senators, governors, and literary figures on its executive board. Also listed as former members were such famous men as Daniel Webster, Mark Twain, and Dwight Eisenhower. Less ambitious promotional schemes are common. Almost every charity associated with an illness has its own movie star as chairman, and solicitations for local drives are on letterheads that include prominent local citizens as committee members.

Such appeals are applications of theories about ethos and consistency; they drive subtly at the desire for self-esteem. Who wouldn't like to belong to the same organization as Walter Cronkhite and Justice William O. Douglas? If the mayor and other leading citizens are on the governing board of a charity, surely it must be reputable! The movie star is someone I like; therefore, I like whatever he supports.

For the person preparing a persuasive message, prestige and transfer are valuable strategies. Through devices . . . one enhances his credibility, and through research one locates materials adaptable to the transfer technique. One can quote passages from respected figures supporting his position, and he can list corroborating authorities. "Name dropping" is useful for serious persuasive purposes as well as for conversational one-upsmanship; "I had a rare opportunity when Senator Blank was in our city to discuss my plan with him, and I was pleased when he said that he liked my idea so much that he might introduce a bill founded on it." Through transfer the speaker hopes to shift respect for the senator to respect for the proposal.

An especially interesting example comes from India, where the basis for one campaign was the attempted transfer of reverence for a sacred animal to approval of birth control measures:

> And in India an elephant named Beautiful Flower has been enlisted in the ecological cause as a distributor of contraceptives. Her job is to help reduce the country's suicidal rate of population growth, by plodding from village to village wearing birth control posters on her sides and forehead. As soon as she collects a crowd in a village street, Beautiful Flower (with a little guidance from her mahout) starts to pass out family-planning literature and packets of contraceptives. Since many Indians regard the elephant as a semi-sacred animal, her efforts are more persuasive than those of human propagandists.[3]

GLITTERING GENERALITY AND NAME CALLING

Besides *transfer* the Institute for Propaganda Analysis, a prominent organization in the 1930s, listed six other categories, two being glittering generality and name calling. Both are noninformative, inimical to thoughtful examinations of public issues, and deserving of condemnation; yet they are common enough that educated, responsible citizens should be familiar with their techniques.

[3]John Fischer, "The Easy Chair: Good News, in a Small Way," *Harper's*, 243 (October 1971), 21.

For an example of glittering generalities the critic can look at almost any political campaign. To avoid offending any element within the electorate, the candidate states that he is for law and order, good schools, higher wages, ethics in government, protection of personal freedoms, reduction of pollution, and lower taxes. Whether he is for or against capital punishment, legalized abortion, police review boards, or any other specific proposal often remains in doubt until election day, and he is likely to leave unexplained how he could bring about, if elected, both lower taxes and increased services. Not only is no one offended, but also through wishful thinking voters may conclude that the candidate's true view is the same as theirs.

Likewise short circuiting rational evaluation is name calling. Such appellations as "Tricky Dick," "Thousand Percent George," and "Horsemeat Adlai" express broad evaluations without any reference to the facts and assert relationships between men and events without any analysis of the circumstances. Tidy, often effective, and bringing broader judgments together in concise, memorable form, name calling is a device that one cannot justify ethically.

At times defensible, though, is the glittering generality. In periods of tension, whether the nation, the club, or the family, unity and improved morale may be more important than rational analysis. In such instances the avoidance of the issues may be more useful socially than their identification and examination.

PLAIN FOLKS AND BANDWAGON

Two other effective strategies that obstruct rational analysis are *plain folks* and *bandwagon*. The former, according to Judith Trent's analysis of Nixon's first two presidential campaigns,[4] was a major feature of his speeches in 1960. He referred to working his way through college, toiling on a ranch, taking his daughters to Disneyland, and being vaccinated in a place that made sitting down uncomfortable. "Nixon," Theodore White observes, "seemed obsessed with appearing 'just plain folks.' "[5] In 1968, however, the strategy was significantly different. Using prestige and transfer, he spoke of conferences with famous people and visualized his activities as president. " . . . he never attempted to portray himself as a common man," Dr. Trent summarizes; " . . . the image Nixon seemed to be seeking was that of a world leader, a statesman, a man who was already President."[6]

The preceding example illustrates the danger that the plain folks

[4]"Richard Nixon's Methods of Identification in the Presidential Campaigns of 1960 and 1968," *Today's Speech*, 19 (Fall 1971), 23–30.

[5]*The Making of the President, 1960* (New York: Atheneum, 1961), p. 301.

[6]"Richard Nixon's Methods of Identification in the Presidential Campaigns of 1960 and 1968," p. 27.

device may downgrade a speaker whose ethos is vulnerable. A second example, of a president with unquestioned prestige, is one in which the technique worked well:

> Both Eisenhower and Stevenson were invited to speak at a plowing contest in Newton, Iowa. Although the occasion seemed to call for it, the President chose not to make a major farm policy speech. . . . Ike told the farmers he was not there to make a speech. He just wanted to talk over things. Throughout he sounded a neighborly, bucolic note. He spoke in favor of farmers and farming, of furrow and plow, of casting swords into plow-shares. . . . Everything considered, it was an incredible brush-off, yet the talk proved to be an enormously successful vehicle for projecting the Eisenhower personality.[7]

Quite different from plain folks but also a short-circuiting device is the bandwagon, exemplified in advertising by "Everybody's doing it," "Watch the Fords Go by," and "10 billion hamburgers sold." The assumptions behind this technique are that success is proof of quality and that people like to be associated with a winner.

The bandwagon is easy to use. A speaker can tell how many have joined or donated already, he can cite figures or percentages, and he can repeat names. The aura of success is so supposedly indispensable to victory that in the 1972 presidential campaign George McGovern, though every published poll accurately foretold his decisive defeat, maintained doggedly that he was going to win.

"YES . . . YES" AND "EITHER . . . OR"

Another psychological device is to move by small stages from items that speaker and listener agree on to those that are controversial. In theory— and often in practice—each time that the listener responds affirmatively the easier it is for him to say "yes" to the next question or demand. An example of the "yes . . . yes" strategy appears in an article telling how Norman Jaspan, a private detective, extracts confessions from embezzlers and thieving employees:

> "First, your name and address. Is that a house or apartment? What's the rent? Are you married? Have you children?" Smoothly and implacably he moves along from easy questions to touchier ones such as, "What do you owe on the house? What are your other debts? What do you spend per week on entertainment?" Within five minutes he is blandly asking for information about gambling habits, marital irregularities, and miscellaneous peccadilloes. Astonishingly enough, almost no one ever refuses to answer.

> "It's not so mysterious," Jaspan explained to an assistant a while ago. "I start with easy ones and keep on going, asking as if I had a right to. If you're innocent, what do you care? And if you're guilty, at what point are your

---

[7]Ernest J. Wrage, "Rhetoric and the Campaign of 1956," *Quarterly Journal of Speech,* 43 (February 1957), 51–52.

going to get your back up? By the time the questions get tough, you're afraid to make yourself look bad by backing out."[8]

The example above pertains to interviewing, but the "yes . . . yes" strategy also is adaptable to conversations, discussions, and public speeches.

Also usable in all types of communication is the "either . . . or" device, which creates a false, oversimplified analysis of a problem, puts pressure on the individual to take a stand, and limits the choices to the one advocated and a second one, which is repugnant. Like the other devices, this one may serve either good or bad causes. In one sermon the minister in each section developed the challenge "You are either for God or against him. There can be no middle way." In a conference one businessman, by insisting that the company must either go forward or stagnate, sought to force a choice between his proposal and the spectre of decay. His strategy was to forestall such sensible questions as "Is it true that the status quo means stagnation?" "Is this proposal change for the sake of change?" "Aren't there other new directions besides the one advocated?" and "How well would the plan work?"

The "either . . . or" technique was a favorite of Hitler's, as the following passage indicates. At the end of the quotation Haig A. Bosmajian analyzes the reasons that the strategy was psychologically shrewd:

> Hitler made great use of the "either-or" which appealed to his crowds' desire to escape doubt and uncertainty, their desire for the simple and exaggerated. July 28, 1922: "No! A thousand times No! Here there are only two possibilities: either victory or defeat!" April 12, 1922: "Here, too, there can be no compromise: . . . there are only two possibilities: either victory of the Aryan or annihilation of the Aryan and the victory of the Jew." September, 1923: "That is the mission of our Movement: Swastika or Soviet Star: the despotism of the International or the Holy Empire of German Nationality." . . . Such "either-or" presentations appealed to the crowd mentality simply because of the definiteness and strength in the "either-or" presentation. There is no compromise in "either-or." There is no weakness in "either-or." "Either-or" implies decision and action, not vacillation or weakness. Juxtaposed to the indecisive "palaver" of the Parliamentarians, "either-or" implied direction; juxtaposed to the "double-talk" of the Jews, it implied straightforward honesty; compared to the "cowardly speech" of the pacifist, "either-or" was power and strength.[9]

SCAPEGOAT AND BIG LIE

Two other Hitlerian techniques, both thoroughly despicable, unfortunately appear from time to time in both public and interpersonal controversies. No circumstances can justify the use of these devices, but the educated

[8]Morton M. Hunt, "Private Eye to Industry," *Harper's,* 223 (November 1961), 63.

[9]Haig A. Bosmajian, "Nazi Persuasion and the Crowd Mentality," *Western Speech,* 29 (Spring 1965), 73–74.

man should be prepared to detect them. Scapegoating is the procedure of uniting followers by making them fearful of some individual or group— in Hitler's case, the German Jews. Through fear and suspicion, often fed by lies and invented or manipulated incidents, the communicator portrays himself as the savior of those he seeks as followers. Whenever fear appeals involve attacks on a person or a group, the prospective persuadee should inquire about the motives of the communicator and look critically at the allegations.

The person who uses the scapegoat technique is morally capable of the Big Lie. One precept of the Nazi propagandists was that the Big Lie, if told often enough, will be believed.

SUMMARY

The devices mentioned in this section are not the only ones that are available for the persuader to use and for the respondent to view warily. Appearing all too often in both interpersonal and public discourse are repetition, prestige and transfer, glittering generality and name calling, plain folks and bandwagon, "yes . . . yes" and "either . . . or," and scapegoating and the Big Lie.

FOR DISCUSSION

1. All of the persuasive devices discussed by Thompson may be found in current advertisements. Locate an advertisement which uses each of these devices and analyze the specific methods used by the advertiser to make the product or service more appealing. Are these devices effective? Are they ethical?

2. Read one or more speeches in *Vital Speeches of the Day*, in *Representative American Speeches* (both should be in your library), or in any of the numerous other sources and analyze the speech for the persuasive devices noted by Thompson. Discuss your findings with others in the class.

A Decalogue for the Persuader

Wayne Thompson

1. He has a clear notion of his objectives.
2. He analyzes his receivers and adapts to them in message, style, and delivery.
3. He conducts himself so that listeners perceive him as competent, trustworthy, dynamic, and well intentioned.
4. He knows his topic thoroughly.
5. He uses language that is clear, appropriate, and forceful.
6. He speaks fluently, directly, and with vocal variety that creates clarity and emphasis.
7. He forms strategic plans for interpersonal situations, and he makes conscious rhetorical choices in preparation for public addresses.
8. He gains favorable attention at the beginning and directs interest toward his main ideas throughout.
9. He is sophisticated in using the theoretical constructs that have become part of the literature of persuasion. Among the concepts that he understands and applies to practical needs are the enthymeme, rationalization, polarization, stereotypes, reference groups, motivation, consistency theory, suggestion, identification, norms and conformity, and innoculation.
10. By respecting truth and by concern for the best interests of society and its subgroups, he tries to perform ethically.

"A Decalogue for the Persuader," pp. 22-23 in *The Process of Persuasion: Principles and Readings* by Wayne N. Thompson (1975). Reprinted by permission of Harper & Row, Publishers, Inc.

Retortmanship

How to Avoid Answering Questions

Chandler Washburne

At the risk of being considered somewhat Machiavellian, I would like to deal with some practical methods in use today to defend man from the omnipresent question. Our age, in addition to being atomic, contains further dangers to the individual—in that he is continually bombarded with questions. Atomic bombardment is viewed as evil, whereas we have come to accept the deluge of questions, prying into every aspect of our lives, as a natural event. In a democracy this trend is particularly strong. The idea of equality allows anyone, as an equal, to presume to question you and makes you feel compelled to answer. A clear demonstration of this is seen in politics. Even the President is continually subjected to questioning by newsmen. He cannot revert to a position of superiority, from which he could resist being questioned or not feel the need to give answers, as a dictator might.

All this means that various defenses must be built against the question: methods must be developed by which we can keep the questioner from feeling that his question has not been answered. In other words, we appear to cooperate in answering the question; yet somehow he fails to secure the information which we do not wish revealed—without his being fully aware of it, as this would only lead to another question. (Washington, D.C. would be the world's greatest laboratory.) We leave him (1) satisfied or (2) in a position where he is restrained by politeness from further imposition or (3) in a state of confusion, which prevents him from formulating another query.

From Chandler Washburne, "Retortmanship: How to Avoid Answering Questions," *ETC: A Review of General Semantics, 28* (March 1969), 69-75, by permission of The International Society for General Semantics.

A further limitation which has been placed on the methods used here is that the reply should be within the limits of truth. The outright lie is not dealt with here. Distraction and misunderstandings may be exploited, but using the methods that follow should prevent one from being faced later with contradictory "facts." This is because these methods are really ways of not responding to what the question is asking about—primarily by throwing roadblocks in the questioner's way, which hinder his progress or get him off on other roads.

There are two aspects of the subject of questions which we have to look at before we begin to think about the answer that is not an answer.

First, we must determine as closely as possible what meaning the question has for the questioner. This is where people frequently make their first mistake. In psychological terms, they project their own meaning into the question, rather than holding it to the meaning of the person who asked it. "What did you do last night?" is not an attempt to find out about the crime you committed then. The answer can very well be a statement about the delightful supper which preceded the act. We do not have to avoid answering, in many cases, if we interpret the question properly.

The second principle in regard to the question grows out of the first. It is limitation of the question to certain restricted meanings—associated with the intent of the questioner. We often lead others just to the area we don't want them to investigate by responding as if their questions were directed to this area. The neurotic person may feel that all questions are focused on his guilty secret and then is constantly on the defensive. Heavily defended areas are likely to draw fire. We thus do not let our opponent—if I may call him that—know what area we are defending; or, even better, we do not let him know that we are defending any area and that he is our opponent.

If we look at the questioner's meaning and limit the question to this, we may find it harmless to answer. If not, we must then proceed in one of several ways to avoid answering the question.

There are three basic methods of solving the problem of not answering: (1) not answering at all; (2) managing the question; (3) managing the questioner. There is a certain amount of interrelationship among them; but, for the purposes of study, let us look at them separately.

Perhaps it should be pointed out that the methods don't have to be used in a particular order. Feel free to work them in any combination, depending upon circumstances and inclination. Remember that retortmanship is an art; to perfect it, practice the ones that are not familiar.

NOT ANSWERING AT ALL

Some questions can get along in life very well without a mate. Let us not suppose that every question demands an answer. Many people have burned themselves by picking up a hot question which they might well have left lying. Even if the question seems to demand an answer, there are ways of avoiding making any response at all. The simplest is to ignore or apparently not hear the question. This can be done in some circumstances without impoliteness. Sometimes it is best to wait and see if your interrogator is going to force the question into your awareness.

Or you may cope with the question by means of *distraction*. The commonest tactic is related to the use of cigarettes. You may let time lapse—and the more time, the better—by lighting a cigarette, inhaling, removing ashes, coughing, and choking. If the situation has still not changed, at least you have had time to plan a defense. Pipe smokers have excellent props for delaying action for several minutes. Occasionally one can try things along the line of spilling a glass of water (preferably over the questioner), or the smoker may drop his cigarette into the depths of the sofa. But what if we get beyond all this, into the dangerous quicksands of the evasive answer?

MANAGING THE QUESTION

A method that can be used occasionally is *misunderstanding* the question. Although we have carried out the first step of probing the meaning of the question, we lead the questioner to think that we have misunderstood it. If he asks about Tuesday night, start in by saying: "Well, Monday we had gone . . . ." He waits, thinking you will go to Tuesday, but you never do. It helps if the misunderstanding is not immediately detected and therefore subject to correction. The example starts as if laying background, so you are not stopped. If the questioner asks you to go back to Tuesday after you finish, he seems to be imposing. One can generally count on a question not being repeated, but if it is, additional techniques can be used.

Limitation is closely connected with misunderstandings. Limitation does not call for confirming the question to the interrogator's intent; it requires artfully constructing it to the desired meaning. "How did you like my play?" is answered with, "I particularly noticed the storekeeper's role; it must be extremely difficult." Or, "What did you do Tuesday night?" can be answered with, "We started off with a wonderful dinner. The soup, you can't imagine! It was made of . . . ." Then you discuss foods for half an hour. You have limited the field twice, first to the dinner situation, then to the foods, and you have moved the question into neutral territory.

Another method related to misunderstanding is the *non sequitur*. The politician, when asked about food prices, may end up talking about red-blooded Americans, motherhood, and the Fourth of July. The answer is not logically related to the question. Some when asked a question they can make neither head nor tail of—or do not care to answer—give a five-minute history of aviation or some such thing. In this case, you should usually start in by saying, "As I understand that, it would include . . ." or "I think I can best answer by drawing a parallel example," or "This whole thing seems closely related to . . . ."

In using the non sequitur, it often is advisable to respond with things that have emotional appeal to the questioner. The politician refers to motherhood, and we are drawn up in the associated emotions and forget the question. It helps if the answer is fairly long and wide-ranging, so that the questioner can read his own answer into the material you present.

Another method most useful to the professor, politician, or lecturer, but well adapted to everyday usage, is *restatement*. One takes the question and then, apparently in the interests of clarity, restates it before starting to answer. This is the opportunity to convert the question into one that is easy to answer. The politician may be asked, "Are we going into a depression?" He says, "As I understand your question, you are really asking about the present state of the business cycle. Business income is the highest in history . . . ." He has restated the question and thus secured permission in advance to answer his own version of the question. The questioner is seldom alert enough to notice the skirting of his question when we use restatement and begin by saying, "What you are really asking is . . . ."

A method similar to restatement is that of the *more fundamental question*. When asked, "Are you a socialist?" you can respond that we must first consider a more fundamental question: "What is socialism?" This gives you the opportunity not to answer until you resolve the fundamental issue, and you can avoid this by arguing over the definition. Don't think that what you claim as more fundamental must be so; almost any sort of question can be thrown in as a roadblock, just so you make it seem necessary to deal with the second point before answering the original question.

The *hypothetical answer* or the use of *objectivity* is a method widely used by intellectuals. When asked a question, you answer, "Well, now, I would like to respond to that. Supposing you were in this position, then you might feel this; or again, in another position, you might feel that." A senator might be asked, "Should Red China be admitted to the U.N.?" An answer might be, "Let us look at this objectively. There are a number of courses open to the United States. . . . And, of course, is the United States in a position to prevent Red China from entering?" The essence of the method lies in a presenting various alternatives without committing yourself to any specific position.

One of the most interesting operations is the approach I call: *Is this really a question?* Using this method, you proceed to destroy the question. You show that it really consists of three or four questions, or that it sets up a false situation or uses false premises, or that the terms have no fixed meaning. On the question about admitting Red China to the U.N., one answers, "That is really several questions: What is the purpose of the U.N.? What government represents China? What do U.N. members feel?" Take the question, "Do you believe in evolution?" Your answer, "It is not really a question of belief, but of the meaning of certain pieces of evidence . . . ." After you break the question down into three or four others, from the various parts you select one you want to expand upon, and you keep from having the question put back together again.

A somewhat similar method is the *moot* question approach. Whether the question is answerable or not, you assert that it is really a point that can't be answered. Taking the Red China question, we answer: "One should not really speculate upon a question of that type, because of the imponderable elements. We cannot know what the future will bring or what position we will be in, and crossing bridges before we come to them is foolhardy."

The *assertion-of-nothing* is often most satisfactory in answering. The proud mother asks what you think of her ugly baby, and you answer, "That *is* a baby!" (But not: *"That* is a baby?"*) A display of strong feeling and emphasis is necessary to carry this method off, as you seem to be saying something so strongly the questioner feels you must be answering.

MANAGING THE QUESTIONER

This is the counterattack approach. Not recommended generally is putting the original questioner on the defensive, so that he becomes engaged in defending himself. You can point out what profound ignorance such a question reveals, or you can say you feel sorry for anyone who does not understand these things. This is likely to silence him in regard to further questions, but it will also make him angry and vengeful. This technique can be most effective when a friendly manner is used—for example, "You probably didn't mean to ask that, what you would really like to know is . . . ."

Another typical form of counterattack is to answer with *another question*. Question: "What do you think of the Republicans?" Answer: "First we should look at political parties; what do you think of them?" Question: "What did you do Tuesday night?" Answer: "I never do much. You probably had a much more interesting time; what did you do?" Any good evasive technique should always end with a question. As long as you are talking, you are safe. When stopping, pick the topic for the other person in safe territory.

Already in the preceding example we are moving on to an excellent and very subtle counterattack. This is the method of *compliment*. Question: "What do you feel about Marie?" Answer: "How penetrating that you should ask such a question. You seem to have a wonderful understanding of what people are feeling. How did you ever develop this ability?" (Or: "I have long wanted your opinion of her.") Praise is one of the most disarming of methods. That is why the questioner, unless he is particularly alert, is likely to be so absorbed in feelings of gratification that it will be difficult for him to recognize a smokescreen for operations of another kind.

You are now on your own. You will discover many subtle variations and combinations as you work on this. The future of this much-needed science is in your hands.

FOR DISCUSSION

1. One of the most difficult sentences to learn to say is "I don't know," though clearly there are many times when we simply do not know. What psychological and sociological factors might be responsible for our tendency to avoid confessing ignorance or lack of knowledge?

2. Evaluate the effectiveness of the satire in Washburne's article. Would his argument have been more or less effective if he had simply stated his position and defended it and had avoided the satire? Why?

3. Listen to a question and answer session (for example, press conferences, debates, class lectures) with particular reference to Washburne's techniques of retortmanship. Does the speaker utilize any of these techniques? Are the listeners aware of this retortmanship or do they feel that the questions have been answered satisfactorily?

4. What are some of the factors that might motivate people to avoid answering questions and to employ the techniques of retortmanship?

5. What responsibilities or obligations does a communicator have when, after stating his position, he is confronted with questions? Put differently, what ethical standards should govern answering questions?

6. Does the questioner have any responsibilities concerning the questions he asks or the way in which he asks them? That is, what are the ethical considerations that should apply to the questioner and to the questions?

Index

A

Active listening, 137
Adjustment, 65
Advisement, 32
Affinity, as motive in communication, 36
Aggressive behavior, 135
Ambiguous communication, 160
Apprehension, 38–48
   causes of, 46
   effects of, 40
   nature of, 40
   test of, 43–45
Arbitrariness, 62
Audience analysis, 225
Audience psychology, 225
Avoidance of communication, 134

B

Bales, Robert Freed, 190–97
Bandwagon technique in persuasion, 233
Barker, Larry L., 148–52
Barriers to communication, 29–33, 155
Big lie technique in persuasion, 235
Bois, J. S., 27–28
Bypassing, 172

C

Certainty in communication, 54
Clothing as communication, 99
Coherence in organization, 221
Communication:
   definition, 3, 11
   elements of, 3
   learned nature of, 11
   by listening, 143
   models of, 3–9
Confirmation as motive in
   communication, 37
Conflict:
   coping with, 158
   handling, 156
   nature of, 132, 153
   skills in conflict management, 162
   societal views of, 153
Connotation, 172

Control in communication, 51
Cross-cultural communication, 98
Cultural transmission, 62
Cuthill, Rowland, 105–11

D

Decision-making discussions, 200
Decisions as motives in communication, 37
Decode, 4
Defensiveness, 49, 133, 146
Denotation, 172
Description in communication, 50
Destination, definition of, 3
Determinism, 63
DeVito, Joseph A., 59–67, 198–99,
   213–14
Displacement, 61, 63

E

Eakins, Barbara Westbrook, 77–87
Eakins, R. Gene, 77–87
Educatorese, 74
Effectiveness, 27–28
Empathy in communication, 53
Emphasis in organization, 221
Encode, 4
Equality in communication, 54
Evaluation in communication, 50
Eye contact, 99

F

Family communication, 17
Farson, Richard E., 137–47
Feedback:
   definition, 8, 148
   effective, 151
   effects of, 150
   examples of, 8
   exercises in, 11
   functions of, 149
   types of, 149
Feelings in communication, 29, 33, 129,
   142, 145
Field of experience, 5

245